CATWOMAN

FEAR STATE

VOL. **6**

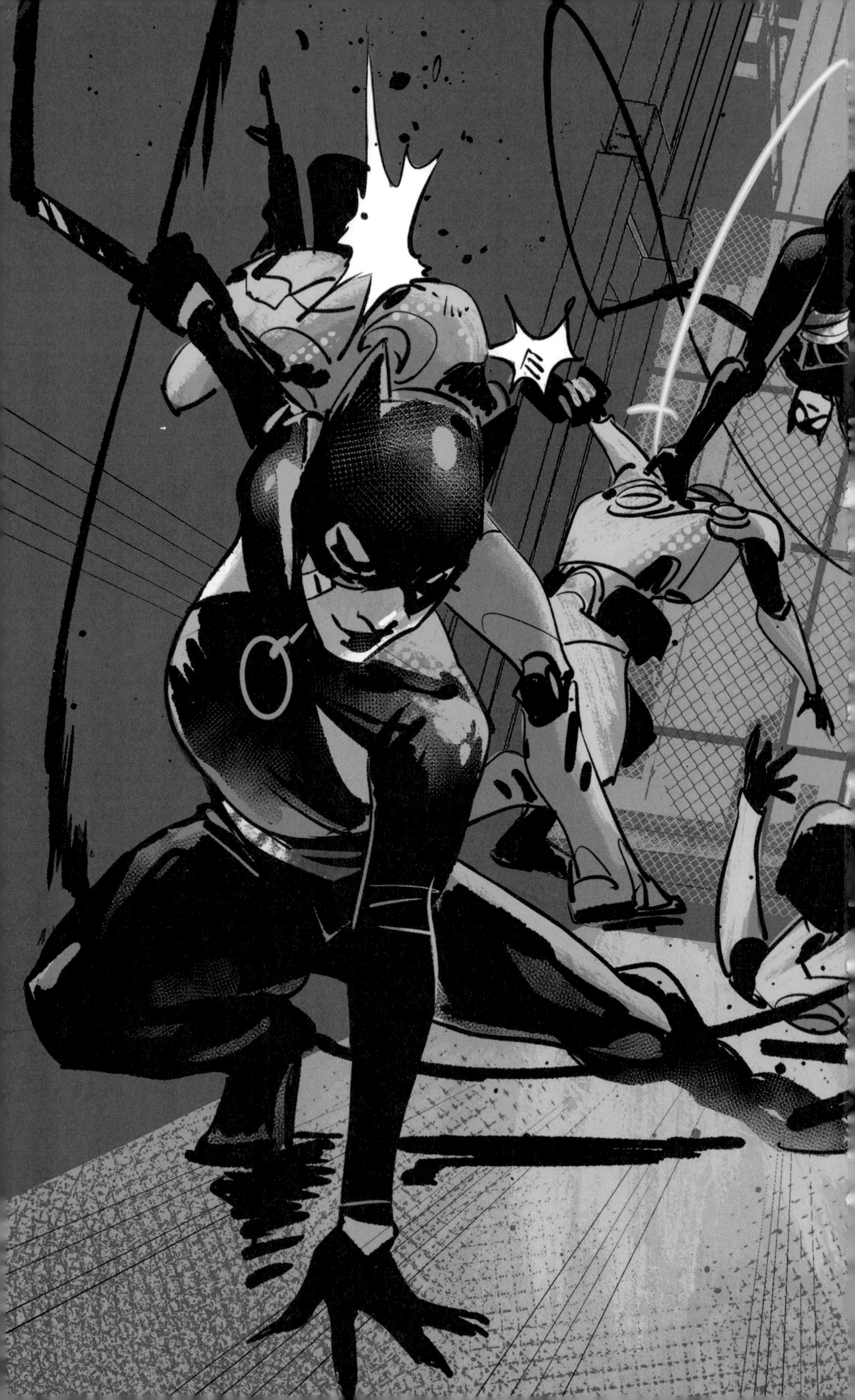

CATWOMAN
FEAR STATE

writer
RAM V

artists
NINA VAKUEVA
FERNANDO BLANCO
CASPAR WIJNGAARD
LAURA BRAGA
GERALDO BORGES

colorist
JORDIE BELLAIRE
CASPAR WIJNGAARD

letterer
TOM NAPOLITANO

collection cover artist
YANICK PAQUETTE
with **NATHAN FAIRBAIRN**

VOL.
6

JESSICA CHEN	Editor – Original Series & Collected Edition
BEN MEARES	Associate Editor – Original Series
STEVE COOK	Design Director – Books
LOUIS PRANDI	Publication Design
ERIN VANOVER	Publication Production
MARIE JAVINS	Editor-in-Chief, DC Comics
ANNE DePIES	Senior VP – General Manager
JIM LEE	Publisher & Chief Creative Officer
DON FALLETTI	VP – Manufacturing Operations & Workflow Management
LAWRENCE GANEM	VP – Talent Services
ALISON GILL	Senior VP – Manufacturing & Operations
JEFFREY KAUFMAN	VP – Editorial Strategy & Programming
NICK J. NAPOLITANO	VP – Manufacturing Administration & Design
NANCY SPEARS	VP - Revenue

DC Comics, 2900 West Alameda Ave., Burbank, CA 91505
Printed by Solisco Printers, Scott, QC, Canada. 4/8/21. First Printing.
ISBN: 978-1-77951-529-2

Library of Congress Cataloging-in-Publication Data is available.

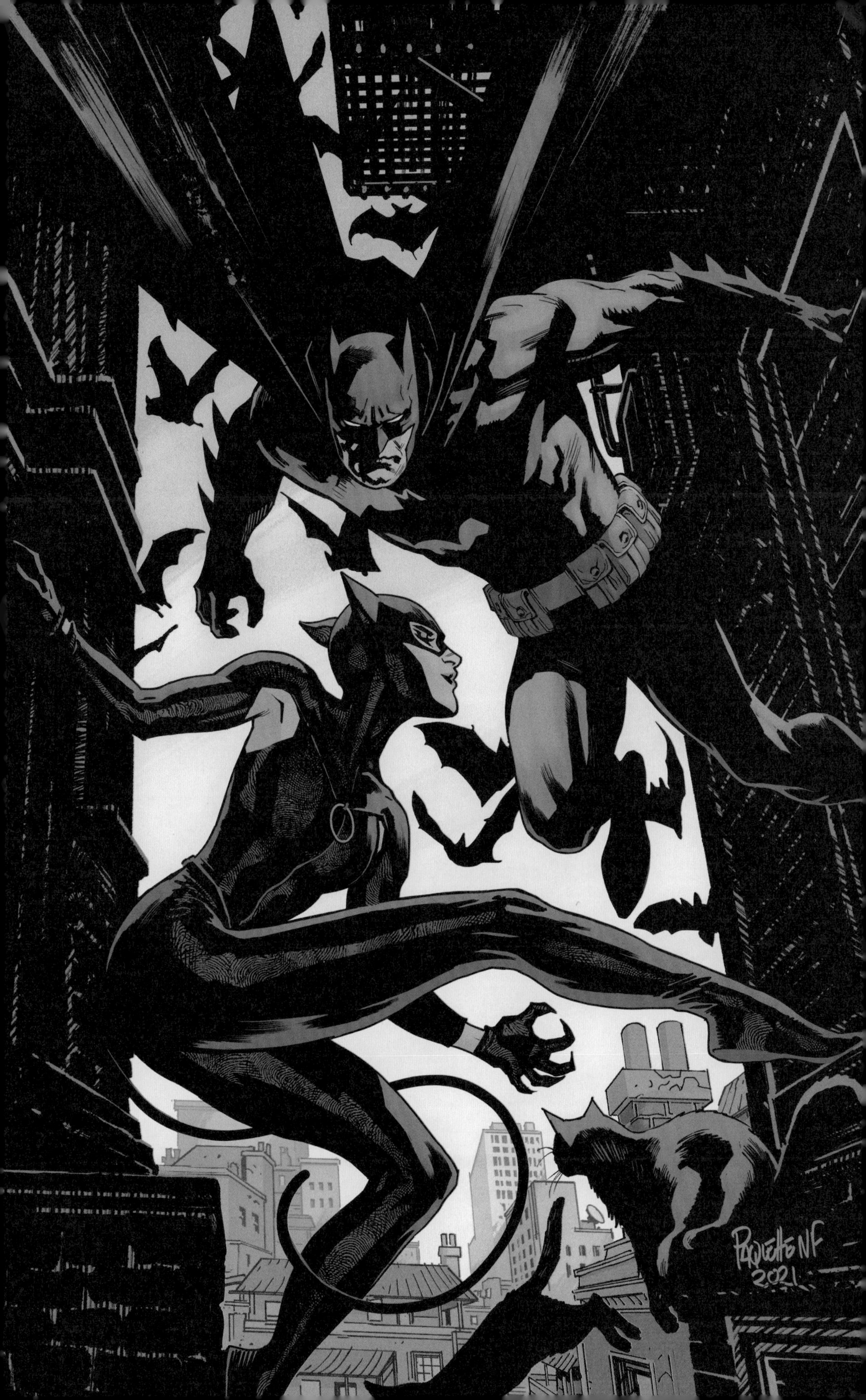
PAQUETTE NF
2021

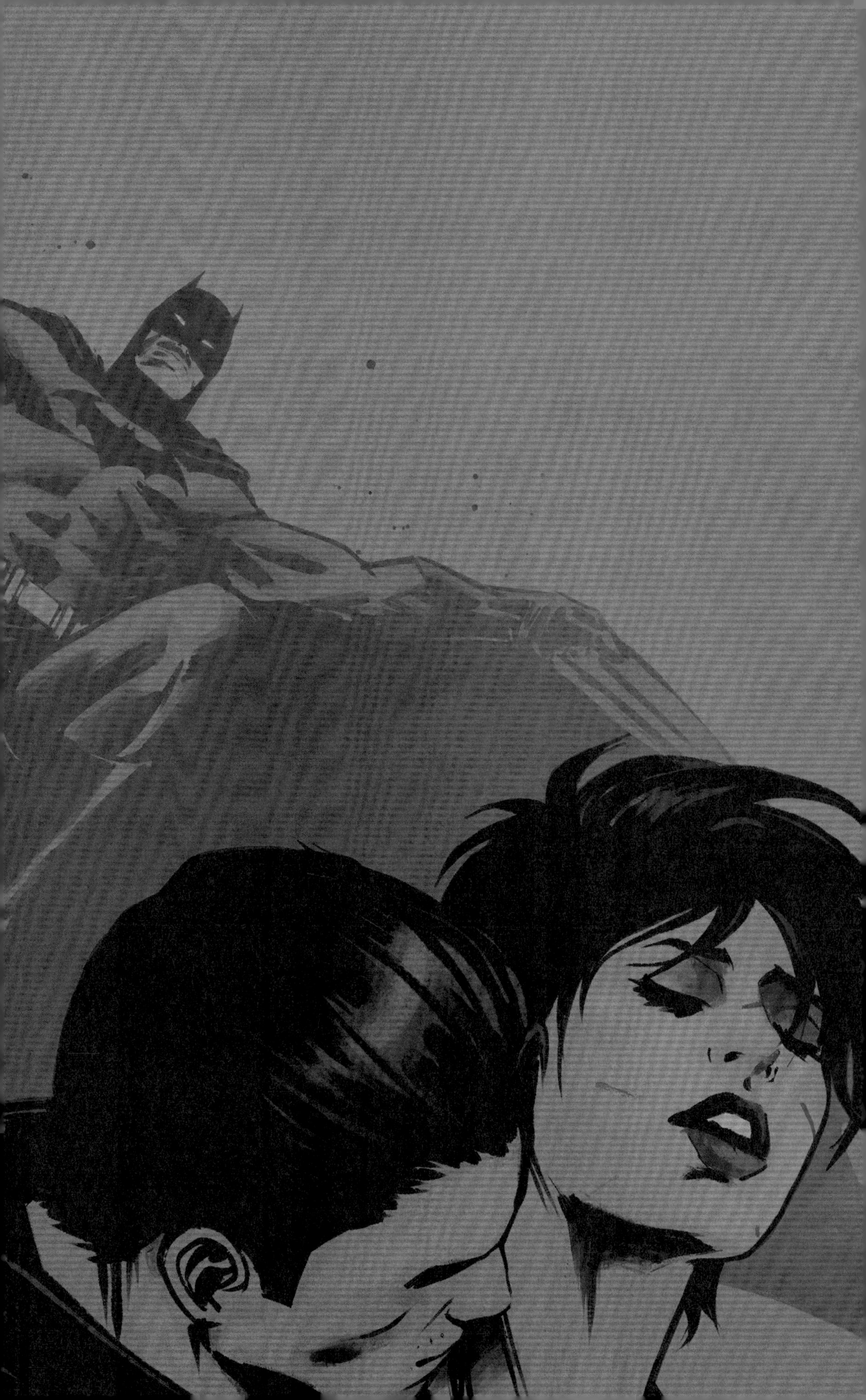

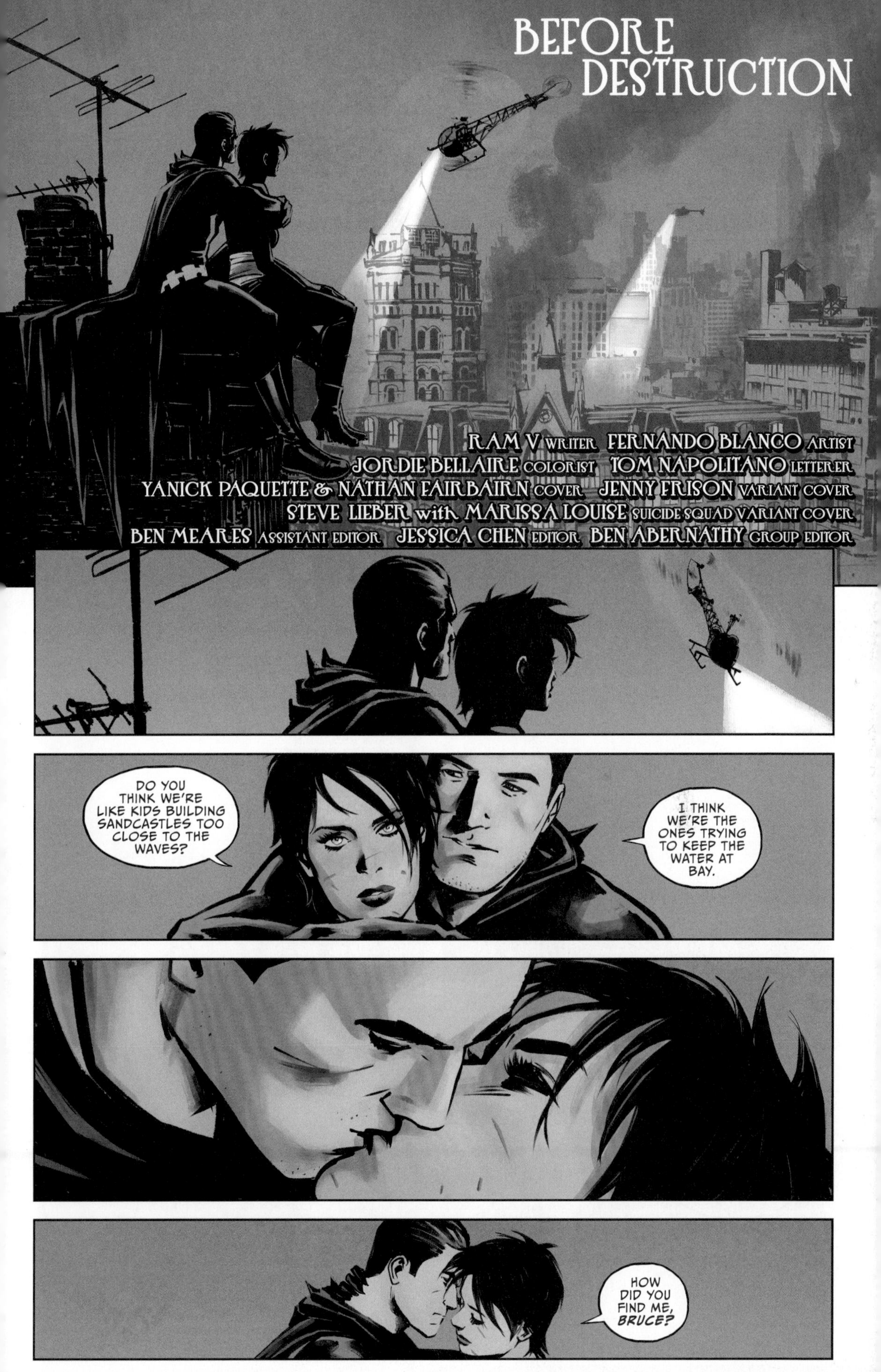
BEFORE DESTRUCTION
RAM V WRITER FERNANDO BLANCO ARTIST
JORDIE BELLAIRE COLORIST TOM NAPOLITANO LETTERER
YANICK PAQUETTE & NATHAN FAIRBAIRN COVER JENNY FRISON VARIANT COVER
STEVE LIEBER with MARISSA LOUISE SUICIDE SQUAD VARIANT COVER
BEN MEARES ASSISTANT EDITOR JESSICA CHEN EDITOR BEN ABERNATHY GROUP EDITOR
DO YOU THINK WE'RE LIKE KIDS BUILDING SANDCASTLES TOO CLOSE TO THE WAVES?
I THINK WE'RE THE ONES TRYING TO KEEP THE WATER AT BAY.
HOW DID YOU FIND ME, *BRUCE?*

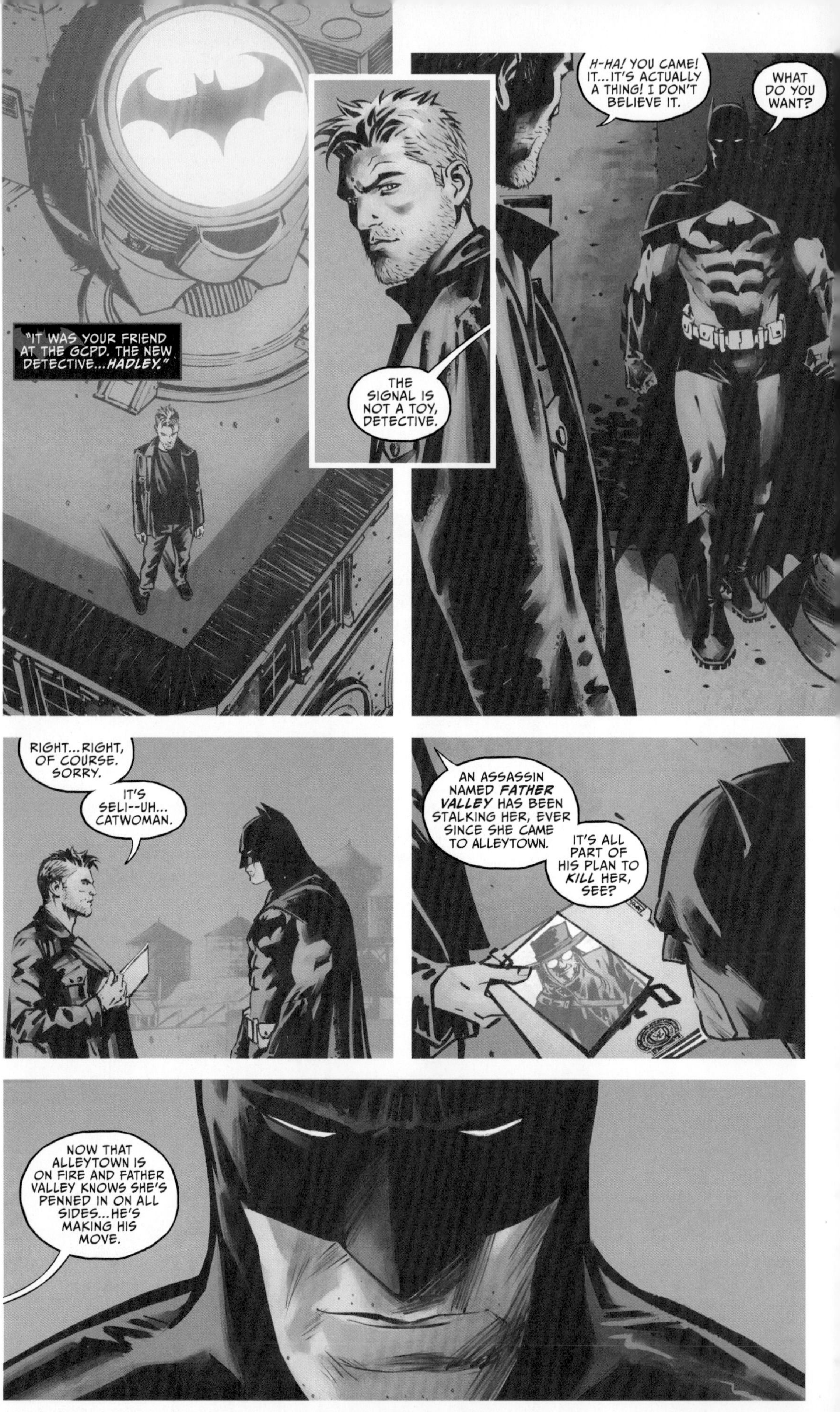
"IT WAS YOUR FRIEND AT THE GCPD. THE NEW DETECTIVE...HADLEY."
THE SIGNAL IS NOT A TOY, DETECTIVE.
H-HA! YOU CAME! IT...IT'S ACTUALLY A THING! I DON'T BELIEVE IT.
WHAT DO YOU WANT?
RIGHT...RIGHT, OF COURSE. SORRY.
IT'S SELI--UH... CATWOMAN.
AN ASSASSIN NAMED FATHER VALLEY HAS BEEN STALKING HER, EVER SINCE SHE CAME TO ALLEYTOWN.
IT'S ALL PART OF HIS PLAN TO KILL HER, SEE?
NOW THAT ALLEYTOWN IS ON FIRE AND FATHER VALLEY KNOWS SHE'S PENNED IN ON ALL SIDES...HE'S MAKING HIS MOVE.

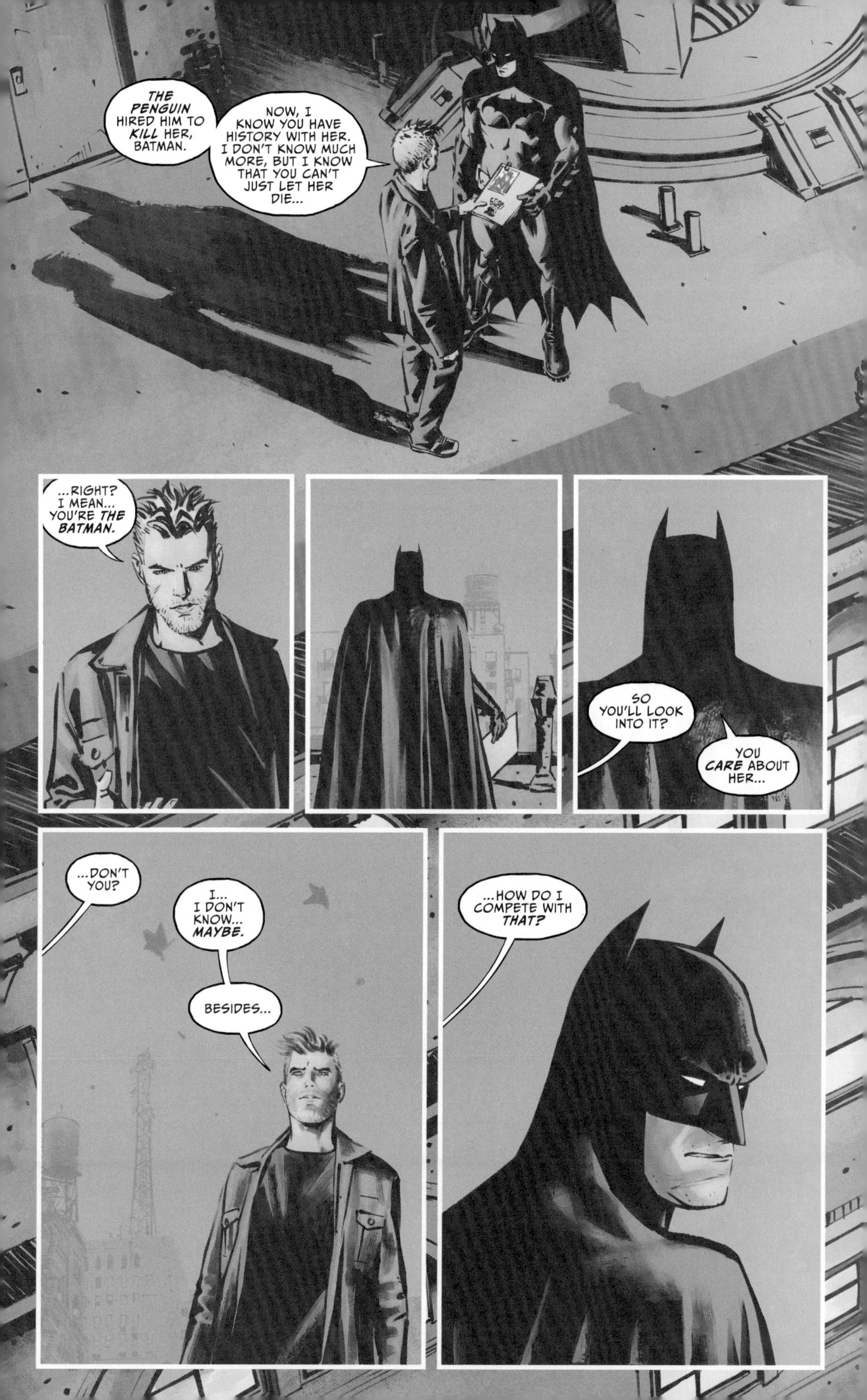
THE PENGUIN HIRED HIM TO KILL HER, BATMAN.
NOW, I KNOW YOU HAVE HISTORY WITH HER. I DON'T KNOW MUCH MORE, BUT I KNOW THAT YOU CAN'T JUST LET HER DIE...
...RIGHT? I MEAN... YOU'RE THE BATMAN.
SO YOU'LL LOOK INTO IT?
YOU CARE ABOUT HER...
...DON'T YOU?
I... I DON'T KNOW... MAYBE.
BESIDES...
...HOW DO I COMPETE WITH THAT?

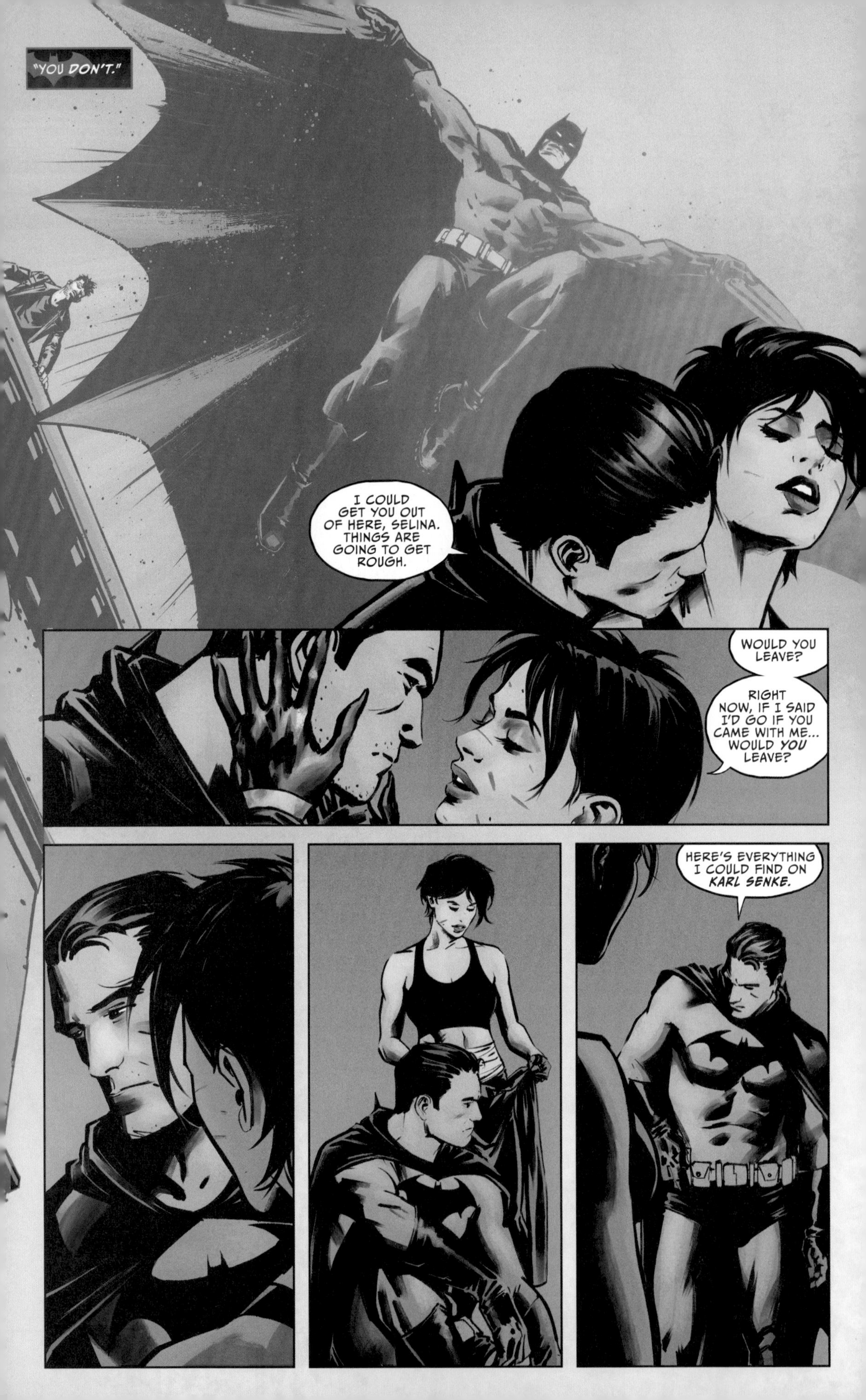
"YOU DON'T."
I COULD GET YOU OUT OF HERE, SELINA. THINGS ARE GOING TO GET ROUGH.
WOULD YOU LEAVE?
RIGHT NOW, IF I SAID I'D GO IF YOU CAME WITH ME... WOULD YOU LEAVE?
HERE'S EVERYTHING I COULD FIND ON KARL SENKE.

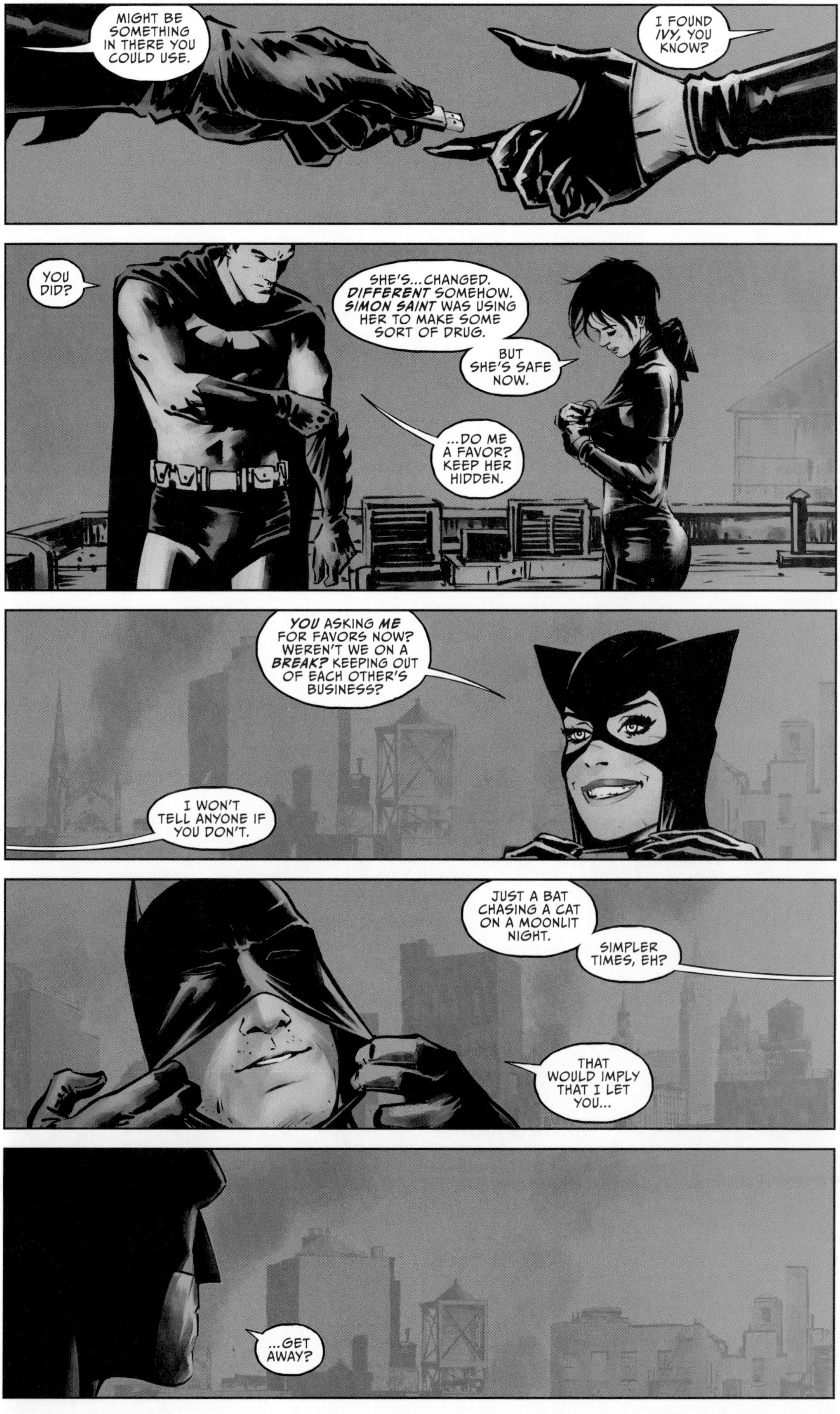
MIGHT BE SOMETHING IN THERE YOU COULD USE.
I FOUND *IVY*, YOU KNOW?
YOU DID?
SHE'S...CHANGED. ***DIFFERENT*** SOMEHOW. ***SIMON SAINT*** WAS USING HER TO MAKE SOME SORT OF DRUG.
BUT SHE'S SAFE NOW.
...DO ME A FAVOR? KEEP HER HIDDEN.
YOU ASKING ***ME*** FOR FAVORS NOW? WEREN'T WE ON A ***BREAK?*** KEEPING OUT OF EACH OTHER'S BUSINESS?
I WON'T TELL ANYONE IF YOU DON'T.
JUST A BAT CHASING A CAT ON A MOONLIT NIGHT.
SIMPLER TIMES, EH?
THAT WOULD IMPLY THAT I LET YOU...
...GET AWAY?

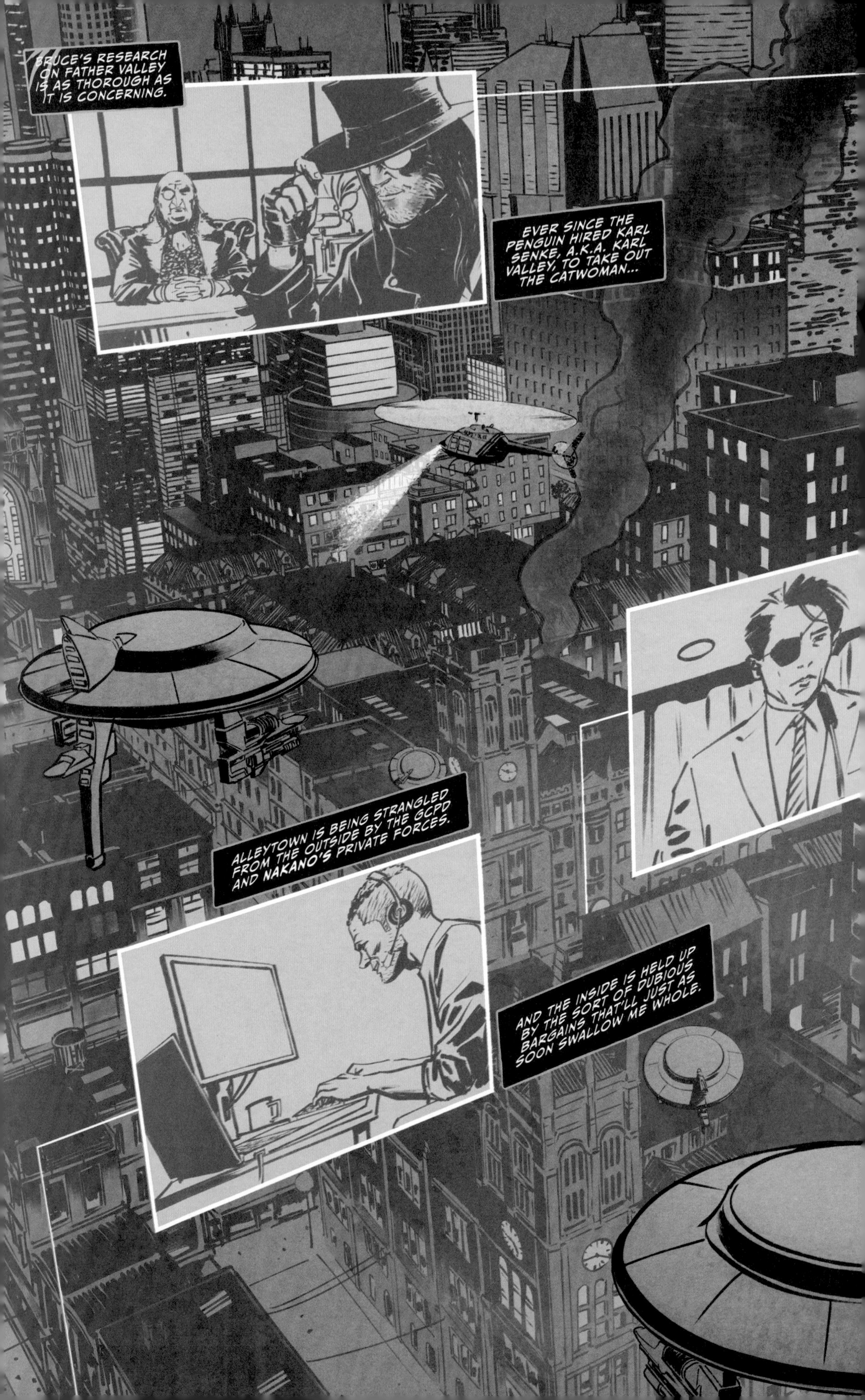
BRUCE'S RESEARCH ON FATHER VALLEY IS AS THOROUGH AS IT IS CONCERNING.
EVER SINCE THE PENGUIN HIRED KARL SENKE, A.K.A. KARL VALLEY, TO TAKE OUT THE CATWOMAN...
ALLEYTOWN IS BEING STRANGLED FROM THE OUTSIDE BY THE GCPD AND NAKANO'S PRIVATE FORCES.
AND THE INSIDE IS HELD UP BY THE SORT OF DUBIOUS BARGAINS THAT'LL JUST AS SOON SWALLOW ME WHOLE.

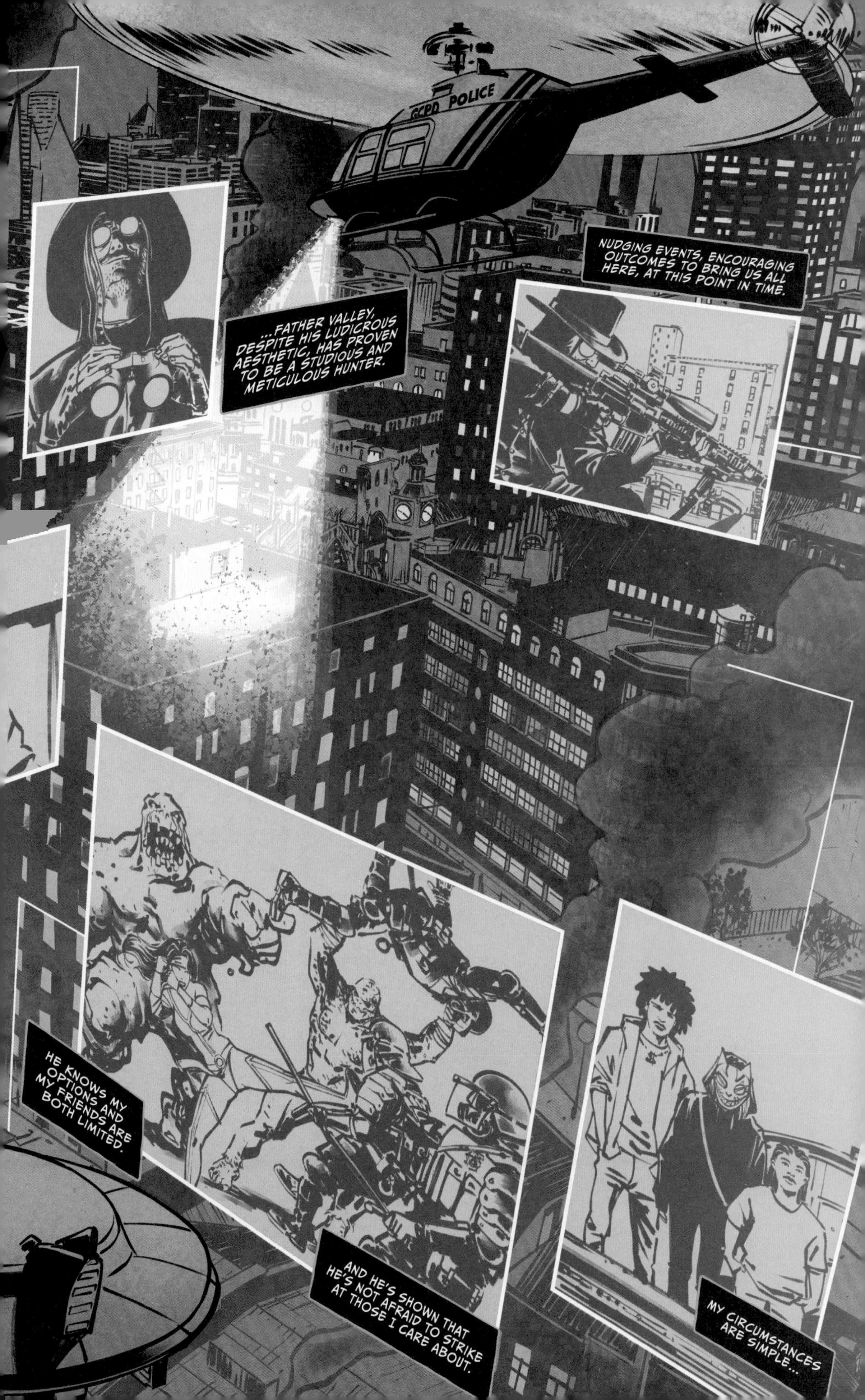
GCPD POLICE
...FATHER VALLEY, DESPITE HIS LUDICROUS AESTHETIC, HAS PROVEN TO BE A STUDIOUS AND METICULOUS HUNTER.
NUDGING EVENTS, ENCOURAGING OUTCOMES TO BRING US ALL HERE, AT THIS POINT IN TIME.
HE KNOWS MY OPTIONS AND MY FRIENDS ARE BOTH LIMITED.
AND HE'S SHOWN THAT HE'S NOT AFRAID TO STRIKE AT THOSE I CARE ABOUT.
MY CIRCUMSTANCES ARE SIMPLE...

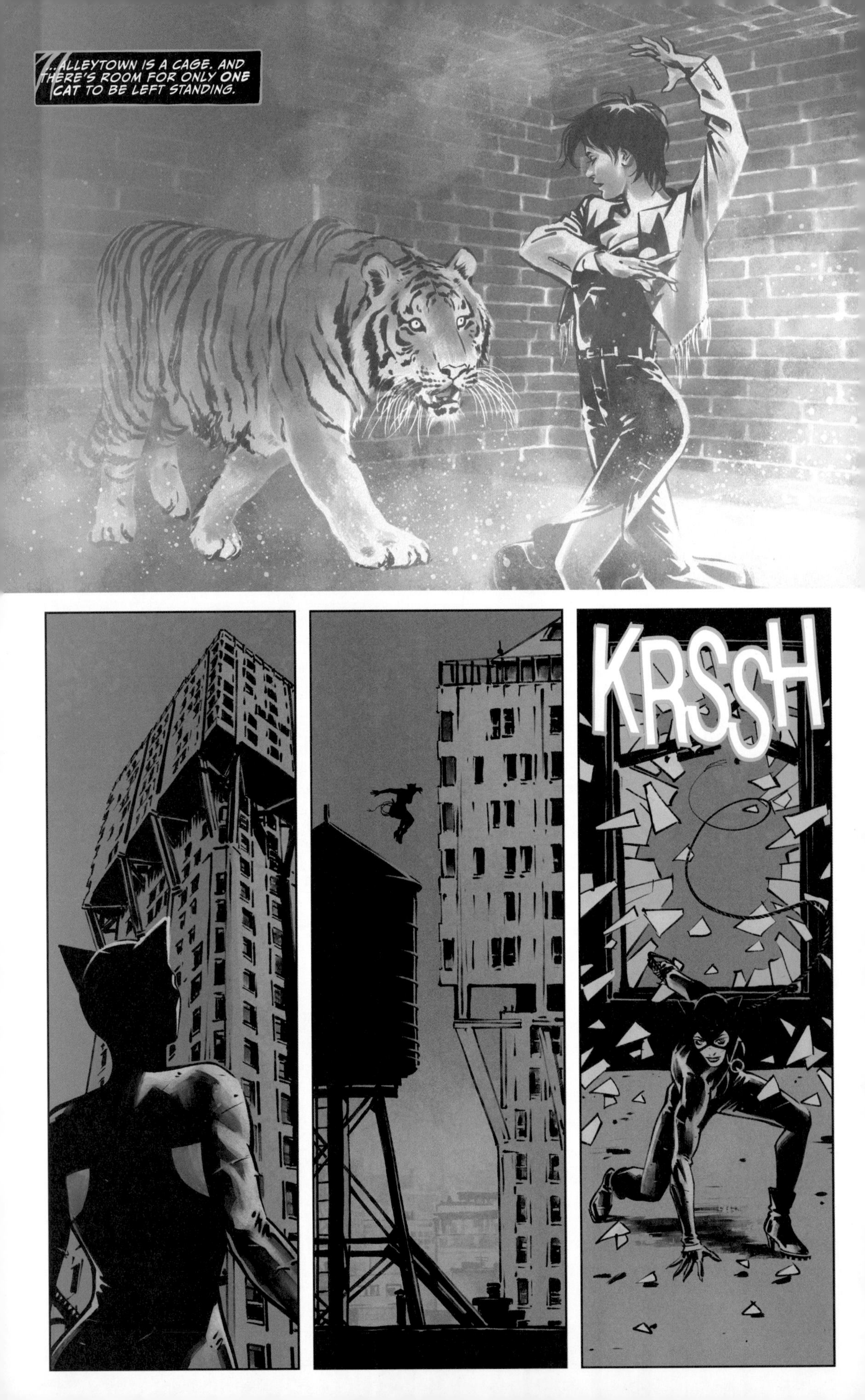
...ALLEYTOWN IS A CAGE. AND THERE'S ROOM FOR ONLY ONE CAT TO BE LEFT STANDING.
KRSSH

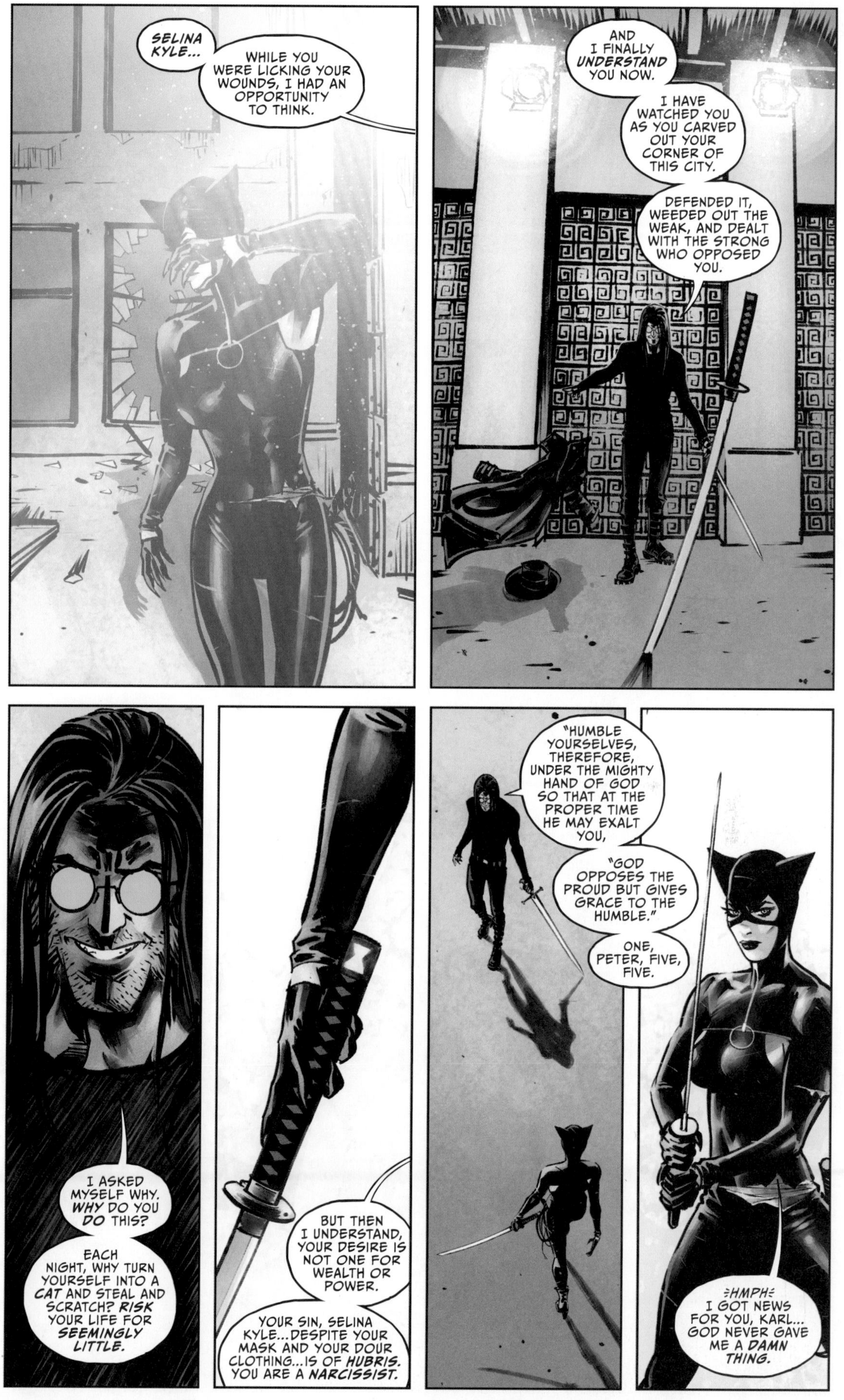
SELINA KYLE...
WHILE YOU WERE LICKING YOUR WOUNDS, I HAD AN OPPORTUNITY TO THINK.
AND I FINALLY UNDERSTAND YOU NOW.
I HAVE WATCHED YOU AS YOU CARVED OUT YOUR CORNER OF THIS CITY.
DEFENDED IT, WEEDED OUT THE WEAK, AND DEALT WITH THE STRONG WHO OPPOSED YOU.
I ASKED MYSELF WHY. WHY DO YOU DO THIS?
EACH NIGHT, WHY TURN YOURSELF INTO A CAT AND STEAL AND SCRATCH? RISK YOUR LIFE FOR SEEMINGLY LITTLE.
BUT THEN I UNDERSTAND, YOUR DESIRE IS NOT ONE FOR WEALTH OR POWER.
YOUR SIN, SELINA KYLE...DESPITE YOUR MASK AND YOUR DOUR CLOTHING...IS OF HUBRIS. YOU ARE A NARCISSIST.
"HUMBLE YOURSELVES, THEREFORE, UNDER THE MIGHTY HAND OF GOD SO THAT AT THE PROPER TIME HE MAY EXALT YOU,
"GOD OPPOSES THE PROUD BUT GIVES GRACE TO THE HUMBLE."
ONE, PETER, FIVE, FIVE.
HMPH I GOT NEWS FOR YOU, KARL... GOD NEVER GAVE ME A DAMN THING.

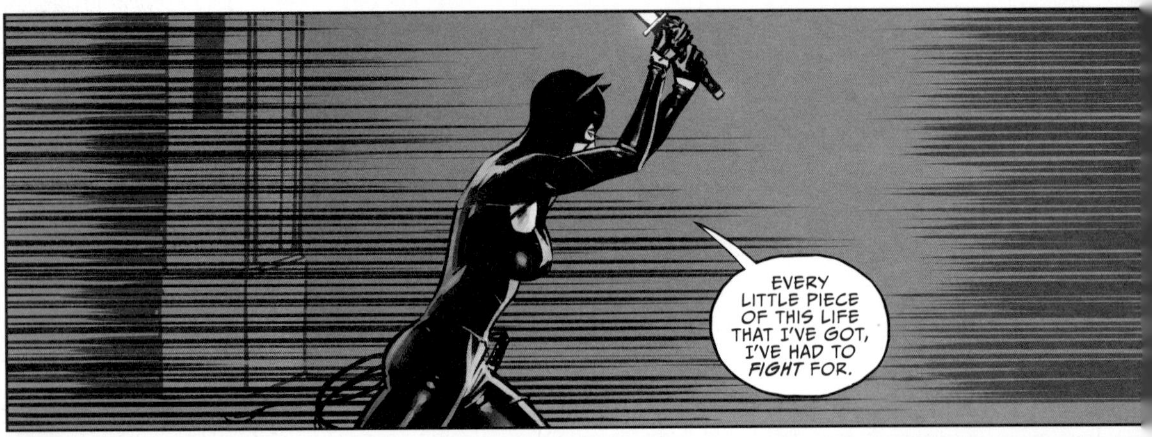
EVERY LITTLE PIECE OF THIS LIFE THAT I'VE GOT, I'VE HAD TO *FIGHT* FOR.

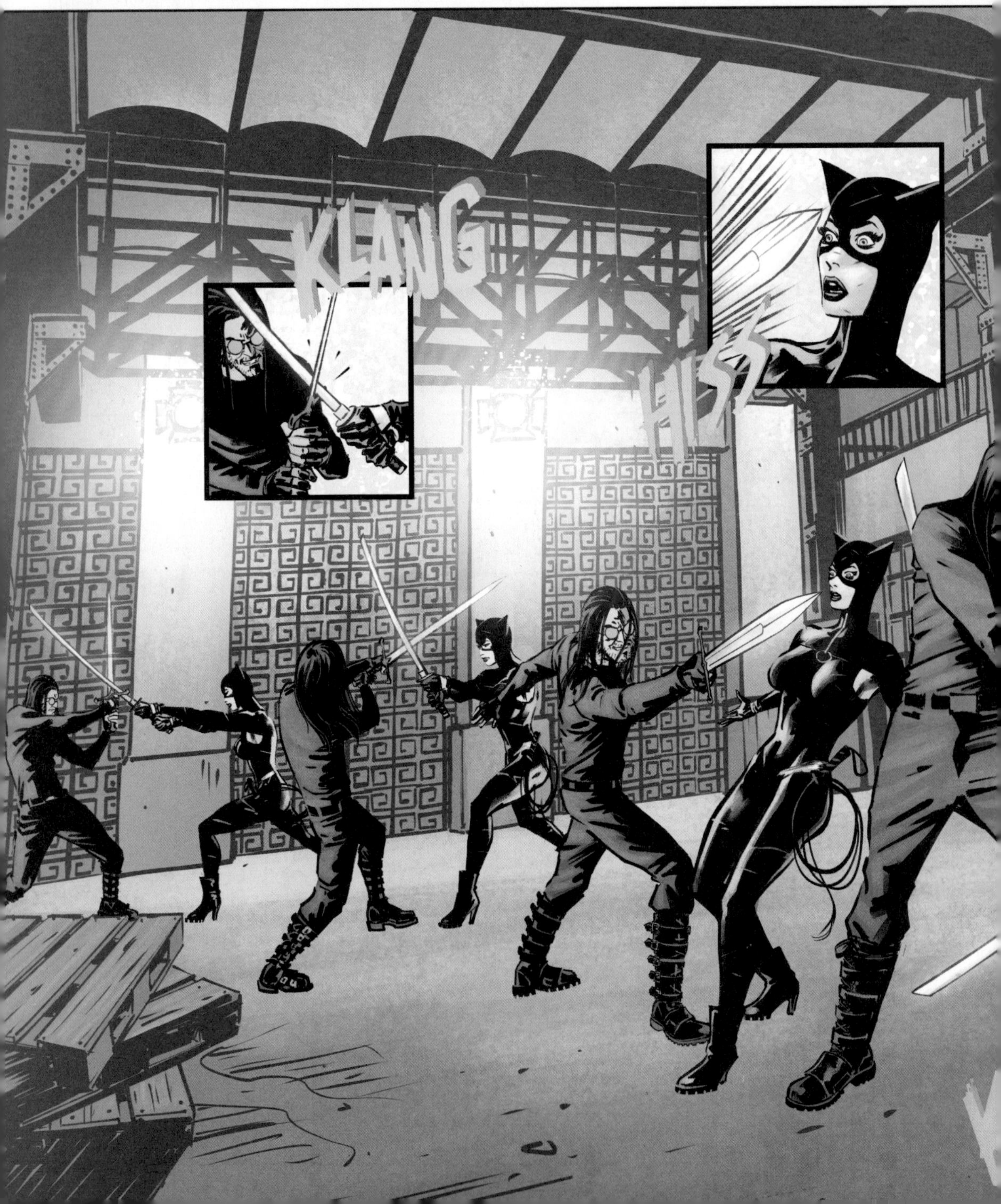
KLANG
HISS

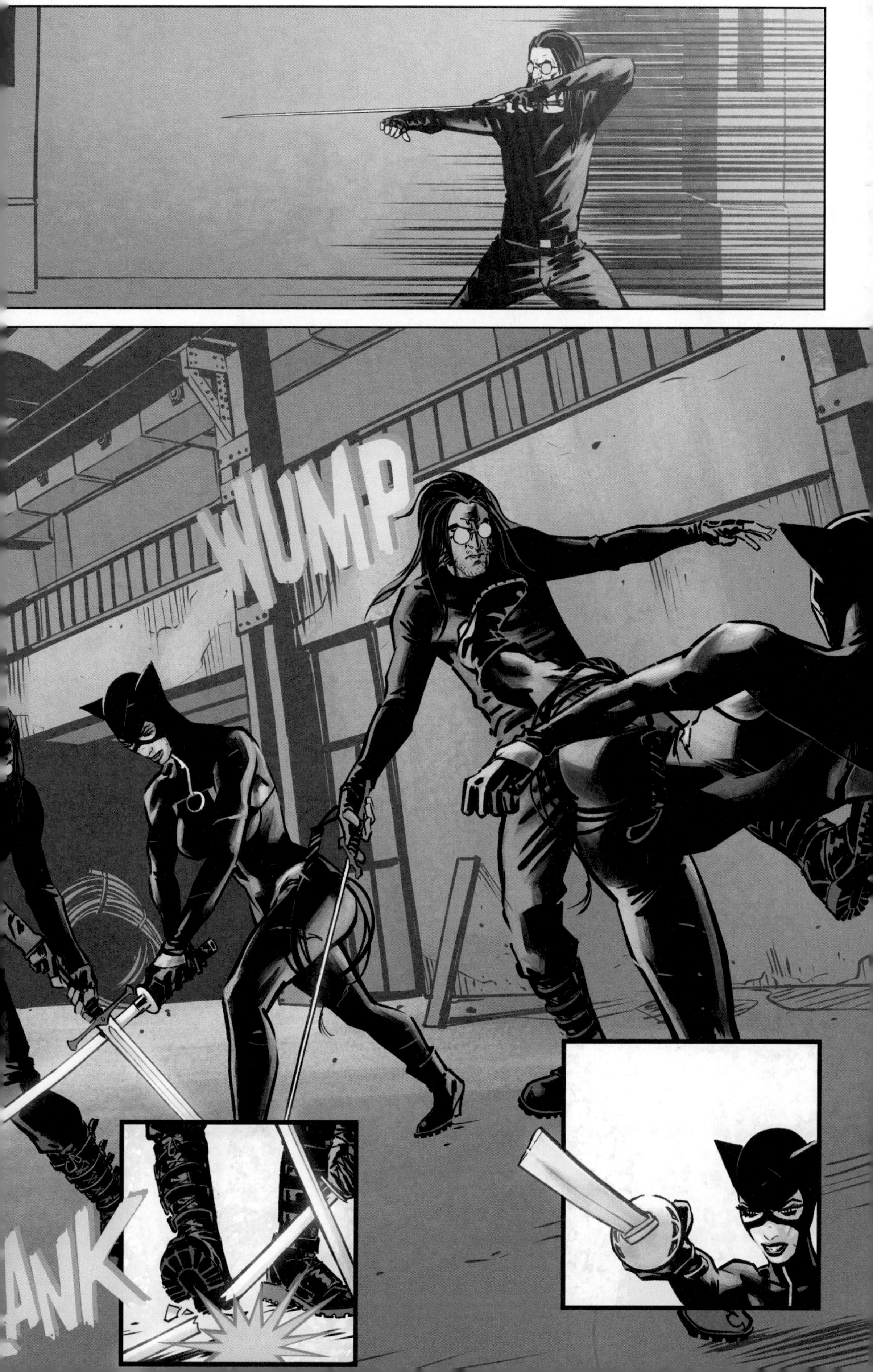
WUMP
ANK

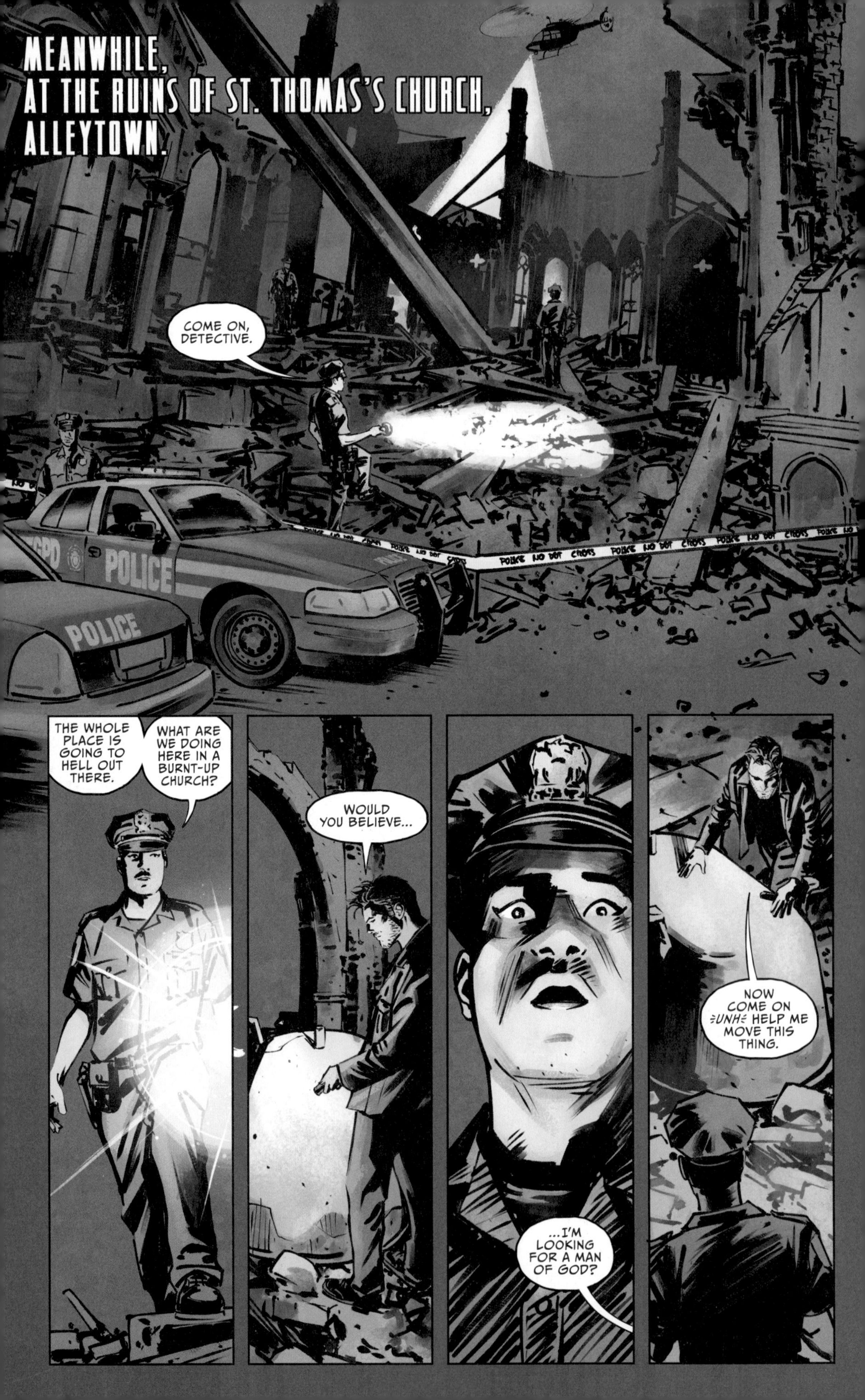
MEANWHILE,
AT THE RUINS OF ST. THOMAS'S CHURCH,
ALLEYTOWN.
COME ON, DETECTIVE.
POLICE
POLICE
THE WHOLE PLACE IS GOING TO HELL OUT THERE.
WHAT ARE WE DOING HERE IN A BURNT-UP CHURCH?
WOULD YOU BELIEVE...
...I'M LOOKING FOR A MAN OF GOD?
NOW COME ON UNH HELP ME MOVE THIS THING.

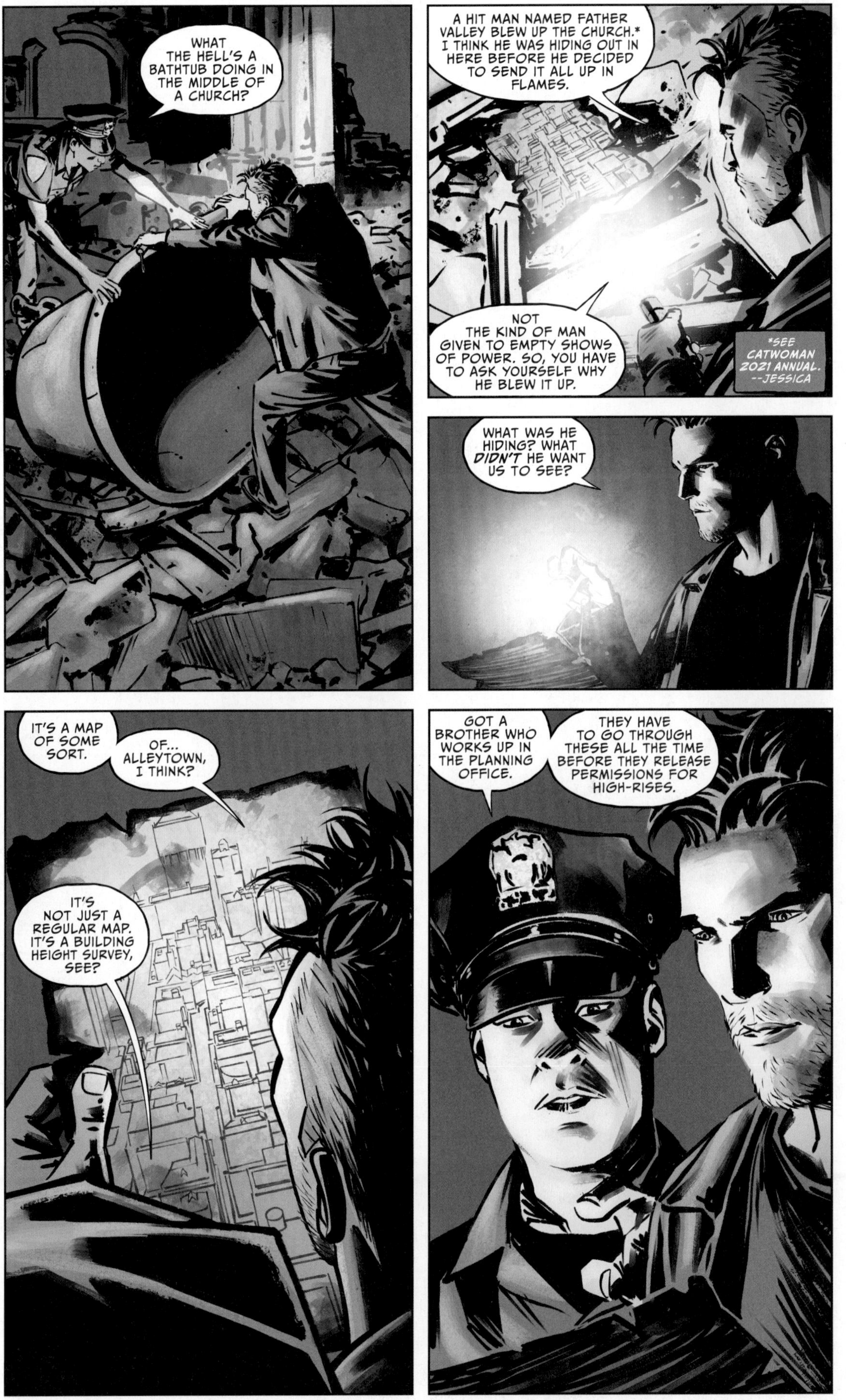
WHAT THE HELL'S A BATHTUB DOING IN THE MIDDLE OF A CHURCH?
A HIT MAN NAMED FATHER VALLEY BLEW UP THE CHURCH.* I THINK HE WAS HIDING OUT IN HERE BEFORE HE DECIDED TO SEND IT ALL UP IN FLAMES.
NOT THE KIND OF MAN GIVEN TO EMPTY SHOWS OF POWER. SO, YOU HAVE TO ASK YOURSELF WHY HE BLEW IT UP.
*SEE CATWOMAN 2021 ANNUAL. --JESSICA
WHAT WAS HE HIDING? WHAT DIDN'T HE WANT US TO SEE?
IT'S A MAP OF SOME SORT.
OF... ALLEYTOWN, I THINK?
IT'S NOT JUST A REGULAR MAP. IT'S A BUILDING HEIGHT SURVEY, SEE?
GOT A BROTHER WHO WORKS UP IN THE PLANNING OFFICE.
THEY HAVE TO GO THROUGH THESE ALL THE TIME BEFORE THEY RELEASE PERMISSIONS FOR HIGH-RISES.

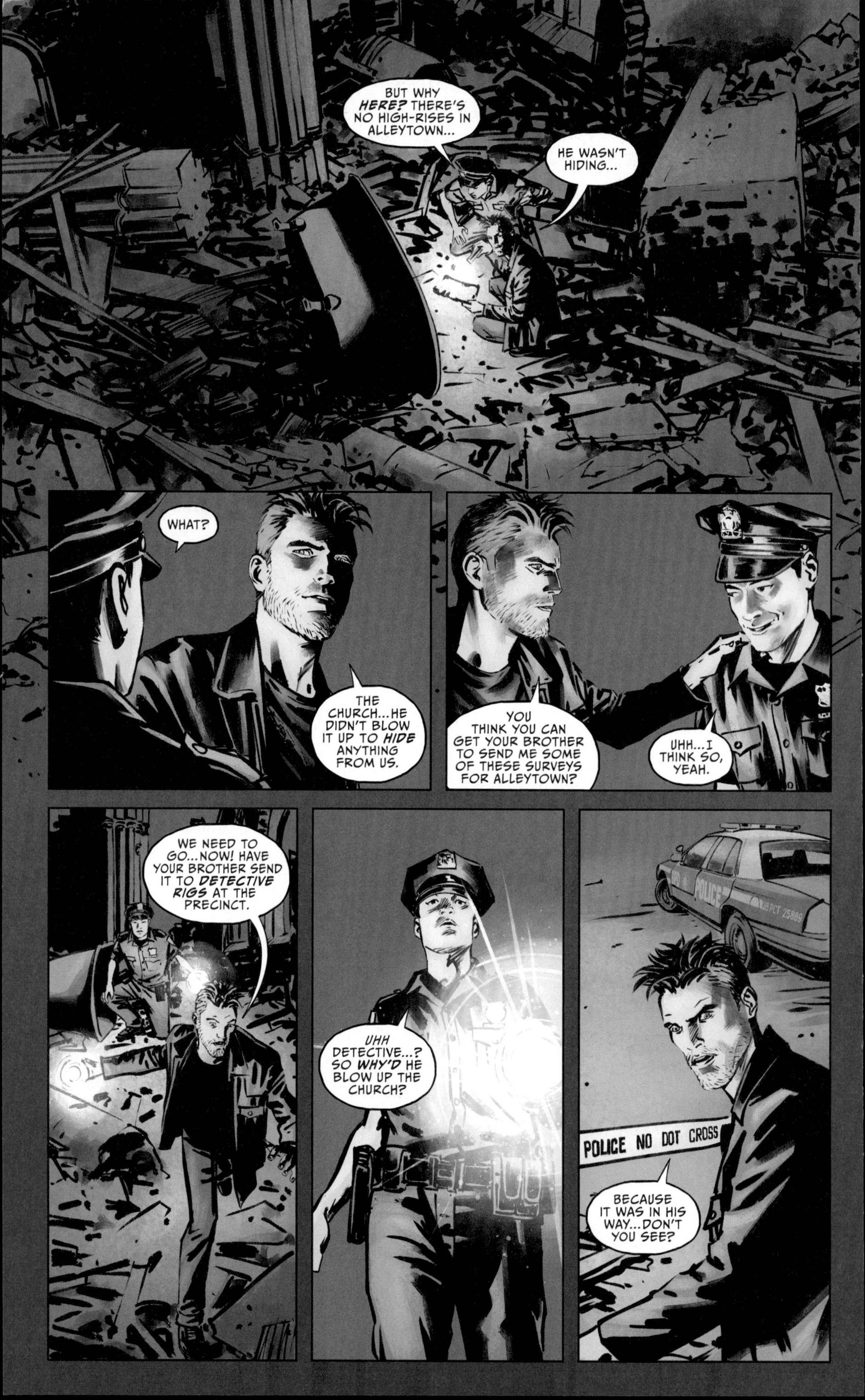
BUT WHY HERE? THERE'S NO HIGH-RISES IN ALLEYTOWN...
HE WASN'T HIDING...
WHAT?
THE CHURCH...HE DIDN'T BLOW IT UP TO HIDE ANYTHING FROM US.
YOU THINK YOU CAN GET YOUR BROTHER TO SEND ME SOME OF THESE SURVEYS FOR ALLEYTOWN?
UHH...I THINK SO, YEAH.
WE NEED TO GO...NOW! HAVE YOUR BROTHER SEND IT TO DETECTIVE RIGS AT THE PRECINCT.
UHH DETECTIVE...? SO WHY'D HE BLOW UP THE CHURCH?
POLICE
28 PCT 25889
POLICE NO DOT CROSS
BECAUSE IT WAS IN HIS WAY...DON'T YOU SEE?

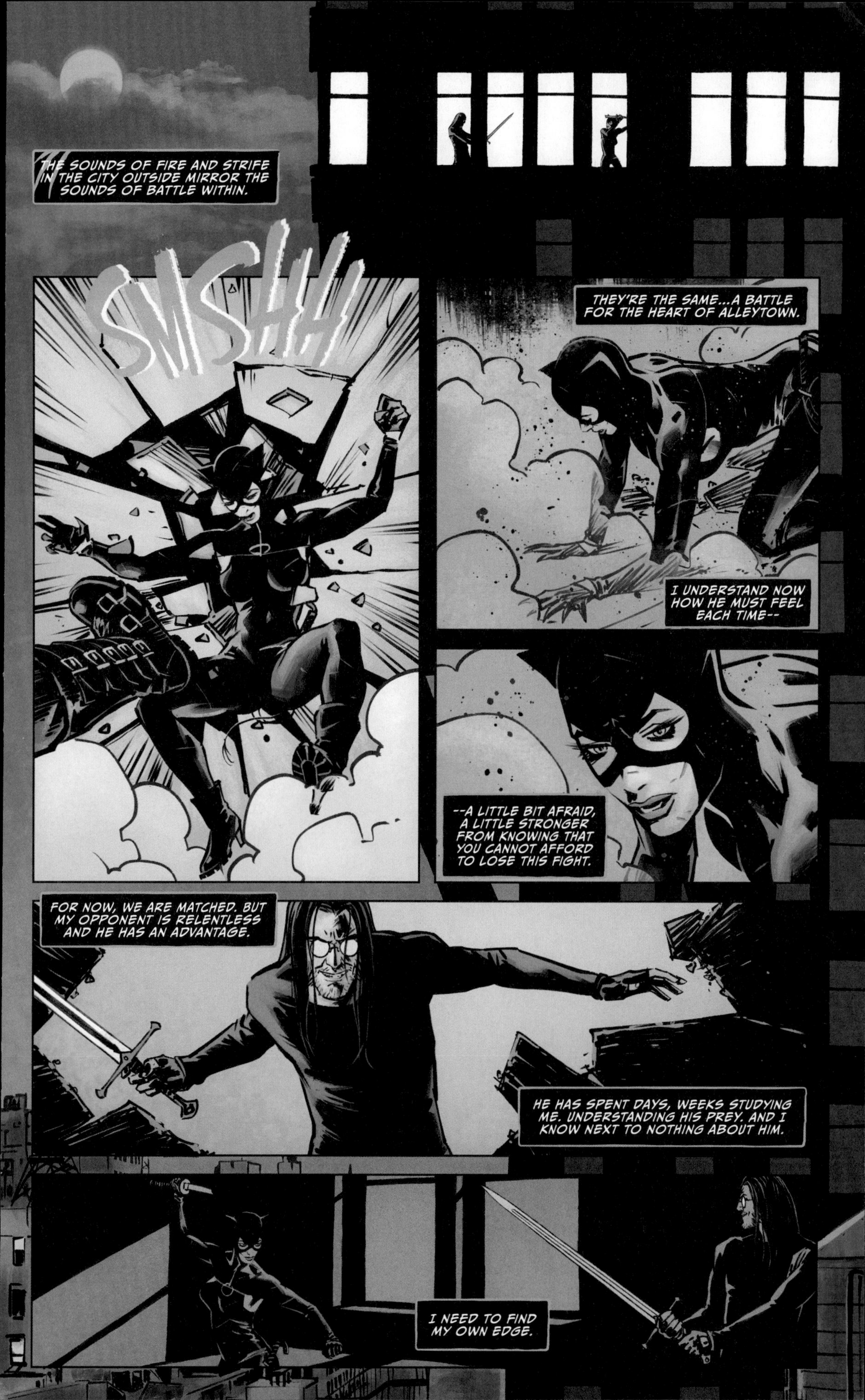
THE SOUNDS OF FIRE AND STRIFE IN THE CITY OUTSIDE MIRROR THE SOUNDS OF BATTLE WITHIN.
SMSHH
THEY'RE THE SAME...A BATTLE FOR THE HEART OF ALLEYTOWN.
I UNDERSTAND NOW HOW HE MUST FEEL EACH TIME--
--A LITTLE BIT AFRAID, A LITTLE STRONGER FROM KNOWING THAT YOU CANNOT AFFORD TO LOSE THIS FIGHT.
FOR NOW, WE ARE MATCHED. BUT MY OPPONENT IS RELENTLESS AND HE HAS AN ADVANTAGE.
HE HAS SPENT DAYS, WEEKS STUDYING ME. UNDERSTANDING HIS PREY. AND I KNOW NEXT TO NOTHING ABOUT HIM.
I NEED TO FIND MY OWN EDGE.

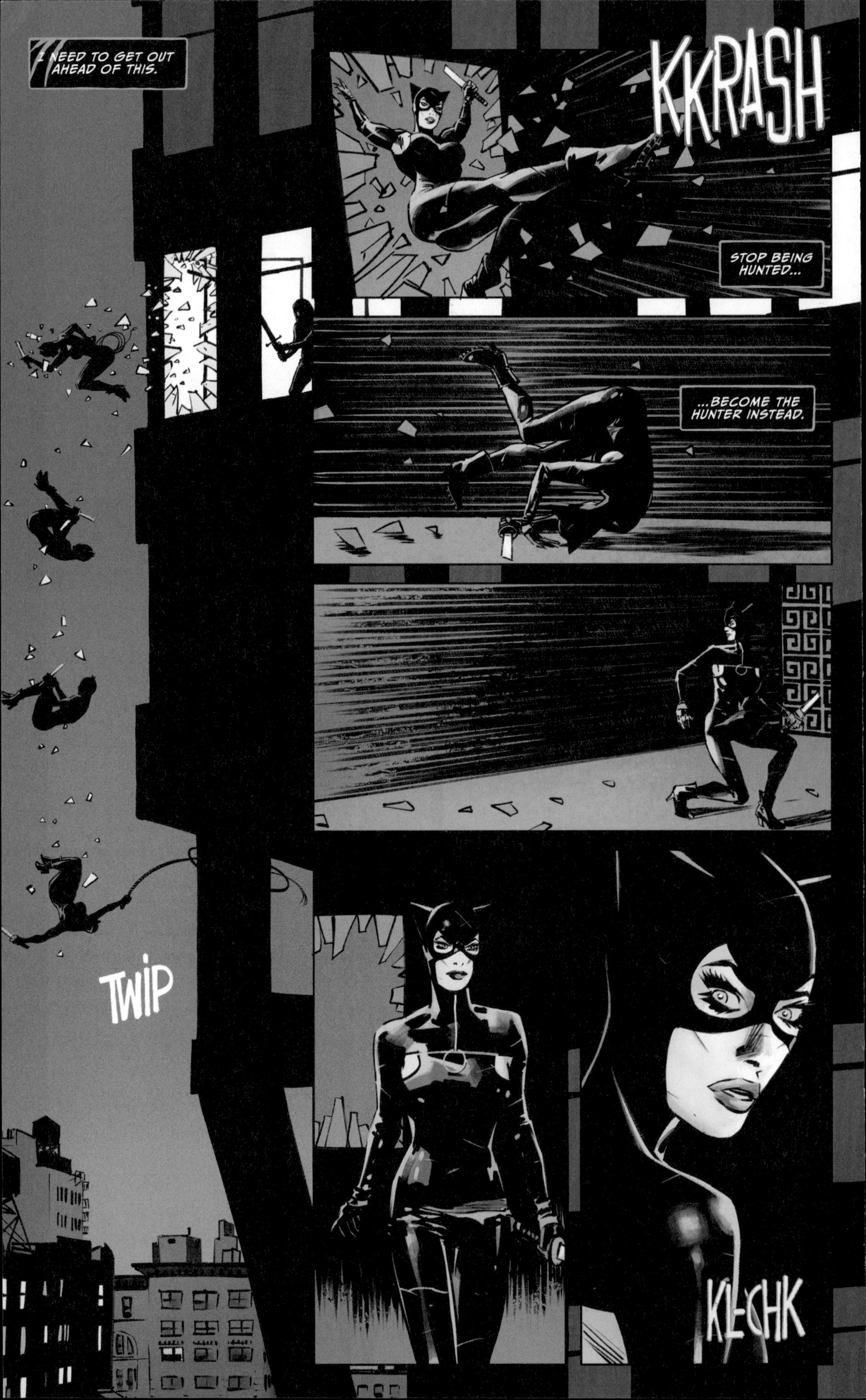
I NEED TO GET OUT AHEAD OF THIS.
KKRASH
STOP BEING HUNTED...
...BECOME THE HUNTER INSTEAD.
TWIP
KL-CHK

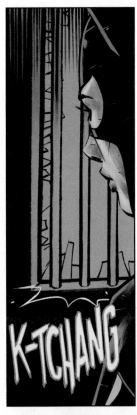

FWOSH

K-TCHANG

DO YOU SEE HOW PREDICTABLE YOU ARE, SELINA KYLE?

CATWOMAN, DARING FEMME FATALE OF THE NIGHT. QUEEN OF ALLEYTOWN.

AND YET EACH TIME YOU ARE FACED WITH ANY REAL DANGER, TRUE STRENGTH-- YOUR INSTINCT IS TO HIDE AND STEAL AND RUN INTO THE SHADOWS.

THERE ARE NO MORE SHADOWS, CATWOMAN. THERE ARE NO MORE HEISTS, NO MORE CLEVER ESCAPES.

THIS RIFLE IS AIMED AT THE BALCONY OF THE NEST WHERE DEAR SISTER MAGGIE HAS HER TEA EACH EVENING...

...ITS CROSSHAIRS PLACED DELICATELY ON HER FOREHEAD.

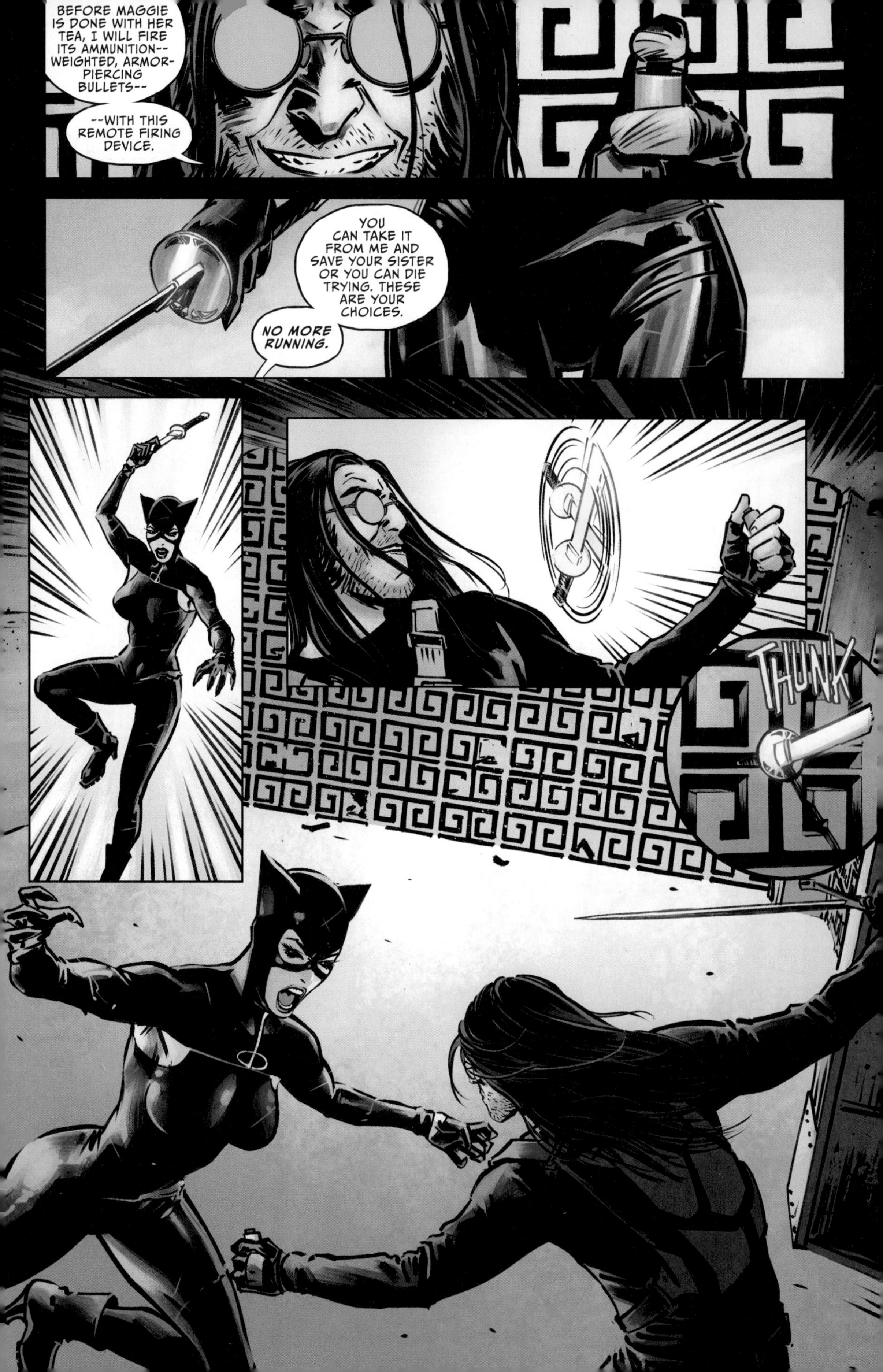
BEFORE MAGGIE IS DONE WITH HER TEA, I WILL FIRE ITS AMMUNITION--WEIGHTED, ARMOR-PIERCING BULLETS--
--WITH THIS REMOTE FIRING DEVICE.
YOU CAN TAKE IT FROM ME AND SAVE YOUR SISTER OR YOU CAN DIE TRYING. THESE ARE YOUR CHOICES.
NO MORE RUNNING.
THUNK

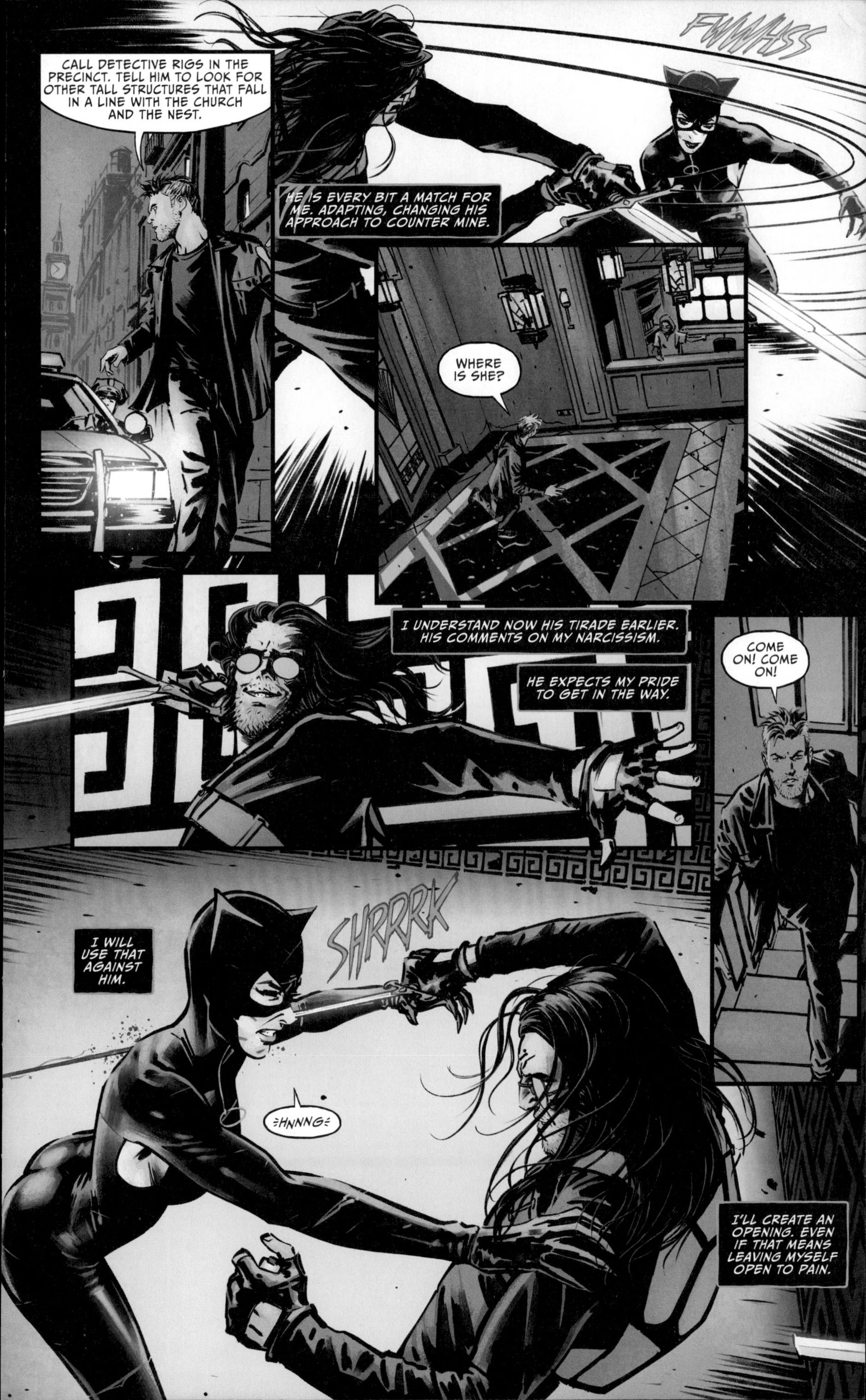
FWWHSS
CALL DETECTIVE RIGS IN THE PRECINCT. TELL HIM TO LOOK FOR OTHER TALL STRUCTURES THAT FALL IN A LINE WITH THE CHURCH AND THE NEST.
HE IS EVERY BIT A MATCH FOR ME. ADAPTING, CHANGING HIS APPROACH TO COUNTER MINE.
WHERE IS SHE?
I UNDERSTAND NOW HIS TIRADE EARLIER. HIS COMMENTS ON MY NARCISSISM.
HE EXPECTS MY PRIDE TO GET IN THE WAY.
COME ON! COME ON!
I WILL USE THAT AGAINST HIM.
SHRRRK
HNNNG
I'LL CREATE AN OPENING. EVEN IF THAT MEANS LEAVING MYSELF OPEN TO PAIN.

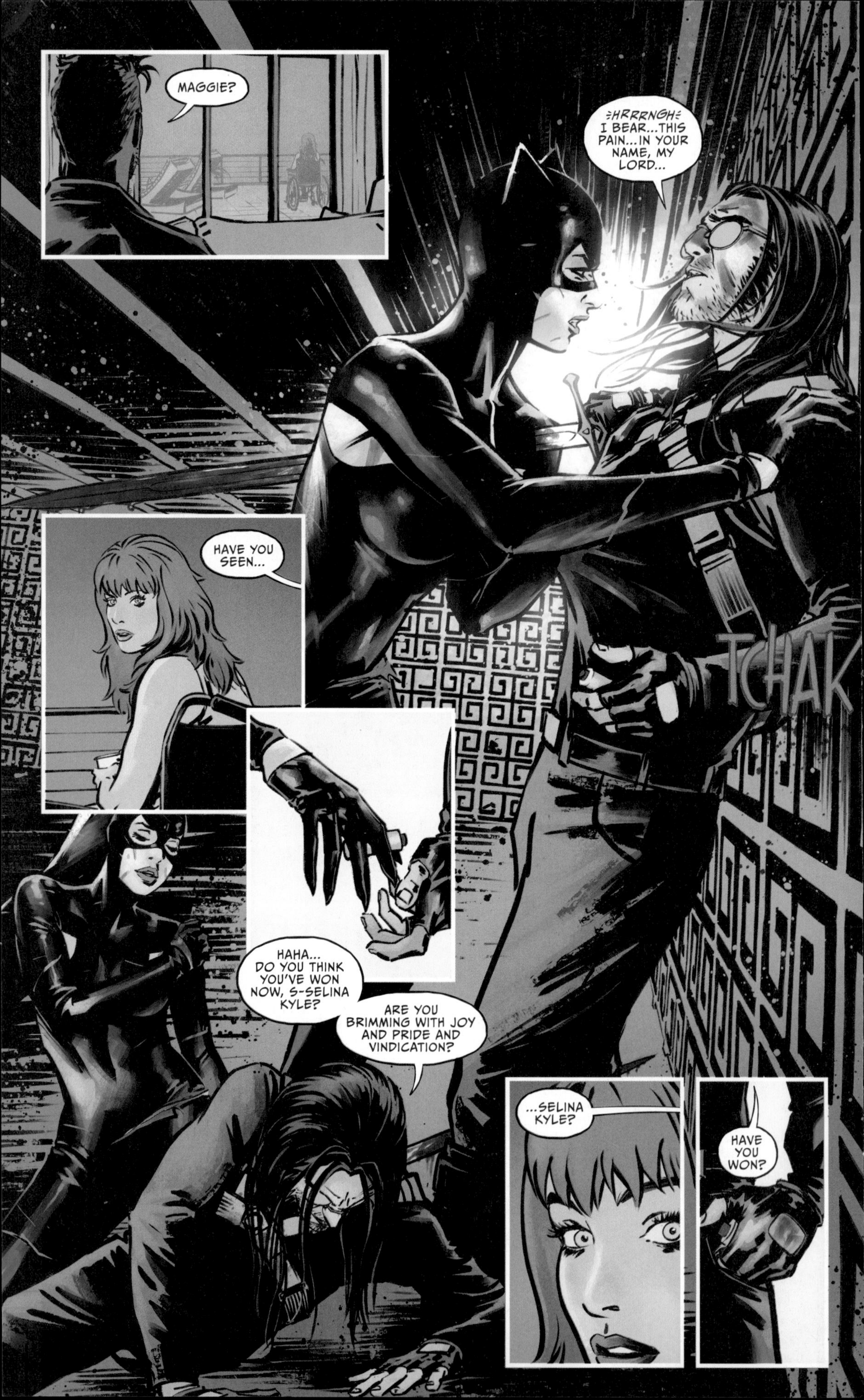
MAGGIE?
HRRRNGH I BEAR...THIS PAIN...IN YOUR NAME, MY LORD...
HAVE YOU SEEN...
TCHAK
HAHA... DO YOU THINK YOU'VE WON NOW, S-SELINA KYLE?
ARE YOU BRIMMING WITH JOY AND PRIDE AND VINDICATION?
...SELINA KYLE?
HAVE YOU WON?

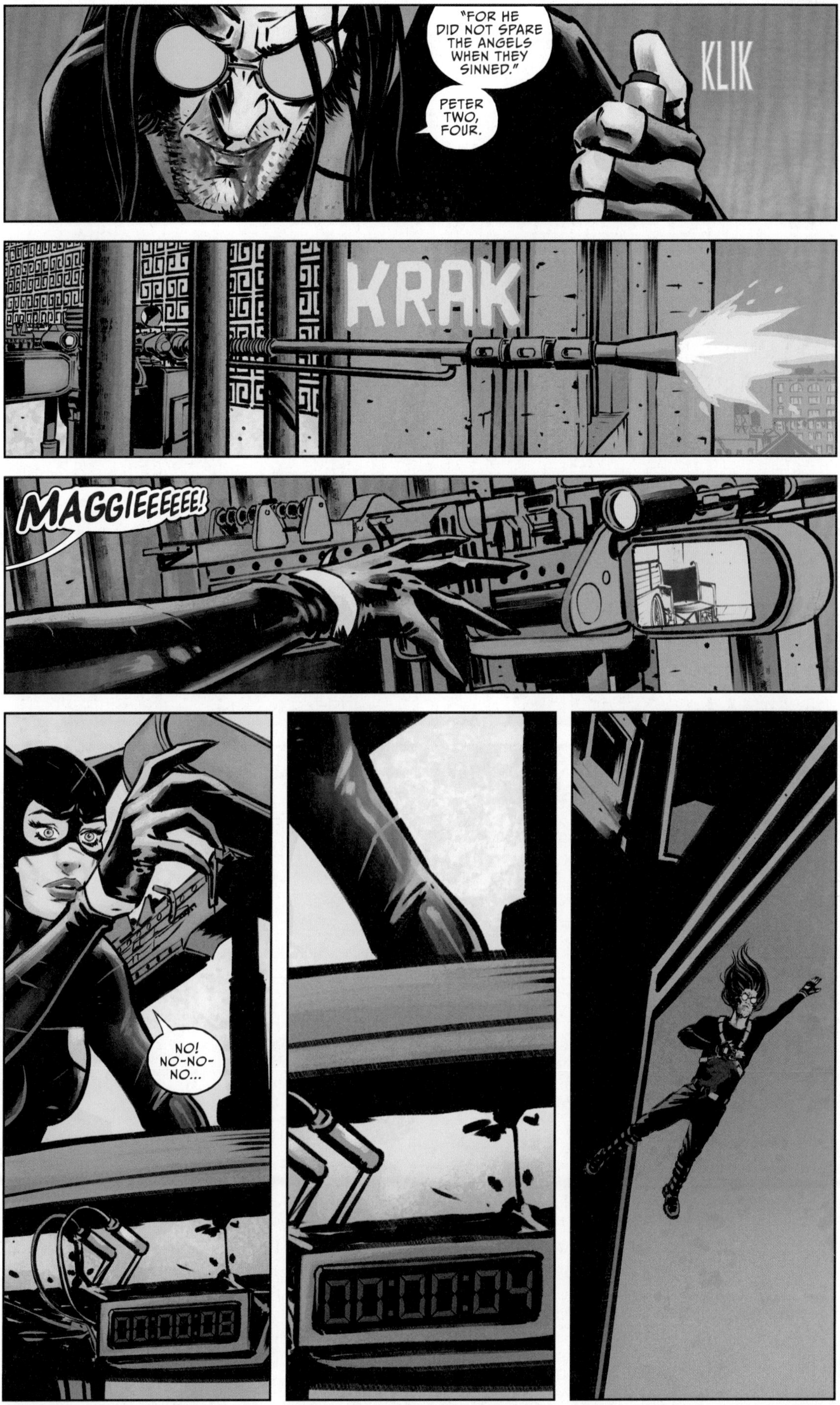
"FOR HE DID NOT SPARE THE ANGELS WHEN THEY SINNED."
PETER TWO, FOUR.
KLIK
KRAK
MAGGIEEEEEE!
NO! NO-NO-NO...
00:00:08
00:00:04

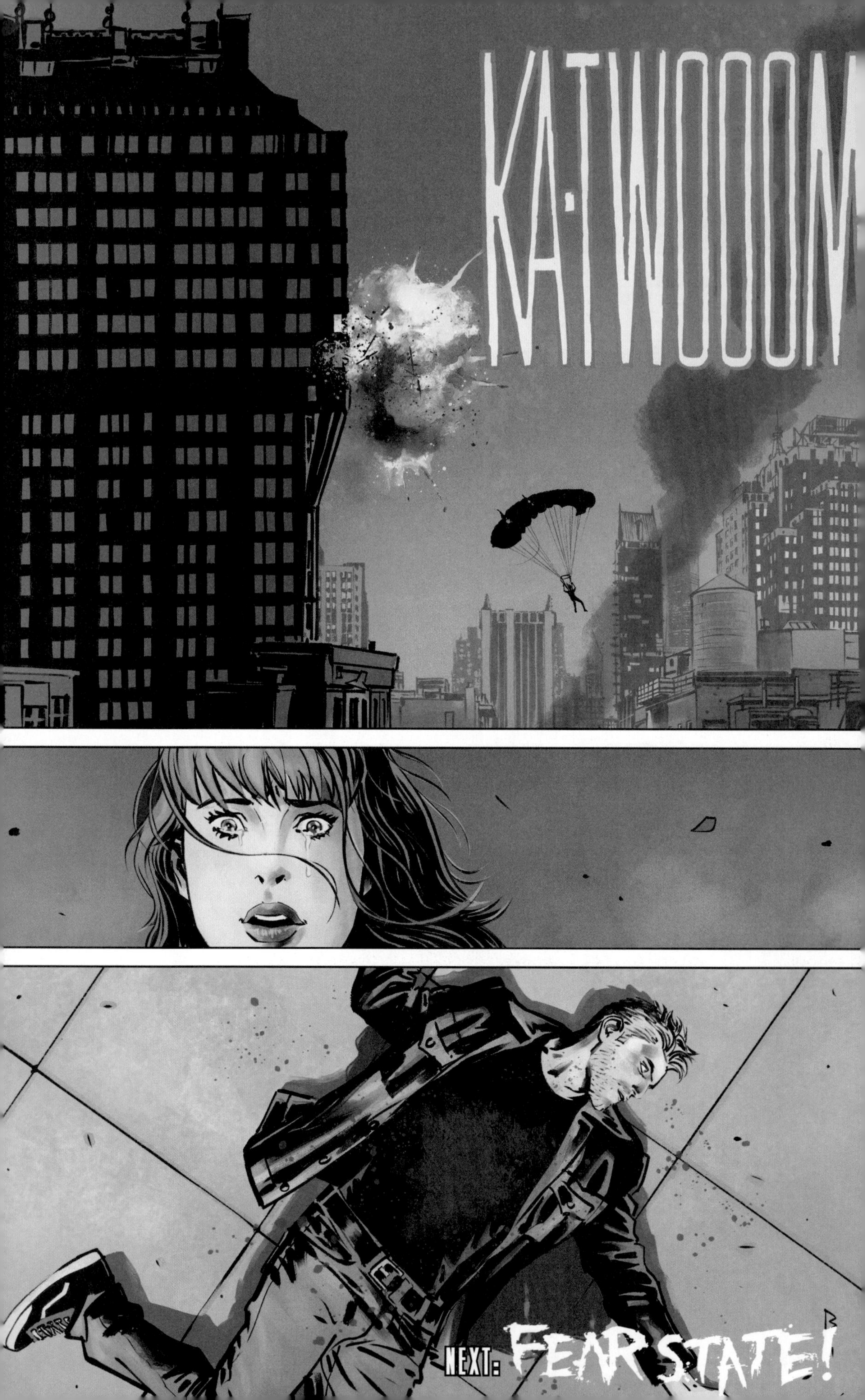
KA-TWOOOM
NEXT: FEAR STATE!

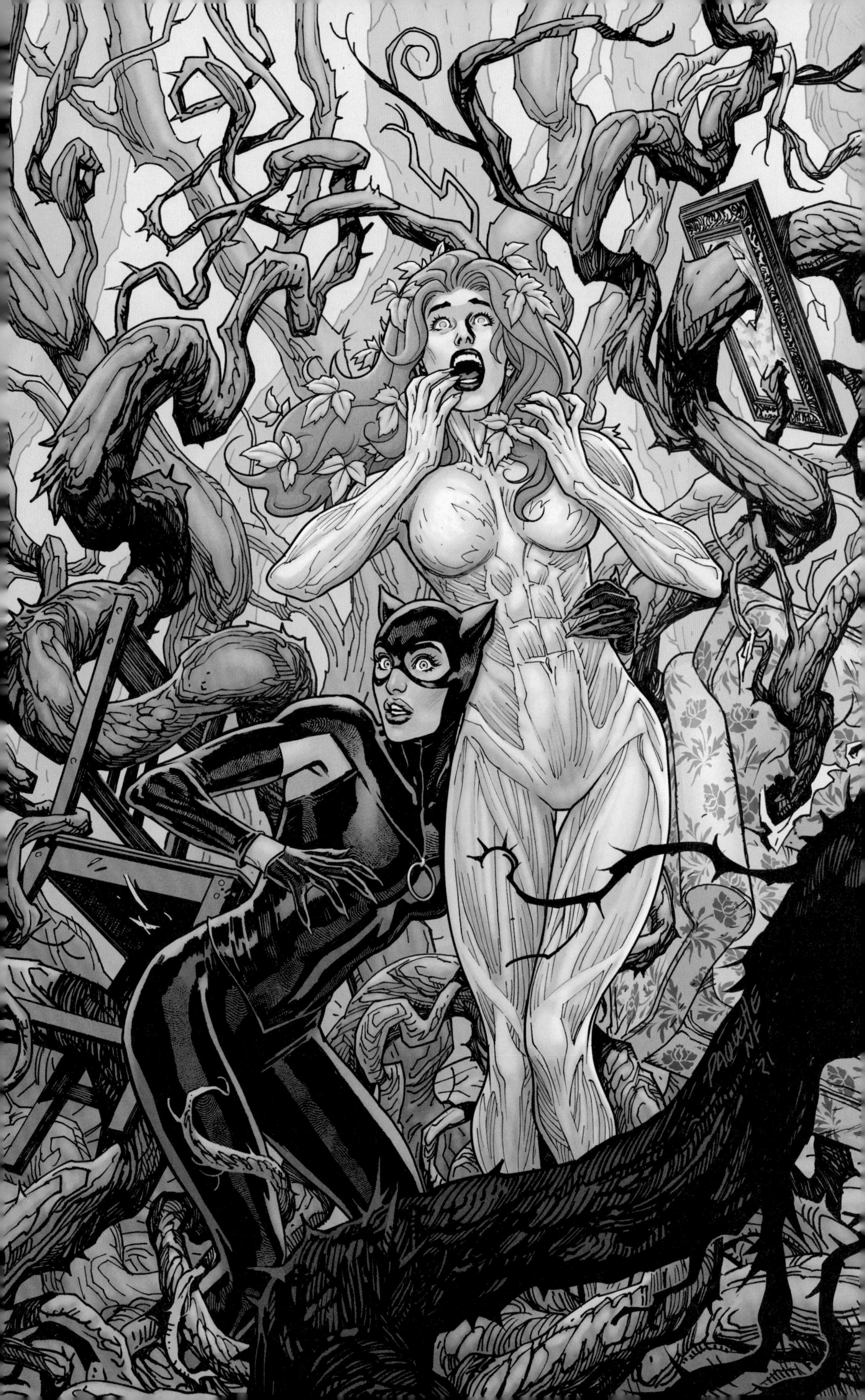

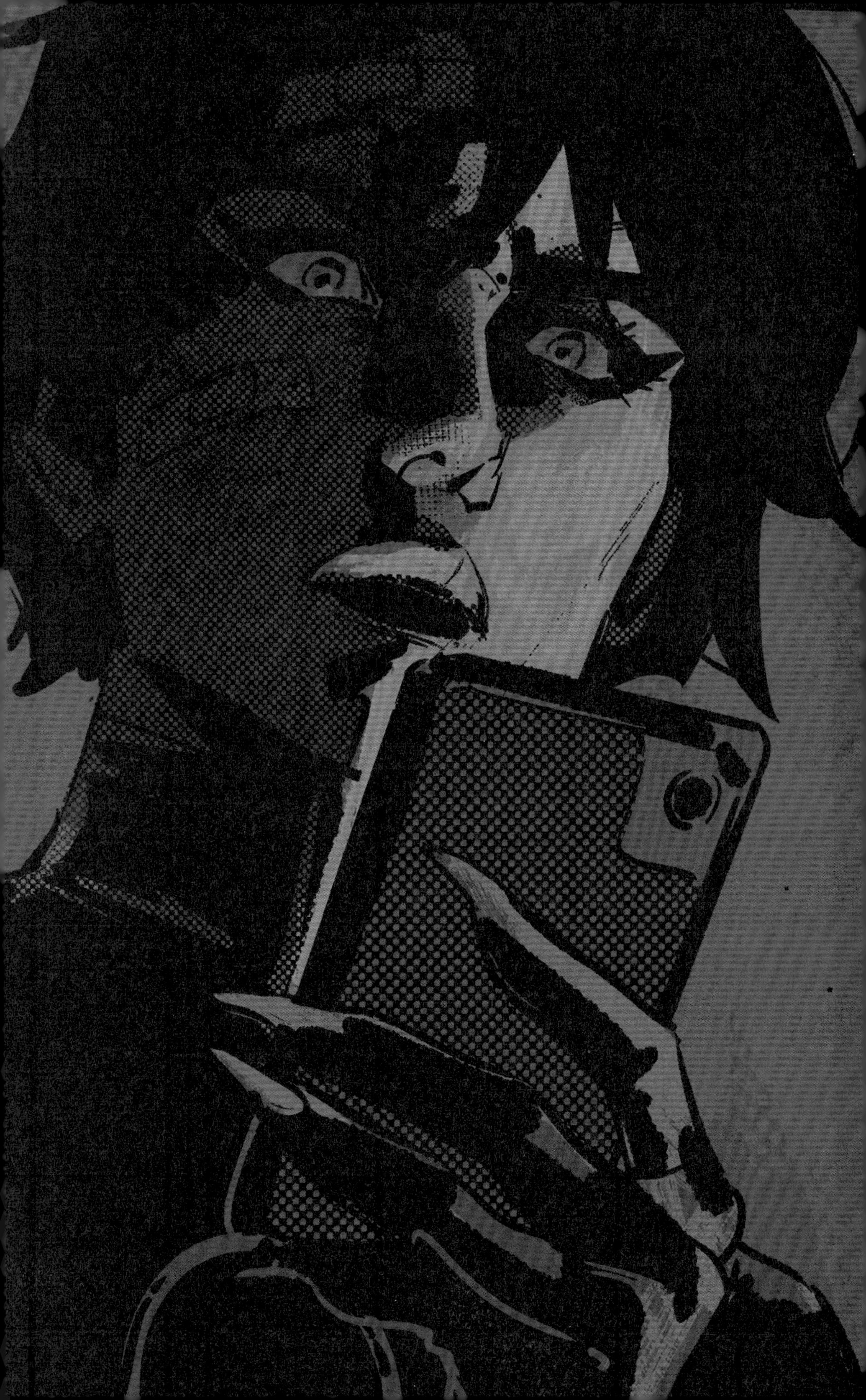

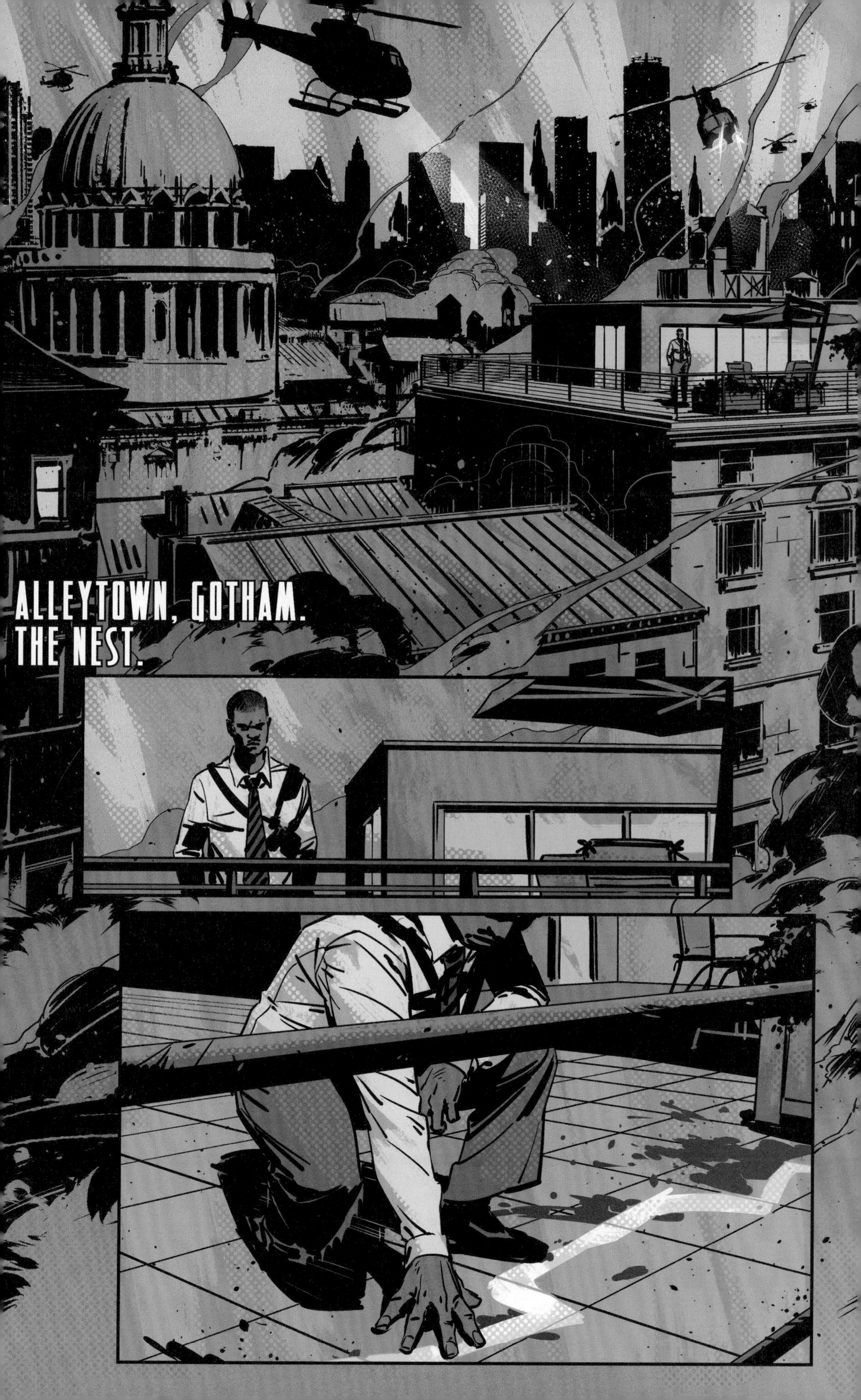
ALLEYTOWN, GOTHAM.
THE NEST.

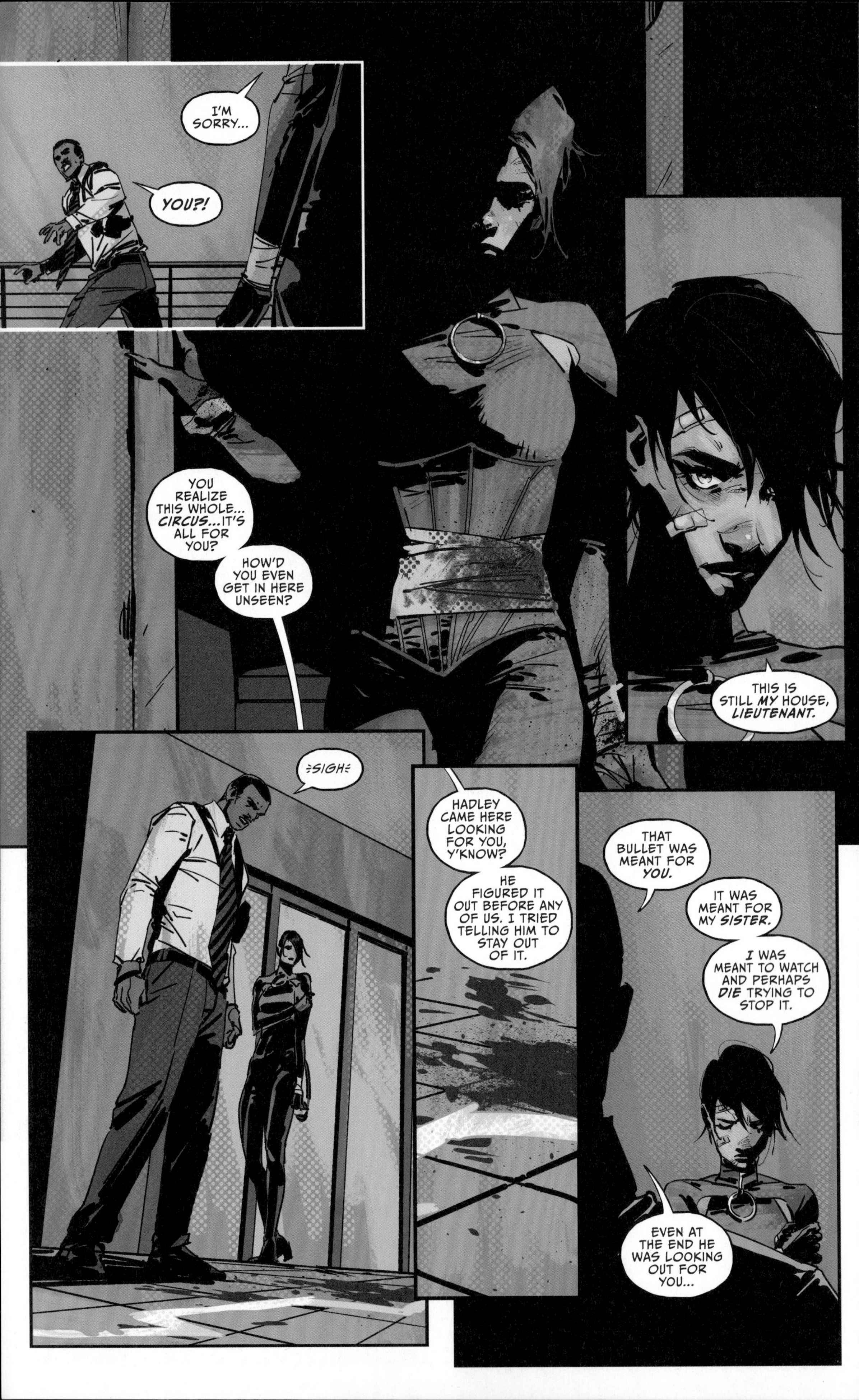
I'M SORRY...
YOU?!
THIS IS STILL MY HOUSE, LIEUTENANT.
YOU REALIZE THIS WHOLE... CIRCUS...IT'S ALL FOR YOU?
HOW'D YOU EVEN GET IN HERE UNSEEN?
SIGH
HADLEY CAME HERE LOOKING FOR YOU, Y'KNOW?
HE FIGURED IT OUT BEFORE ANY OF US. I TRIED TELLING HIM TO STAY OUT OF IT.
THAT BULLET WAS MEANT FOR YOU.
IT WAS MEANT FOR MY SISTER.
I WAS MEANT TO WATCH AND PERHAPS DIE TRYING TO STOP IT.
EVEN AT THE END HE WAS LOOKING OUT FOR YOU...

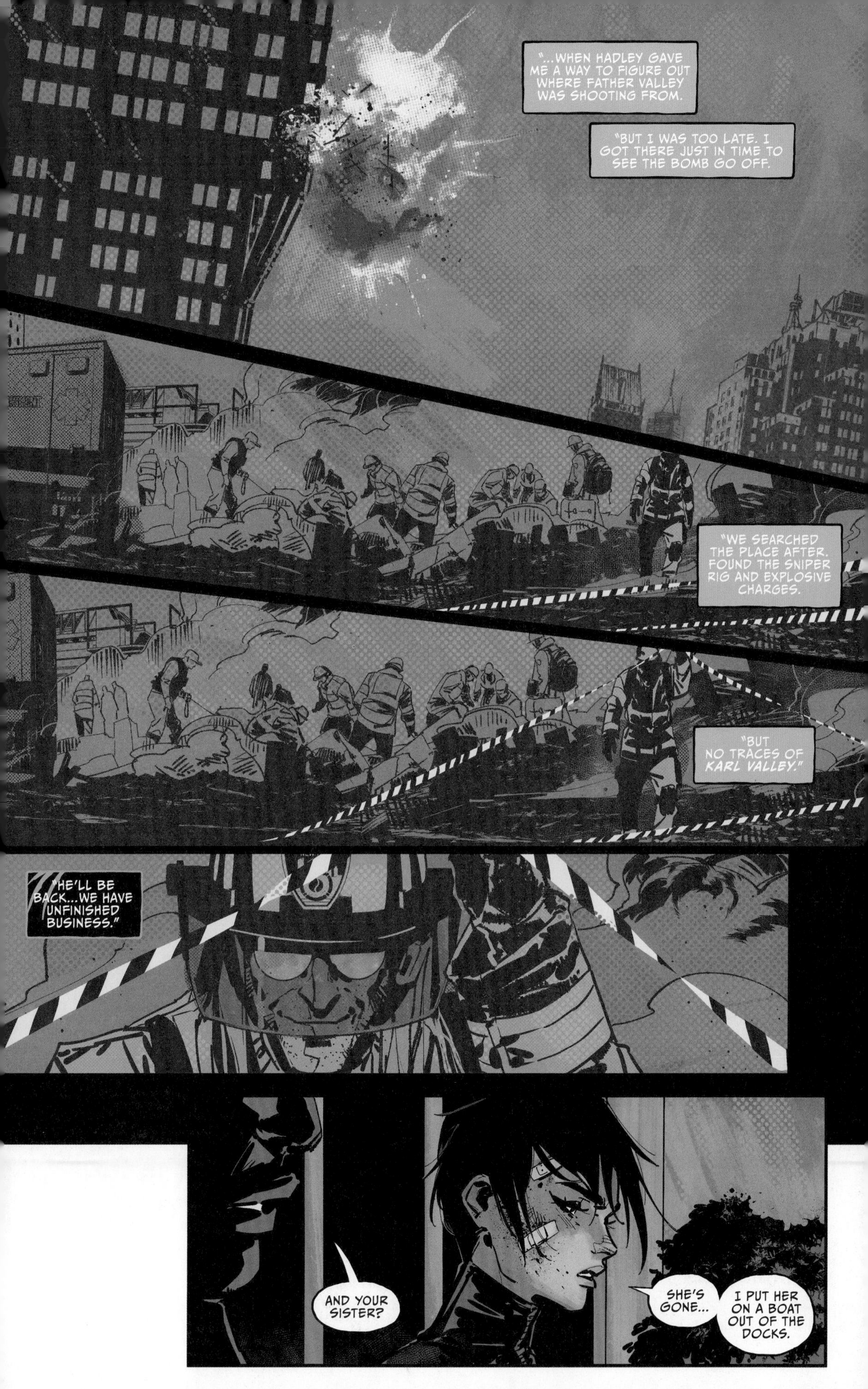
"...WHEN HADLEY GAVE ME A WAY TO FIGURE OUT WHERE FATHER VALLEY WAS SHOOTING FROM.
"BUT I WAS TOO LATE. I GOT THERE JUST IN TIME TO SEE THE BOMB GO OFF.
"WE SEARCHED THE PLACE AFTER. FOUND THE SNIPER RIG AND EXPLOSIVE CHARGES.
"BUT NO TRACES OF *KARL VALLEY.*"
"HE'LL BE BACK...WE HAVE UNFINISHED BUSINESS."
AND YOUR SISTER?
SHE'S GONE...
I PUT HER ON A BOAT OUT OF THE DOCKS.

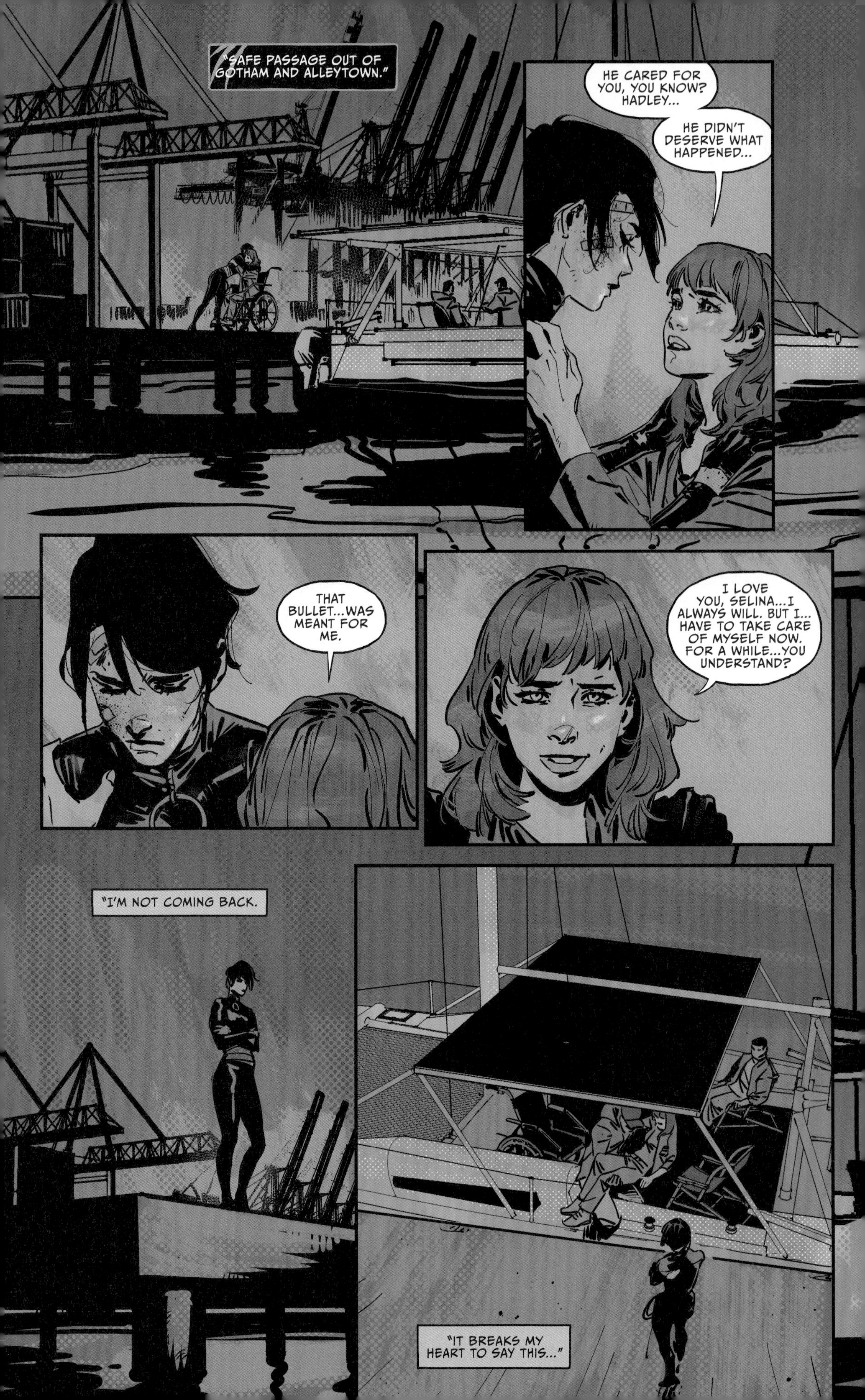
"SAFE PASSAGE OUT OF GOTHAM AND ALLEYTOWN."
HE CARED FOR YOU, YOU KNOW? HADLEY...
HE DIDN'T DESERVE WHAT HAPPENED...
THAT BULLET...WAS MEANT FOR ME.
I LOVE YOU, SELINA...I ALWAYS WILL. BUT I... HAVE TO TAKE CARE OF MYSELF NOW. FOR A WHILE...YOU UNDERSTAND?
"I'M NOT COMING BACK.
"IT BREAKS MY HEART TO SAY THIS..."

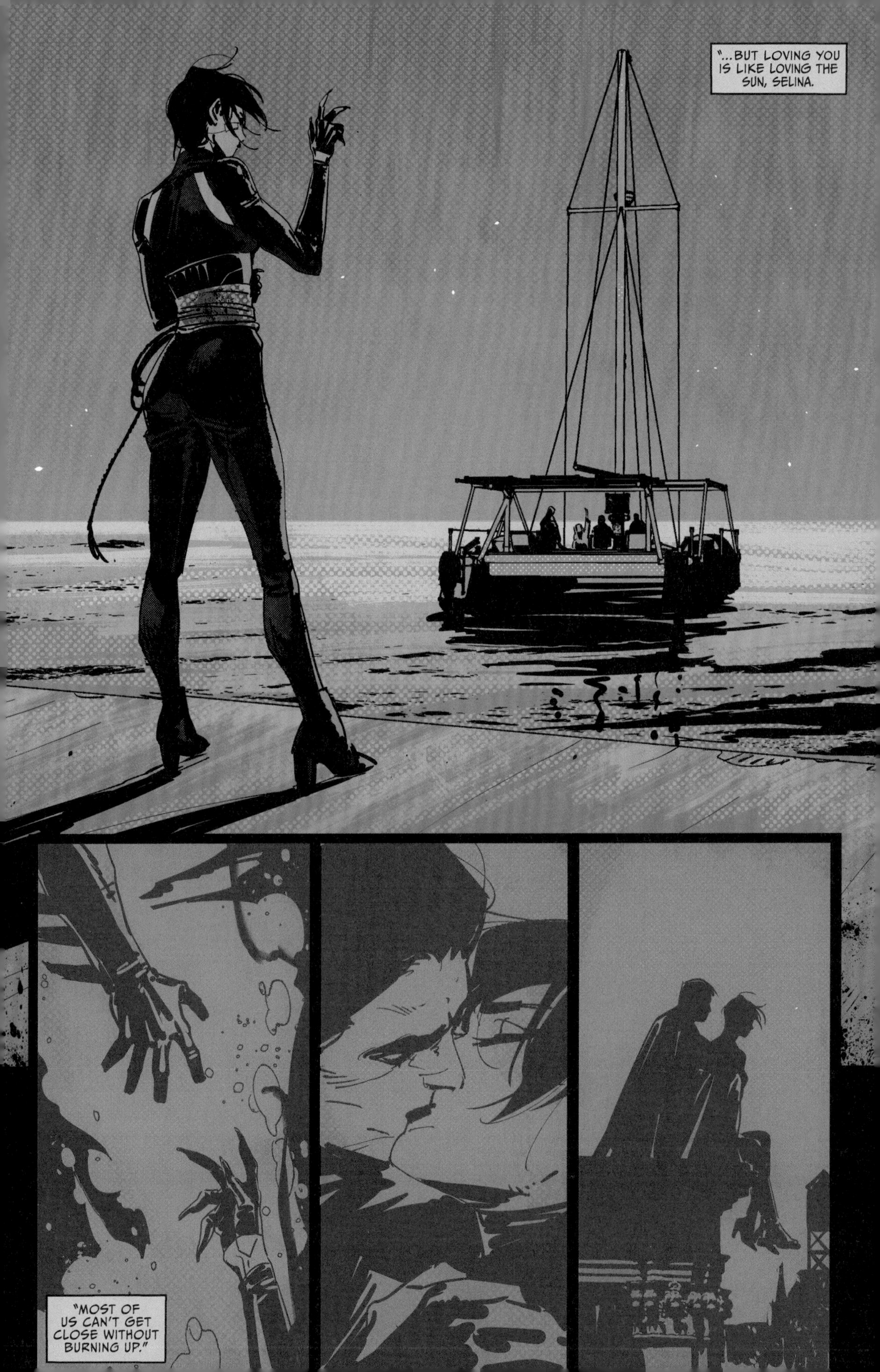
"...BUT LOVING YOU IS LIKE LOVING THE SUN, SELINA.
"MOST OF US CAN'T GET CLOSE WITHOUT BURNING UP."

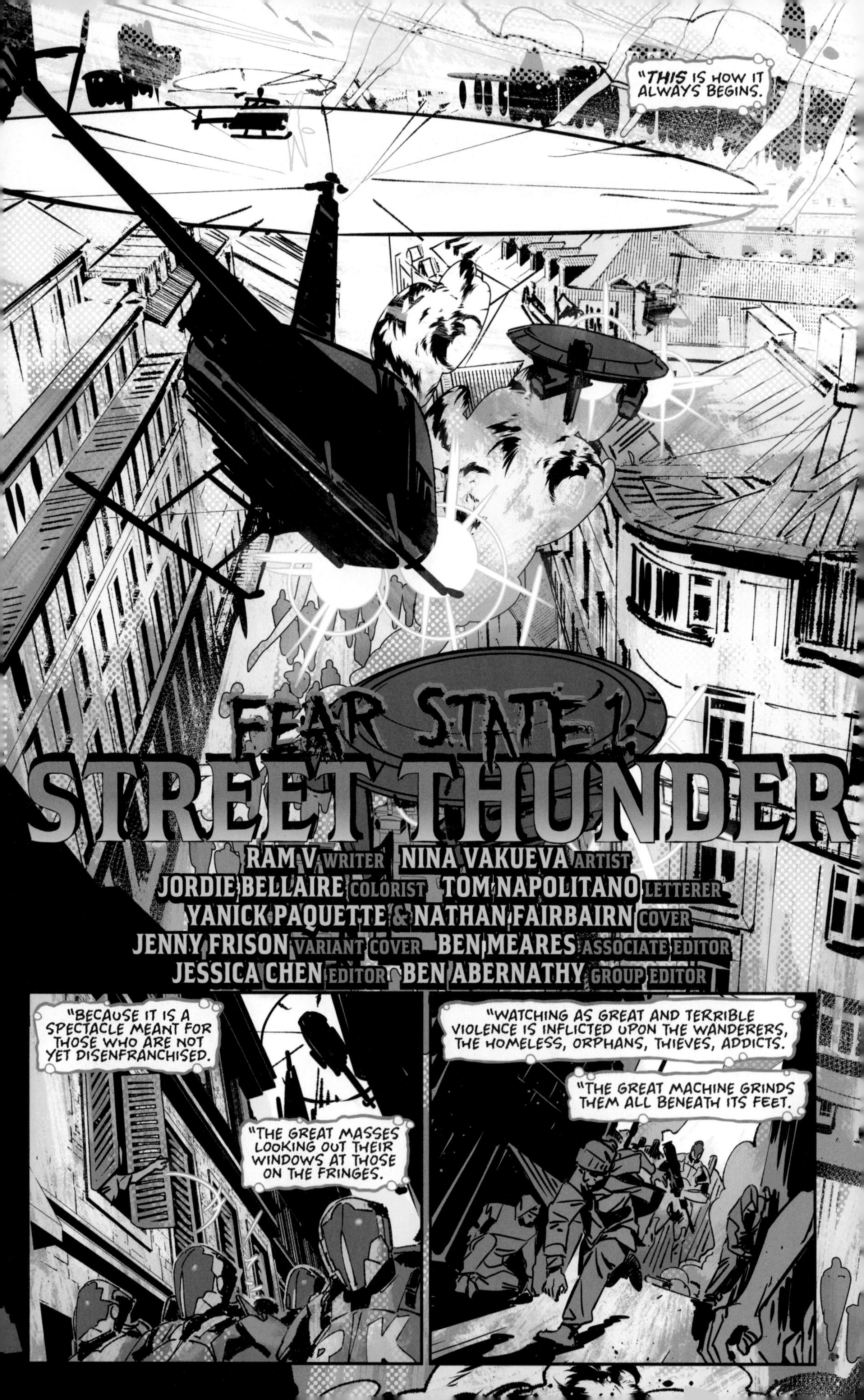
"THIS IS HOW IT ALWAYS BEGINS.
FEAR STATE 1:
STREET THUNDER
RAM V WRITER NINA VAKUEVA ARTIST
JORDIE BELLAIRE COLORIST TOM NAPOLITANO LETTERER
YANICK PAQUETTE & NATHAN FAIRBAIRN COVER
JENNY FRISON VARIANT COVER BEN MEARES ASSOCIATE EDITOR
JESSICA CHEN EDITOR BEN ABERNATHY GROUP EDITOR
"BECAUSE IT IS A SPECTACLE MEANT FOR THOSE WHO ARE NOT YET DISENFRANCHISED.
"THE GREAT MASSES LOOKING OUT THEIR WINDOWS AT THOSE ON THE FRINGES.
"WATCHING AS GREAT AND TERRIBLE VIOLENCE IS INFLICTED UPON THE WANDERERS, THE HOMELESS, ORPHANS, THIEVES, ADDICTS.
"THE GREAT MACHINE GRINDS THEM ALL BENEATH ITS FEET.

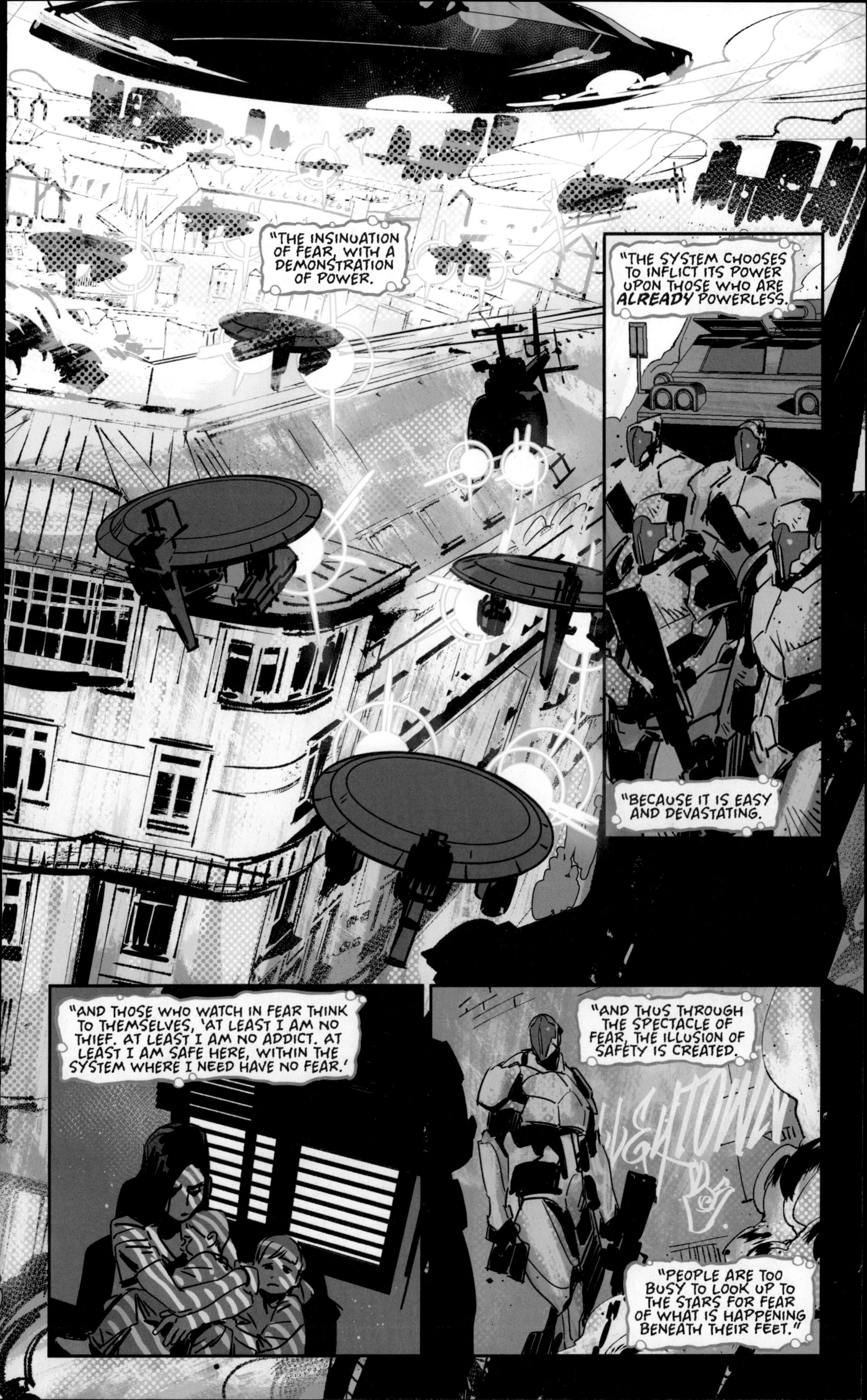
"THE INSINUATION OF FEAR, WITH A DEMONSTRATION OF POWER.
"THE SYSTEM CHOOSES TO INFLICT ITS POWER UPON THOSE WHO ARE ALREADY POWERLESS.
"BECAUSE IT IS EASY AND DEVASTATING.
"AND THOSE WHO WATCH IN FEAR THINK TO THEMSELVES, 'AT LEAST I AM NO THIEF. AT LEAST I AM NO ADDICT. AT LEAST I AM SAFE HERE, WITHIN THE SYSTEM WHERE I NEED HAVE NO FEAR.'
"AND THUS THROUGH THE SPECTACLE OF FEAR, THE ILLUSION OF SAFETY IS CREATED.
"PEOPLE ARE TOO BUSY TO LOOK UP TO THE STARS FOR FEAR OF WHAT IS HAPPENING BENEATH THEIR FEET."

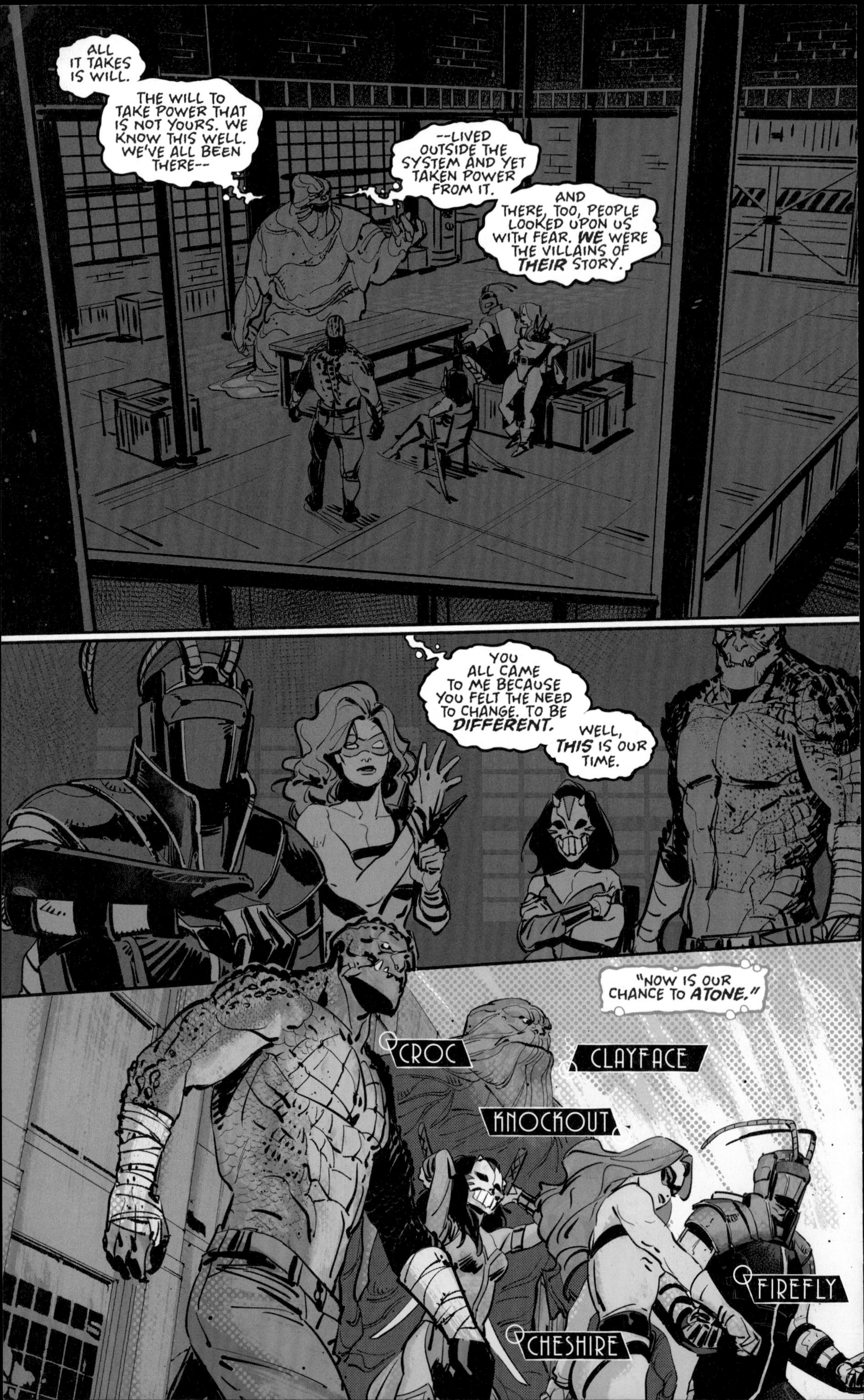
ALL IT TAKES IS WILL.
THE WILL TO TAKE POWER THAT IS NOT YOURS. WE KNOW THIS WELL. WE'VE ALL BEEN THERE--
--LIVED OUTSIDE THE SYSTEM AND YET TAKEN POWER FROM IT.
AND THERE, TOO, PEOPLE LOOKED UPON US WITH FEAR. WE WERE THE VILLAINS OF THEIR STORY.
YOU ALL CAME TO ME BECAUSE YOU FELT THE NEED TO CHANGE. TO BE DIFFERENT.
WELL, THIS IS OUR TIME.
"NOW IS OUR CHANCE TO ATONE."
CROC
CLAYFACE
KNOCKOUT
FIREFLY
CHESHIRE

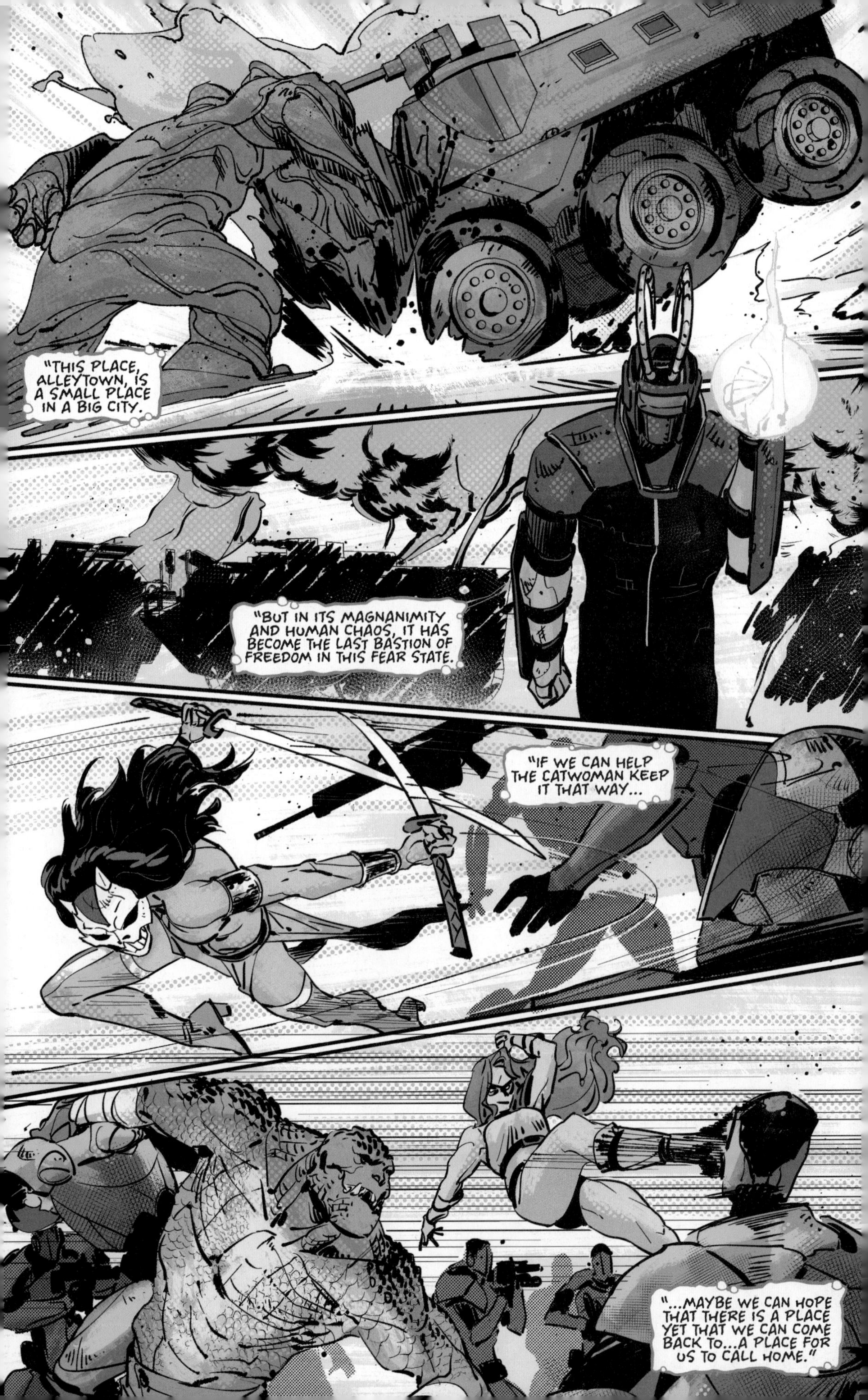
"THIS PLACE, ALLEYTOWN, IS A SMALL PLACE IN A BIG CITY.
"BUT IN ITS MAGNANIMITY AND HUMAN CHAOS, IT HAS BECOME THE LAST BASTION OF FREEDOM IN THIS FEAR STATE.
"IF WE CAN HELP THE CATWOMAN KEEP IT THAT WAY...
"...MAYBE WE CAN HOPE THAT THERE IS A PLACE YET THAT WE CAN COME BACK TO...A PLACE FOR US TO CALL HOME."

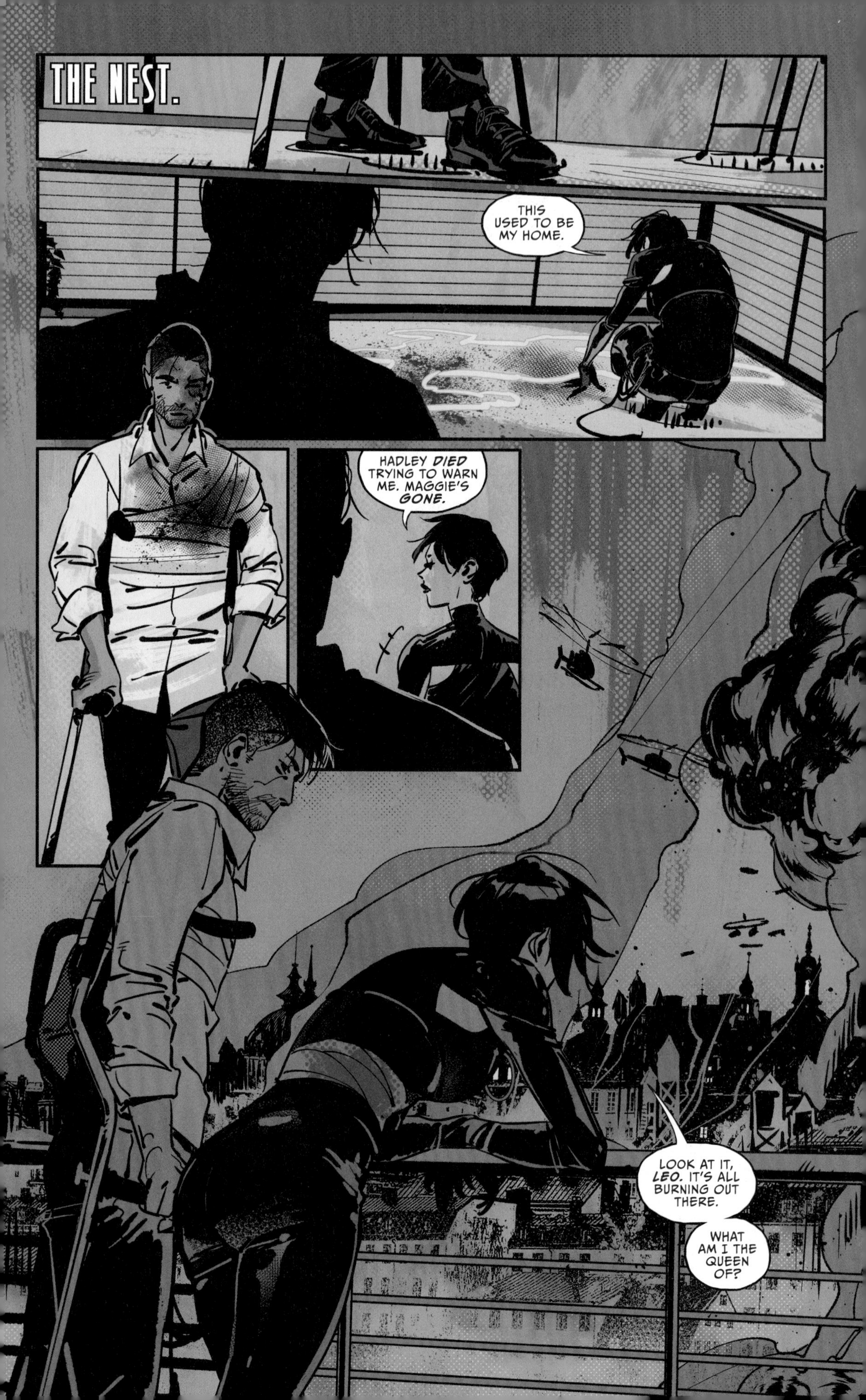
THE NEST.
THIS USED TO BE MY HOME.
HADLEY DIED TRYING TO WARN ME. MAGGIE'S GONE.
LOOK AT IT, LEO. IT'S ALL BURNING OUT THERE.
WHAT AM I THE QUEEN OF?

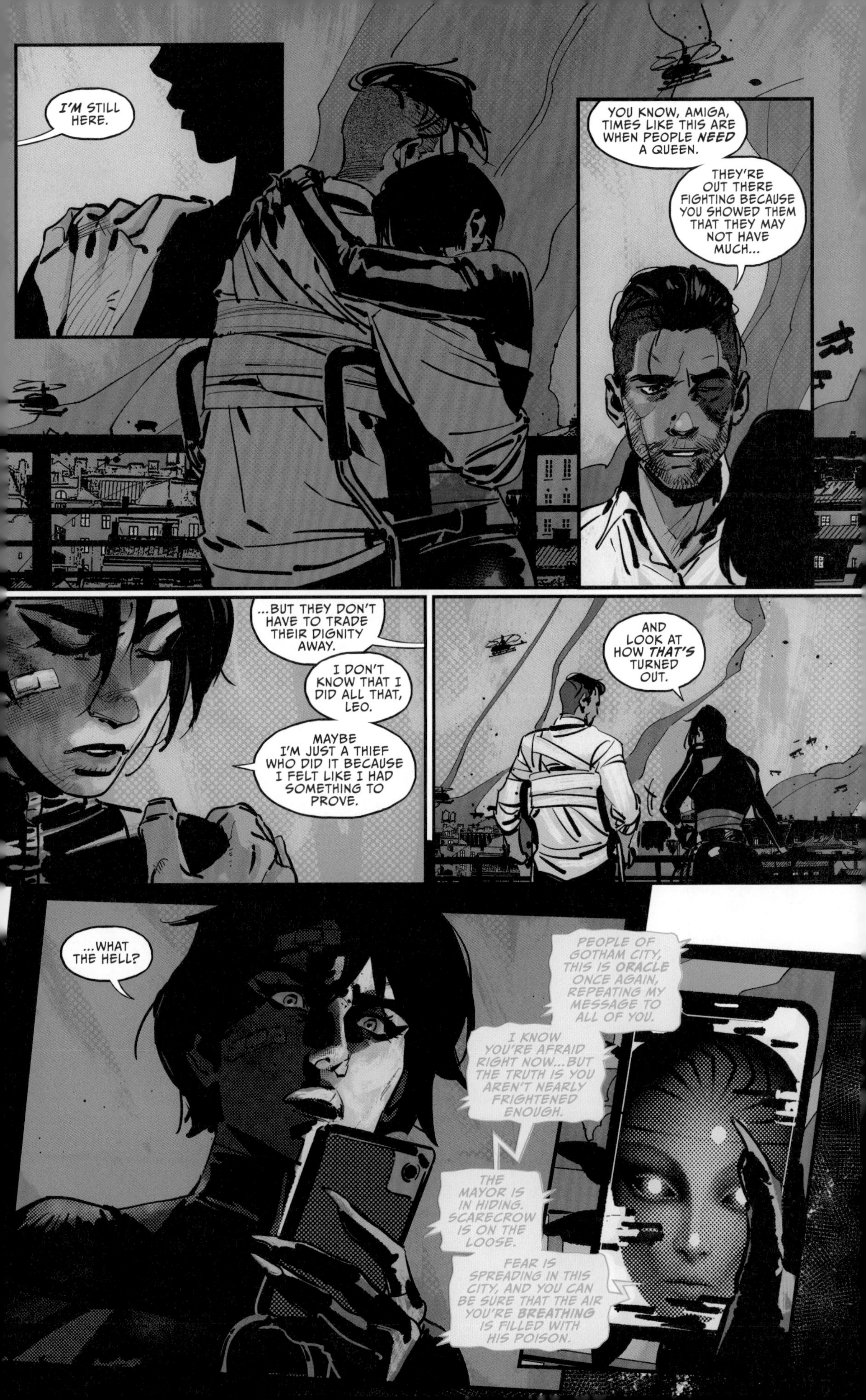
I'M STILL HERE.
YOU KNOW, AMIGA, TIMES LIKE THIS ARE WHEN PEOPLE NEED A QUEEN.
THEY'RE OUT THERE FIGHTING BECAUSE YOU SHOWED THEM THAT THEY MAY NOT HAVE MUCH...
...BUT THEY DON'T HAVE TO TRADE THEIR DIGNITY AWAY.
I DON'T KNOW THAT I DID ALL THAT, LEO.
MAYBE I'M JUST A THIEF WHO DID IT BECAUSE I FELT LIKE I HAD SOMETHING TO PROVE.
AND LOOK AT HOW THAT'S TURNED OUT.
...WHAT THE HELL?
PEOPLE OF GOTHAM CITY, THIS IS ORACLE ONCE AGAIN, REPEATING MY MESSAGE TO ALL OF YOU.
I KNOW YOU'RE AFRAID RIGHT NOW...BUT THE TRUTH IS YOU AREN'T NEARLY FRIGHTENED ENOUGH.
THE MAYOR IS IN HIDING. SCARECROW IS ON THE LOOSE.
FEAR IS SPREADING IN THIS CITY, AND YOU CAN BE SURE THAT THE AIR YOU'RE BREATHING IS FILLED WITH HIS POISON.

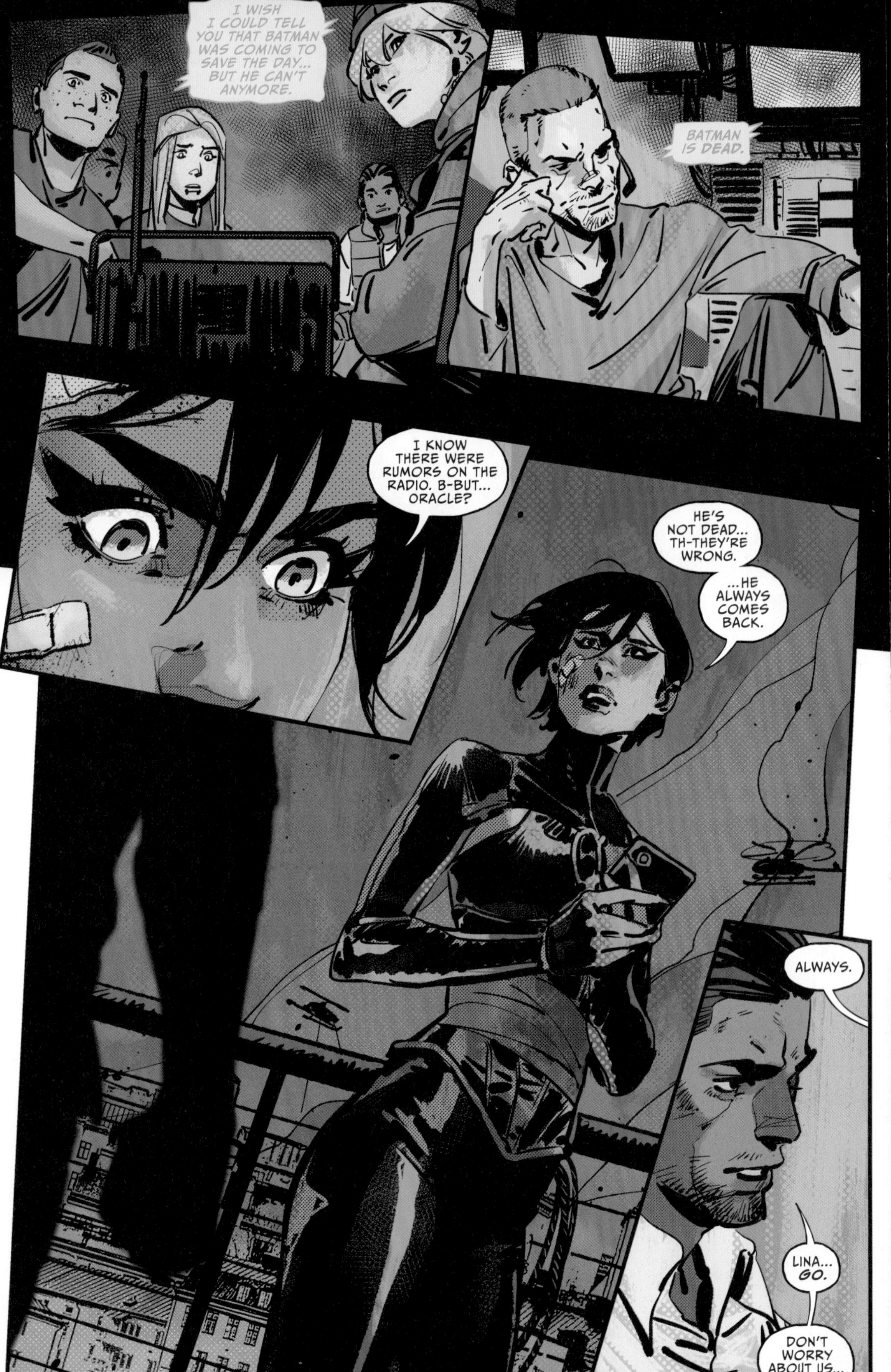
I WISH I COULD TELL YOU THAT BATMAN WAS COMING TO SAVE THE DAY... BUT HE CAN'T ANYMORE.
BATMAN IS DEAD.
I KNOW THERE WERE RUMORS ON THE RADIO. B-BUT... ORACLE?
HE'S NOT DEAD... TH-THEY'RE WRONG.
...HE ALWAYS COMES BACK.
ALWAYS.
LINA... GO.
DON'T WORRY ABOUT US... GO.

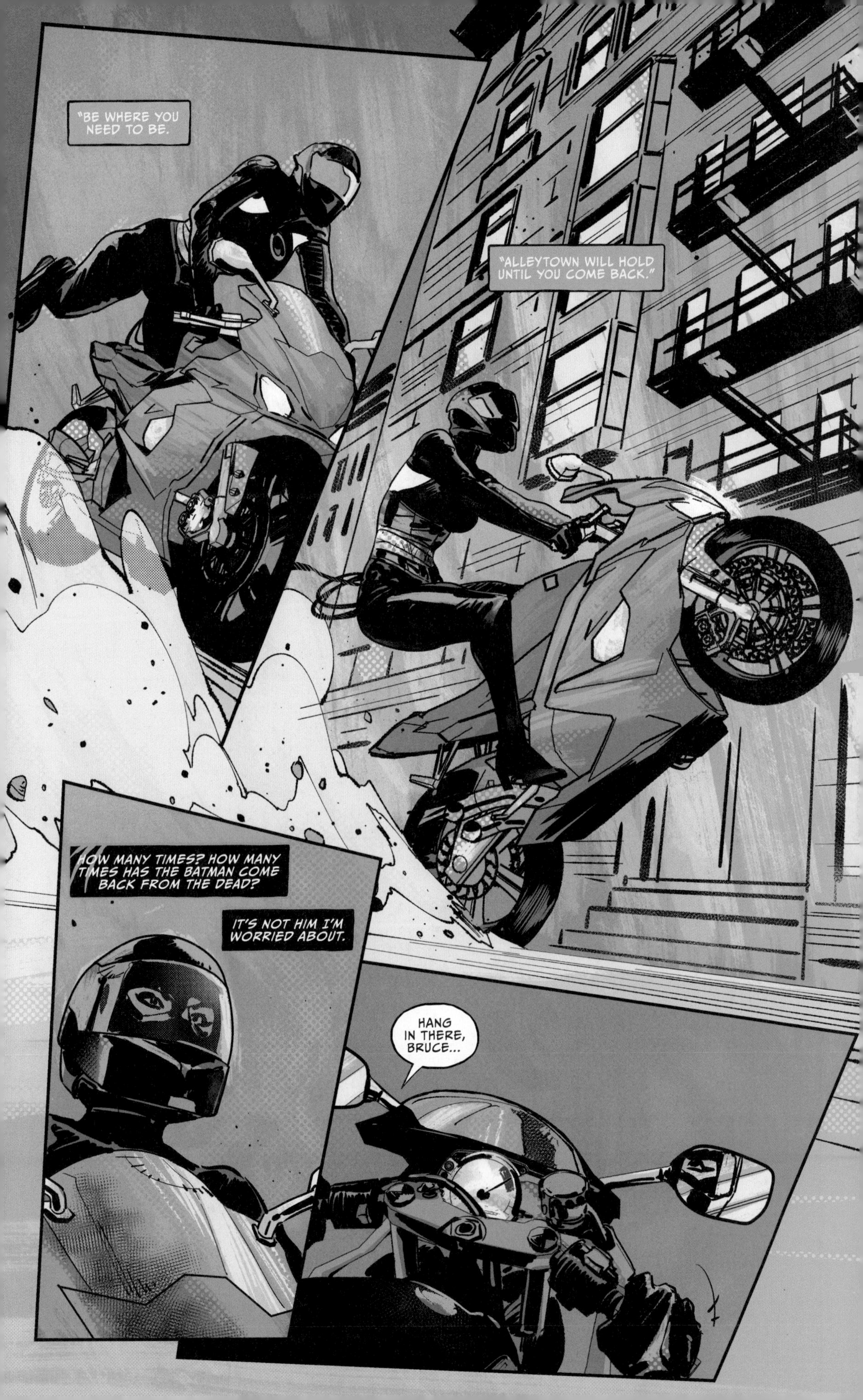
"BE WHERE YOU NEED TO BE.
"ALLEYTOWN WILL HOLD UNTIL YOU COME BACK."
HOW MANY TIMES? HOW MANY TIMES HAS THE BATMAN COME BACK FROM THE DEAD?
IT'S NOT HIM I'M WORRIED ABOUT.
HANG IN THERE, BRUCE...

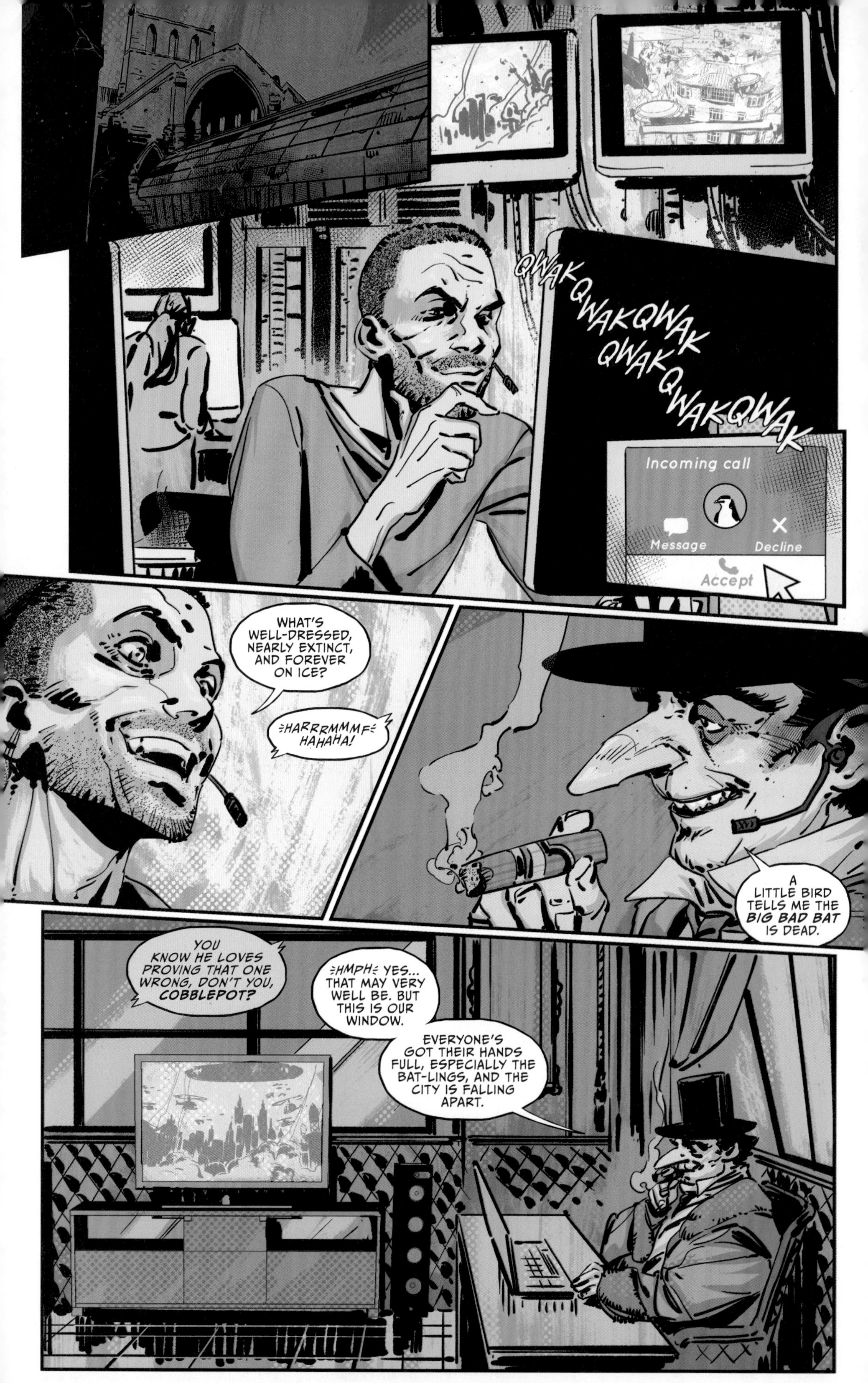
QWAKQWAKQWAK
QWAKQWAKQWAK
Incoming call
Message
Decline
Accept
WHAT'S WELL-DRESSED, NEARLY EXTINCT, AND FOREVER ON ICE?
HARRRMMMF HAHAHA!
A LITTLE BIRD TELLS ME THE BIG BAD BAT IS DEAD.
YOU KNOW HE LOVES PROVING THAT ONE WRONG, DON'T YOU, COBBLEPOT?
HMPH YES... THAT MAY VERY WELL BE. BUT THIS IS OUR WINDOW.
EVERYONE'S GOT THEIR HANDS FULL, ESPECIALLY THE BAT-LINGS, AND THE CITY IS FALLING APART.

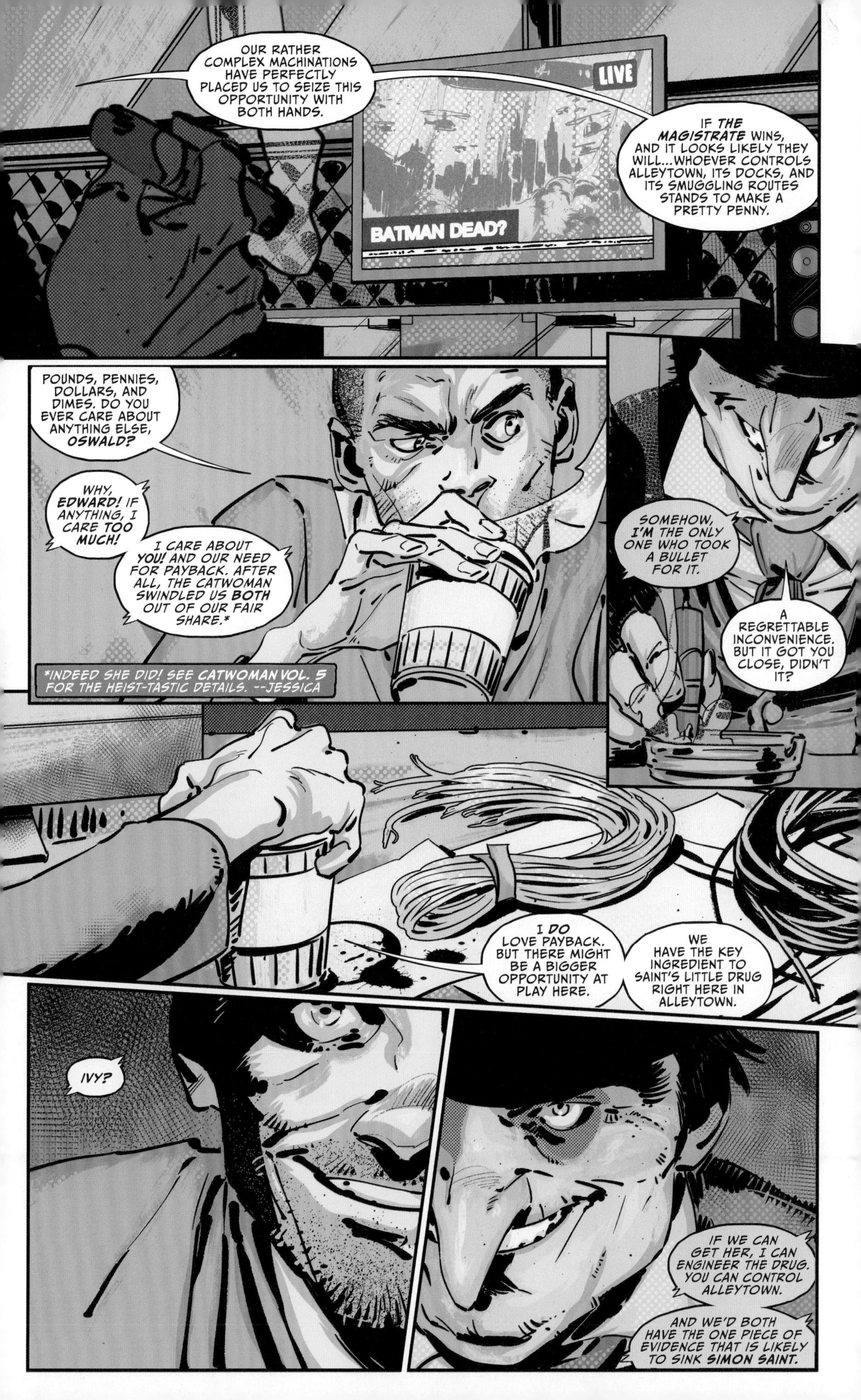
OUR RATHER COMPLEX MACHINATIONS HAVE PERFECTLY PLACED US TO SEIZE THIS OPPORTUNITY WITH BOTH HANDS.
LIVE
BATMAN DEAD?
IF THE MAGISTRATE WINS, AND IT LOOKS LIKELY THEY WILL...WHOEVER CONTROLS ALLEYTOWN, ITS DOCKS, AND ITS SMUGGLING ROUTES STANDS TO MAKE A PRETTY PENNY.
POUNDS, PENNIES, DOLLARS, AND DIMES. DO YOU EVER CARE ABOUT ANYTHING ELSE, OSWALD?
WHY, EDWARD! IF ANYTHING, I CARE TOO MUCH!
I CARE ABOUT YOU! AND OUR NEED FOR PAYBACK. AFTER ALL, THE CATWOMAN SWINDLED US BOTH OUT OF OUR FAIR SHARE.*
*INDEED SHE DID! SEE CATWOMAN VOL. 5 FOR THE HEIST-TASTIC DETAILS. --JESSICA
SOMEHOW, I'M THE ONLY ONE WHO TOOK A BULLET FOR IT.
A REGRETTABLE INCONVENIENCE. BUT IT GOT YOU CLOSE, DIDN'T IT?
I DO LOVE PAYBACK. BUT THERE MIGHT BE A BIGGER OPPORTUNITY AT PLAY HERE.
WE HAVE THE KEY INGREDIENT TO SAINT'S LITTLE DRUG RIGHT HERE IN ALLEYTOWN.
IVY?
IF WE CAN GET HER, I CAN ENGINEER THE DRUG. YOU CAN CONTROL ALLEYTOWN.
AND WE'D BOTH HAVE THE ONE PIECE OF EVIDENCE THAT IS LIKELY TO SINK SIMON SAINT.

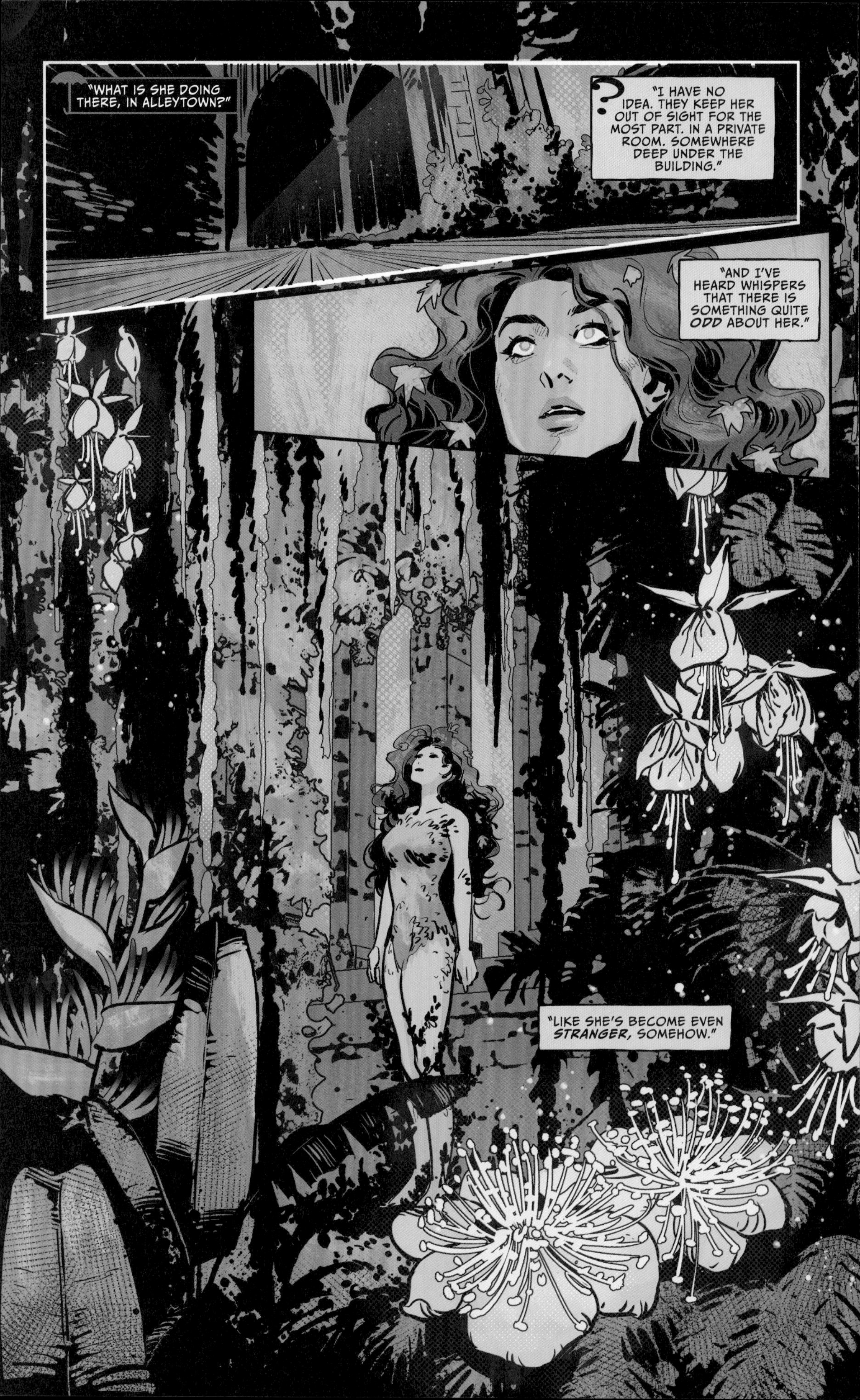
"WHAT IS SHE DOING THERE, IN ALLEYTOWN?"
"I HAVE NO IDEA. THEY KEEP HER OUT OF SIGHT FOR THE MOST PART. IN A PRIVATE ROOM. SOMEWHERE DEEP UNDER THE BUILDING."
"AND I'VE HEARD WHISPERS THAT THERE IS SOMETHING QUITE ODD ABOUT HER."
"LIKE SHE'S BECOME EVEN STRANGER, SOMEHOW."

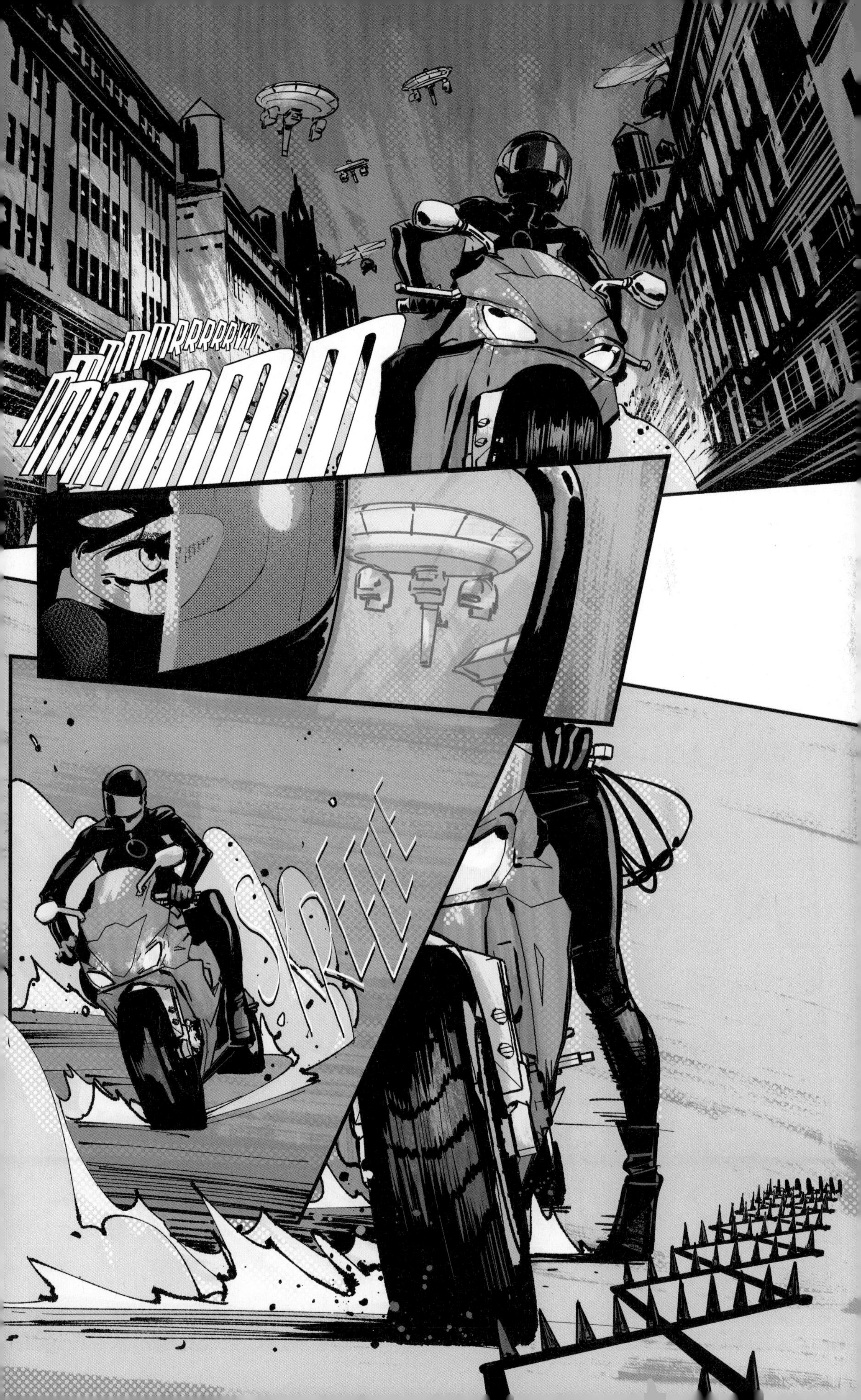
MMMMRRRRRRVV
MMMMMMM
SKREEEE

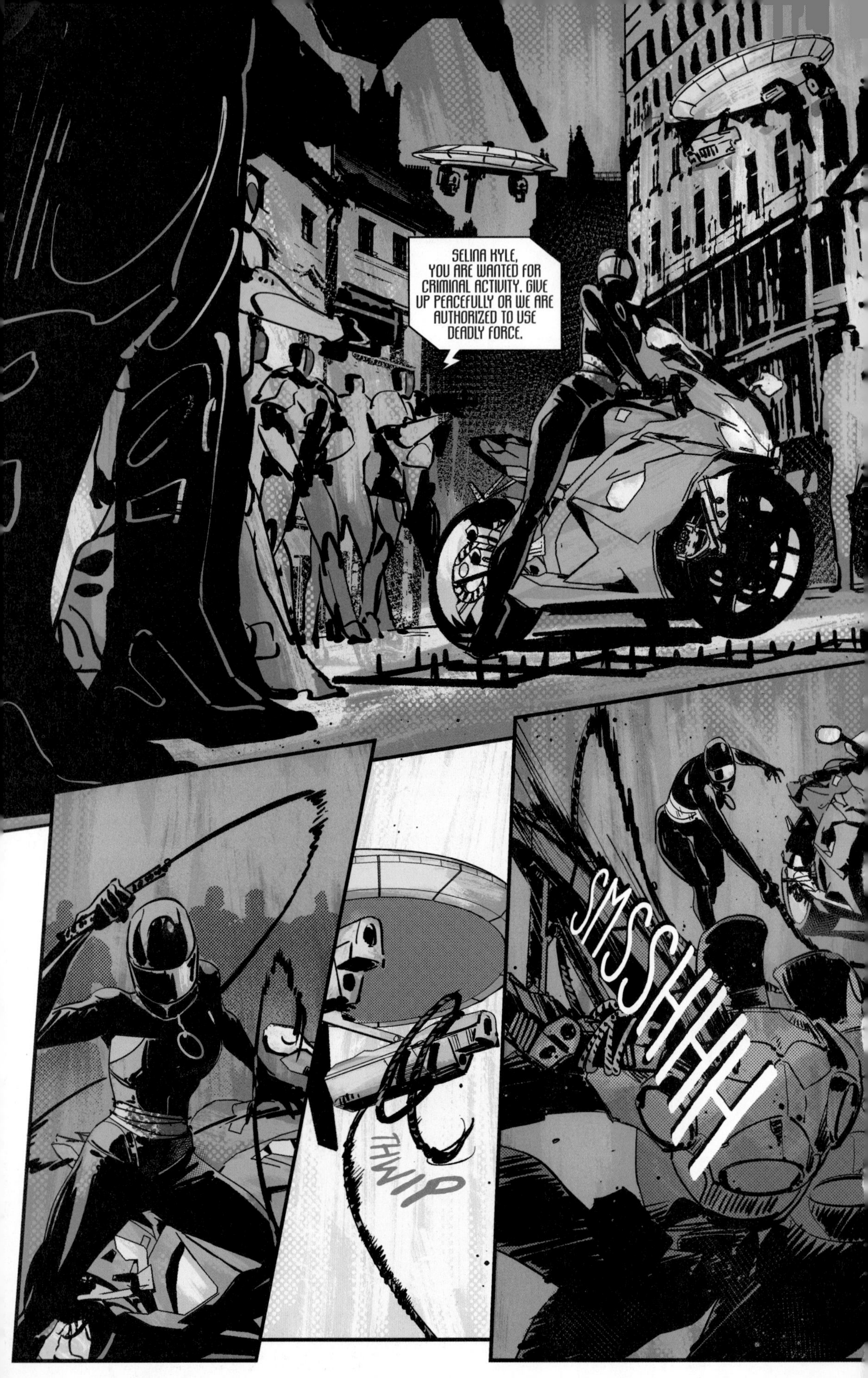
SELINA KYLE, YOU ARE WANTED FOR CRIMINAL ACTIVITY. GIVE UP PEACEFULLY OR WE ARE AUTHORIZED TO USE DEADLY FORCE.
THWIP
SMSSHHHH

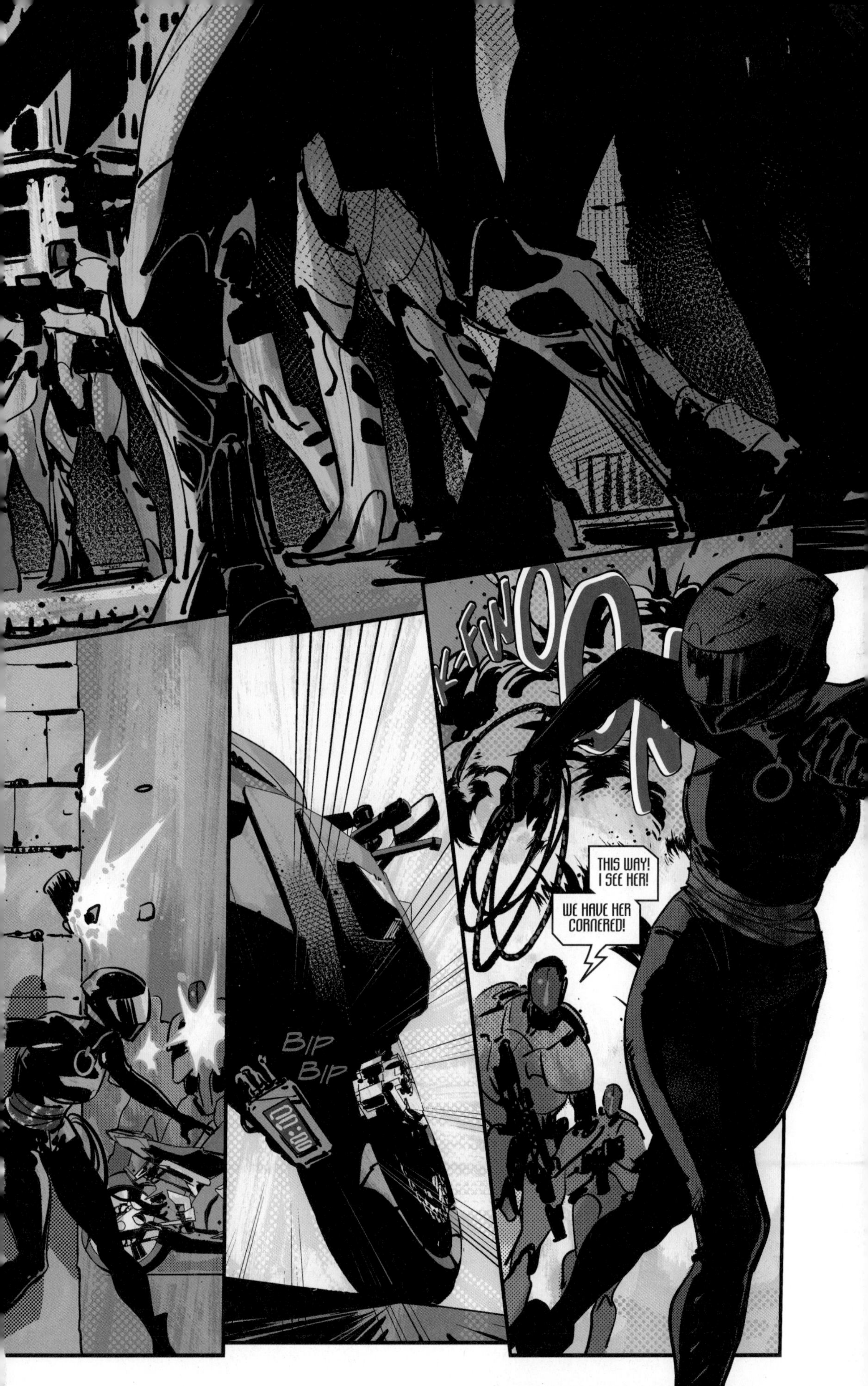
BIP
BIP
K-FWOO
THIS WAY! I SEE HER!
WE HAVE HER CORNERED!

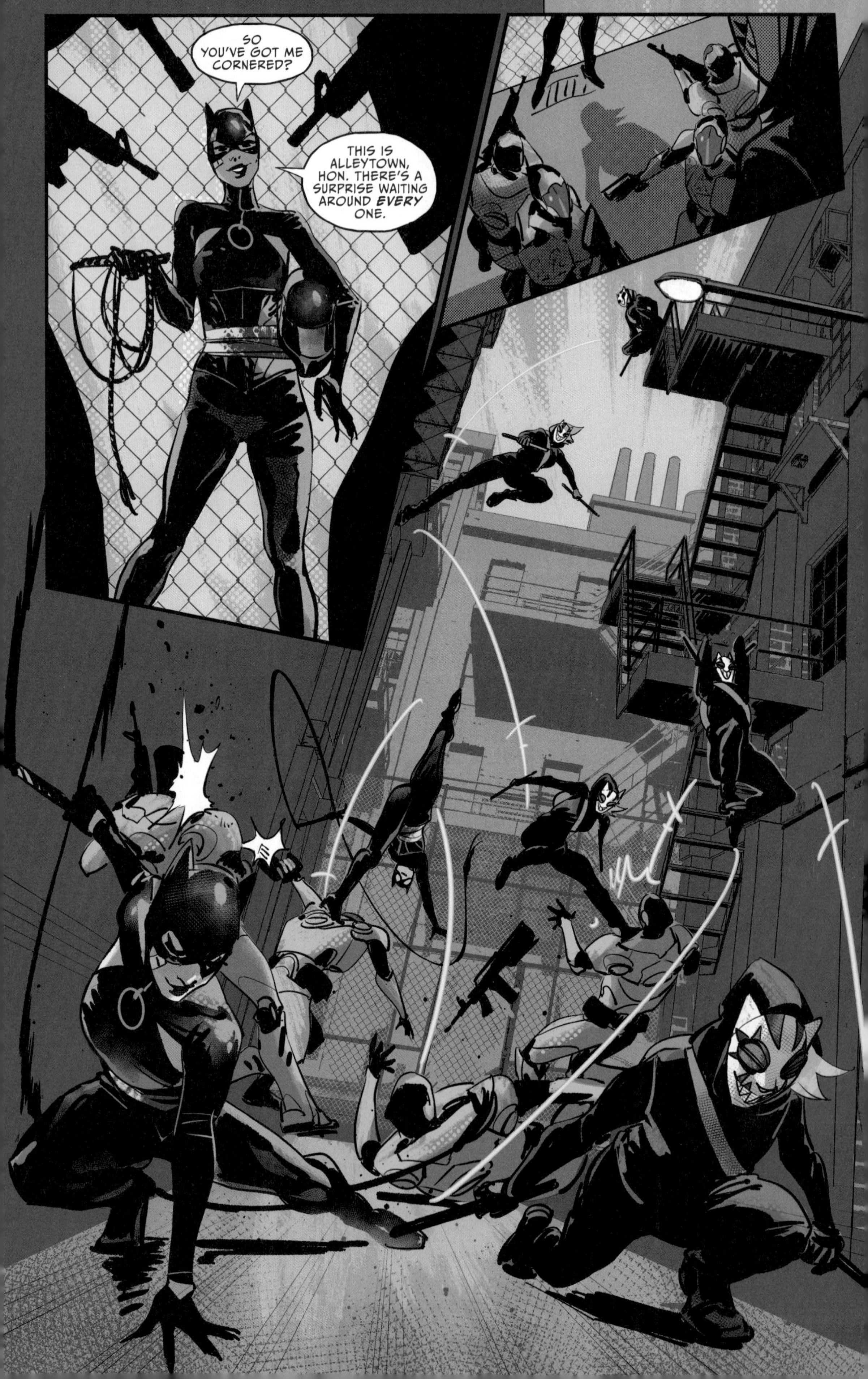
SO YOU'VE GOT ME CORNERED?
THIS IS ALLEYTOWN, HON. THERE'S A SURPRISE WAITING AROUND *EVERY* ONE.

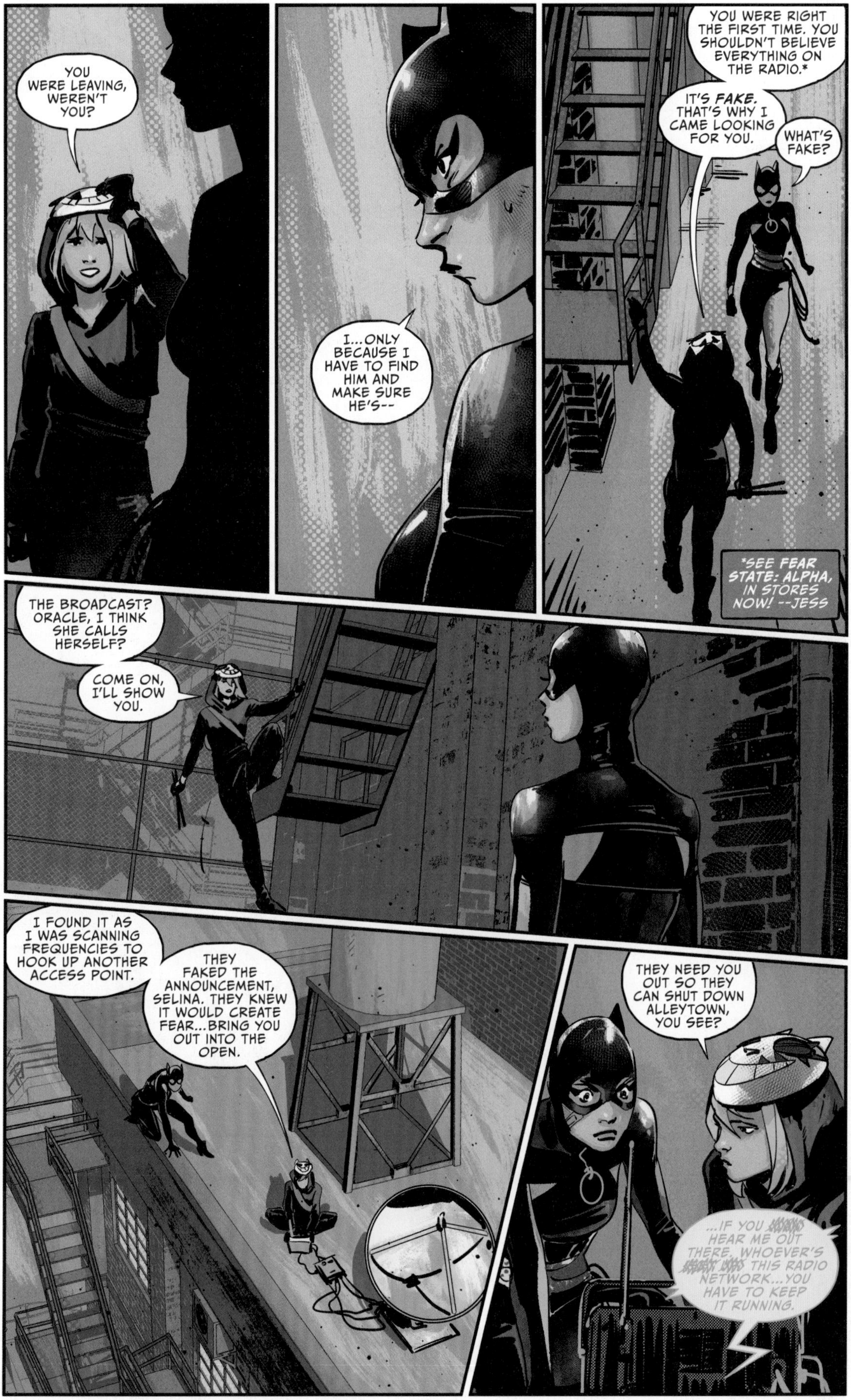

YOU WERE LEAVING, WEREN'T YOU?
I...ONLY BECAUSE I HAVE TO FIND HIM AND MAKE SURE HE'S--
YOU WERE RIGHT THE FIRST TIME. YOU SHOULDN'T BELIEVE EVERYTHING ON THE RADIO.*
IT'S FAKE. THAT'S WHY I CAME LOOKING FOR YOU.
WHAT'S FAKE?
*SEE FEAR STATE: ALPHA, IN STORES NOW! --JESS
THE BROADCAST? ORACLE, I THINK SHE CALLS HERSELF?
COME ON, I'LL SHOW YOU.
I FOUND IT AS I WAS SCANNING FREQUENCIES TO HOOK UP ANOTHER ACCESS POINT.
THEY FAKED THE ANNOUNCEMENT, SELINA. THEY KNEW IT WOULD CREATE FEAR...BRING YOU OUT INTO THE OPEN.
THEY NEED YOU OUT SO THEY CAN SHUT DOWN ALLEYTOWN, YOU SEE?
...IF YOU HEAR ME OUT THERE, WHOEVER'S THIS RADIO NETWORK...YOU HAVE TO KEEP IT RUNNING.

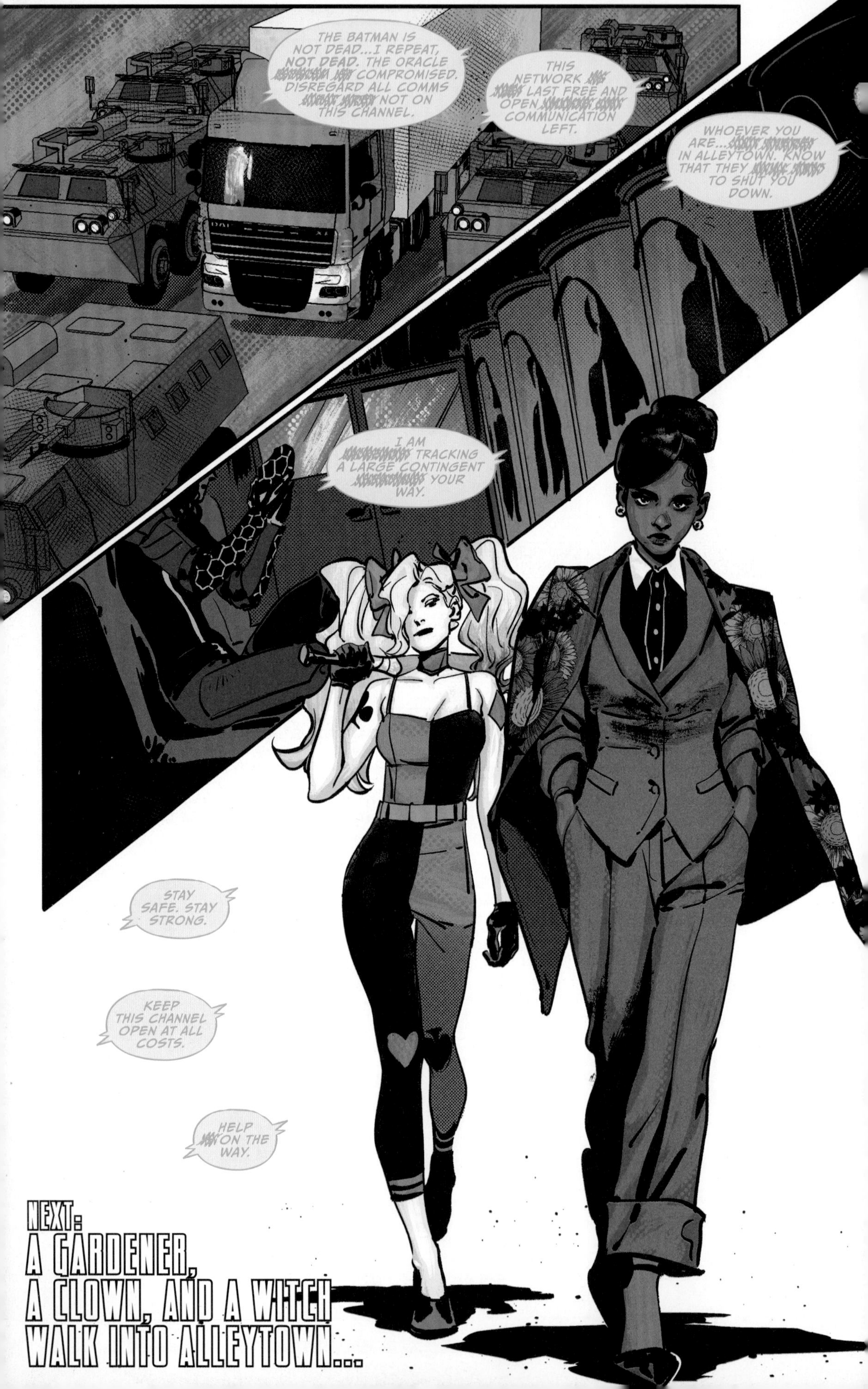
THE BATMAN IS NOT DEAD...I REPEAT, NOT DEAD. THE ORACLE COMPROMISED. DISREGARD ALL COMMS NOT ON THIS CHANNEL.
THIS NETWORK LAST FREE AND OPEN COMMUNICATION LEFT.
WHOEVER YOU ARE... IN ALLEYTOWN. KNOW THAT THEY TO SHUT YOU DOWN.
I AM TRACKING A LARGE CONTINGENT YOUR WAY.
STAY SAFE. STAY STRONG.
KEEP THIS CHANNEL OPEN AT ALL COSTS.
HELP ON THE WAY.
NEXT:
A GARDENER, A CLOWN, AND A WITCH WALK INTO ALLEYTOWN...

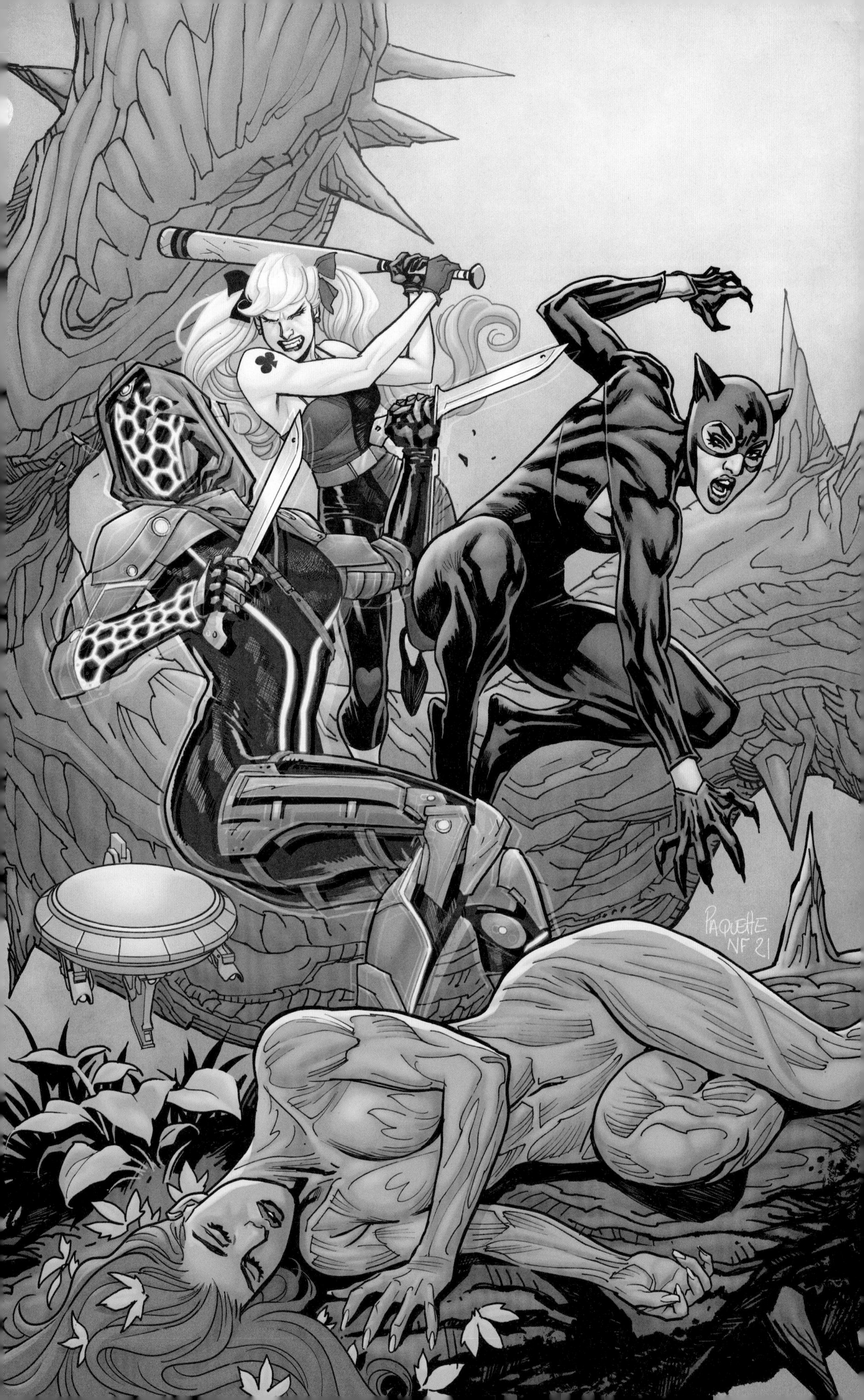
PAQUETTE
NF 21

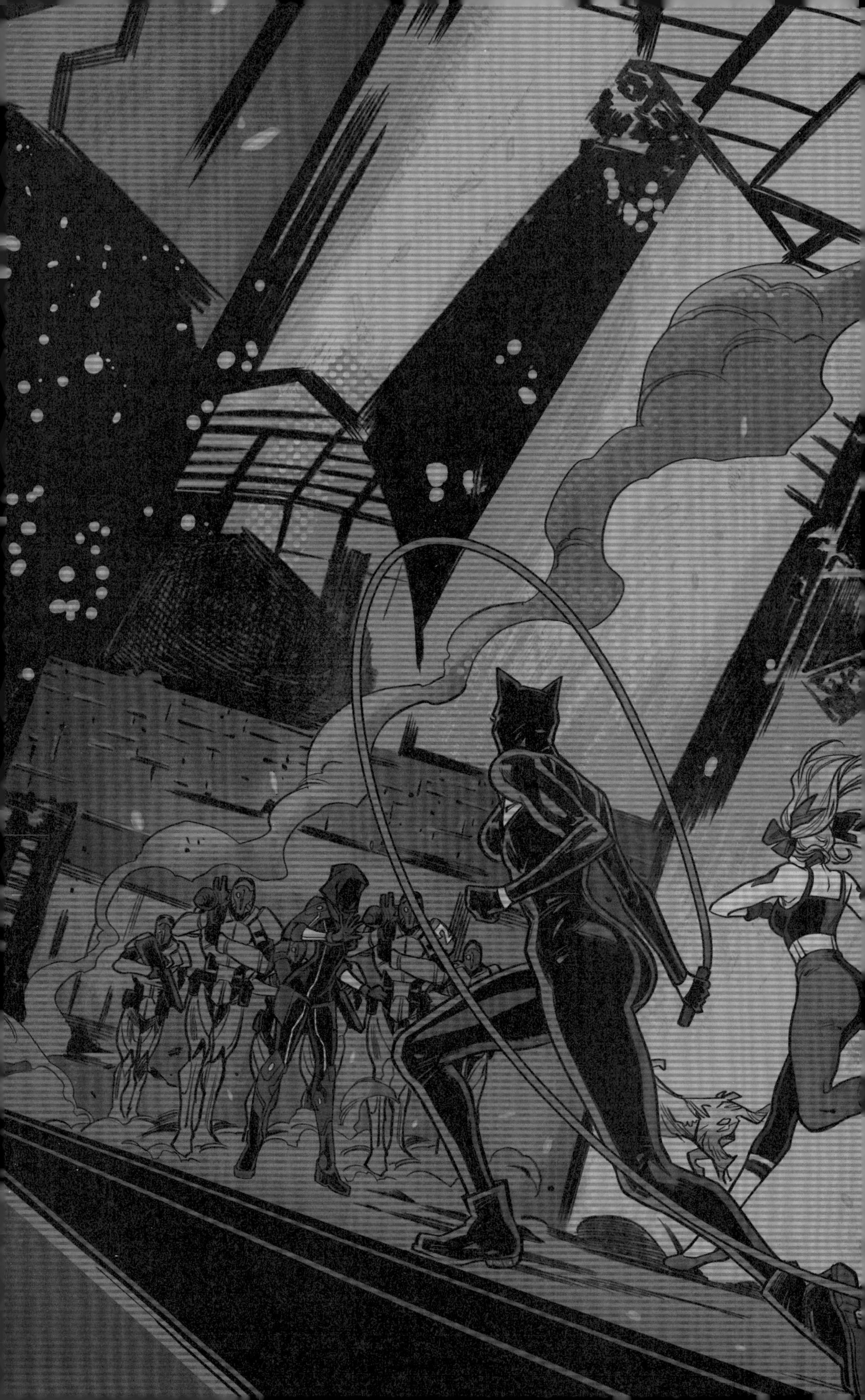

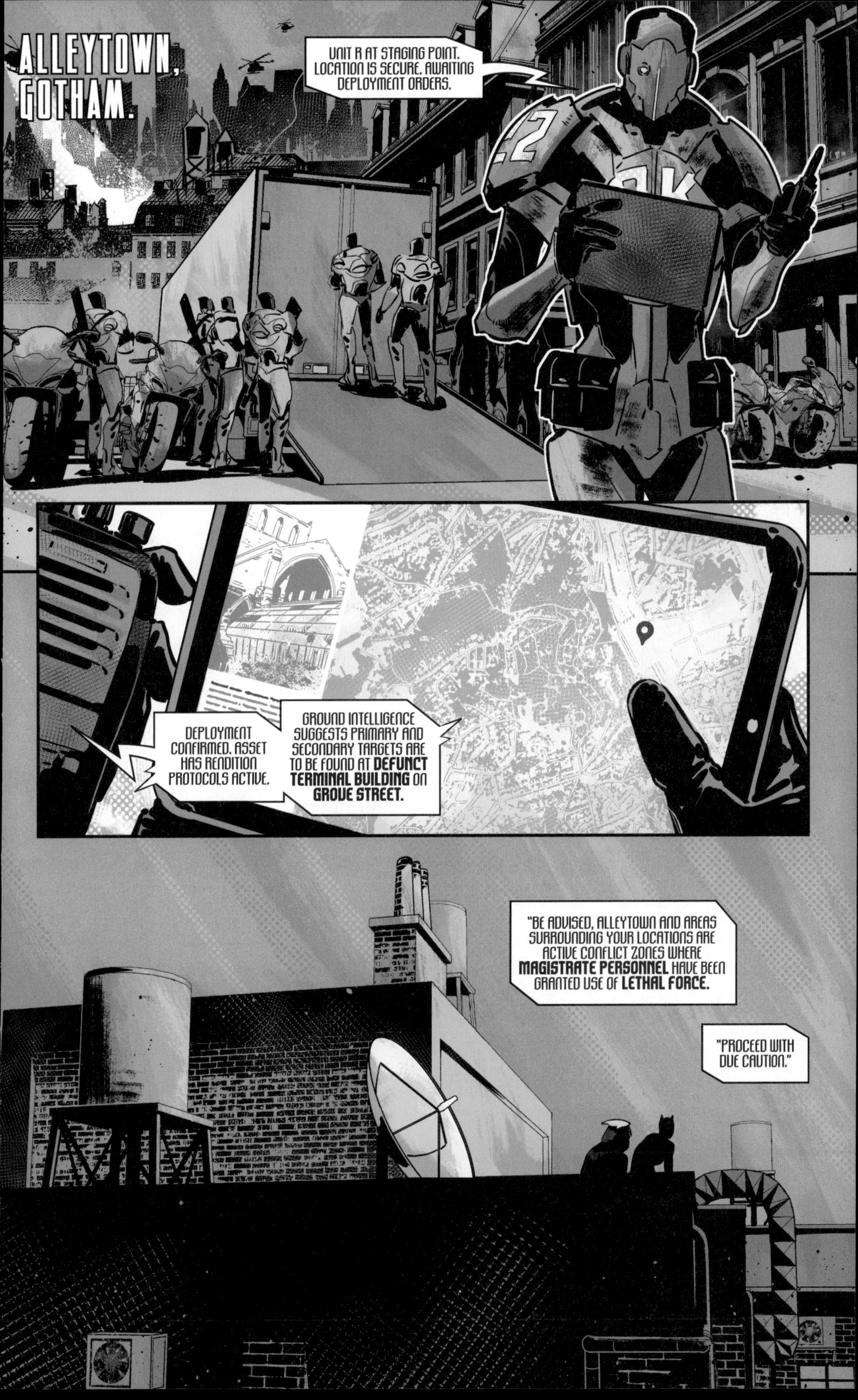

ALLEYTOWN, GOTHAM.
UNIT R AT STAGING POINT. LOCATION IS SECURE. AWAITING DEPLOYMENT ORDERS.
DEPLOYMENT CONFIRMED. ASSET HAS RENDITION PROTOCOLS ACTIVE.
GROUND INTELLIGENCE SUGGESTS PRIMARY AND SECONDARY TARGETS ARE TO BE FOUND AT **DEFUNCT TERMINAL BUILDING** ON **GROVE STREET.**
"BE ADVISED, ALLEYTOWN AND AREAS SURROUNDING YOUR LOCATIONS ARE ACTIVE CONFLICT ZONES WHERE **MAGISTRATE PERSONNEL** HAVE BEEN GRANTED USE OF **LETHAL FORCE.**
"PROCEED WITH DUE CAUTION."

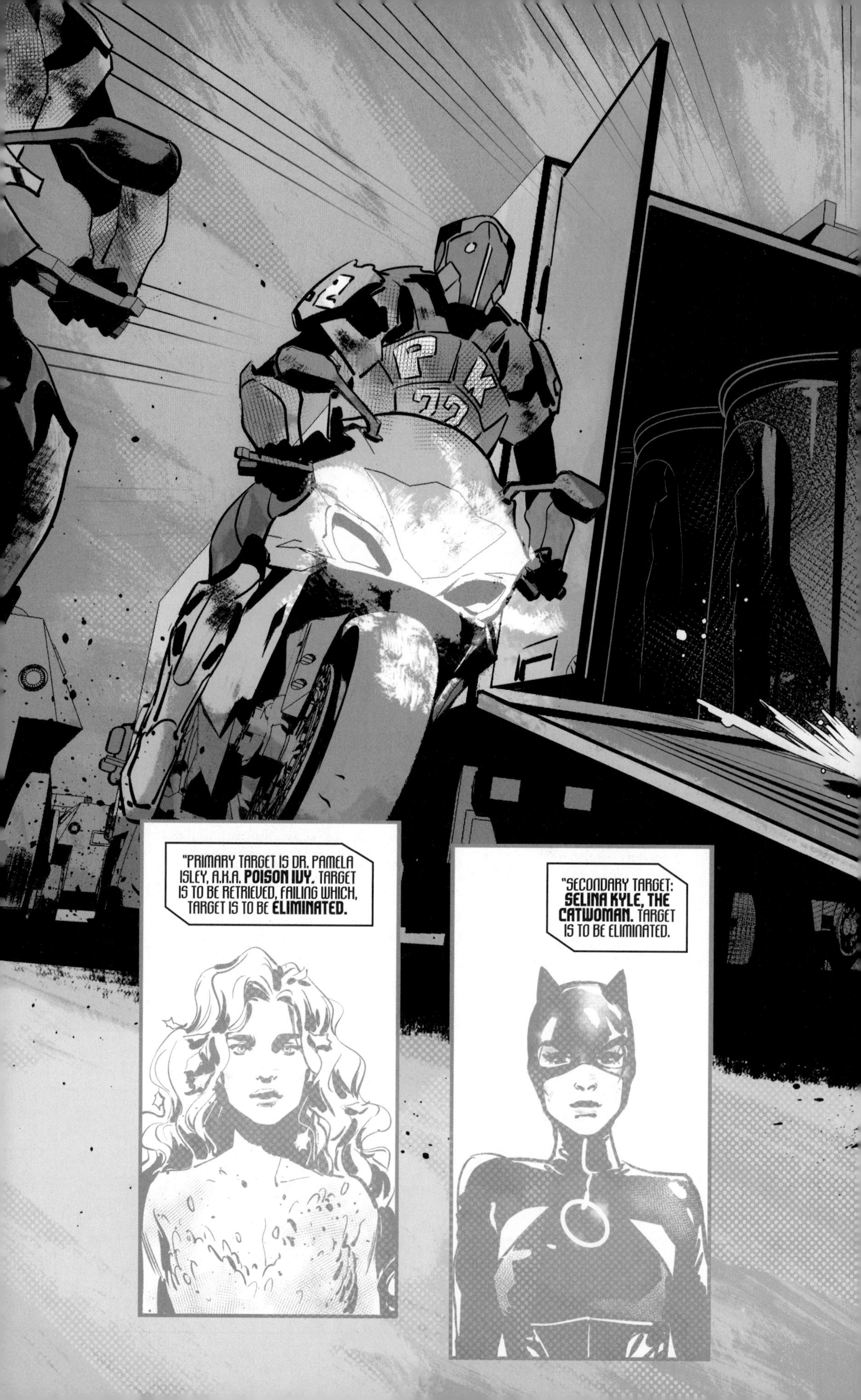
"PRIMARY TARGET IS DR. PAMELA ISLEY, A.K.A. **POISON IVY.** TARGET IS TO BE RETRIEVED, FAILING WHICH, TARGET IS TO BE **ELIMINATED.**
"SECONDARY TARGET: **SELINA KYLE, THE CATWOMAN.** TARGET IS TO BE ELIMINATED.

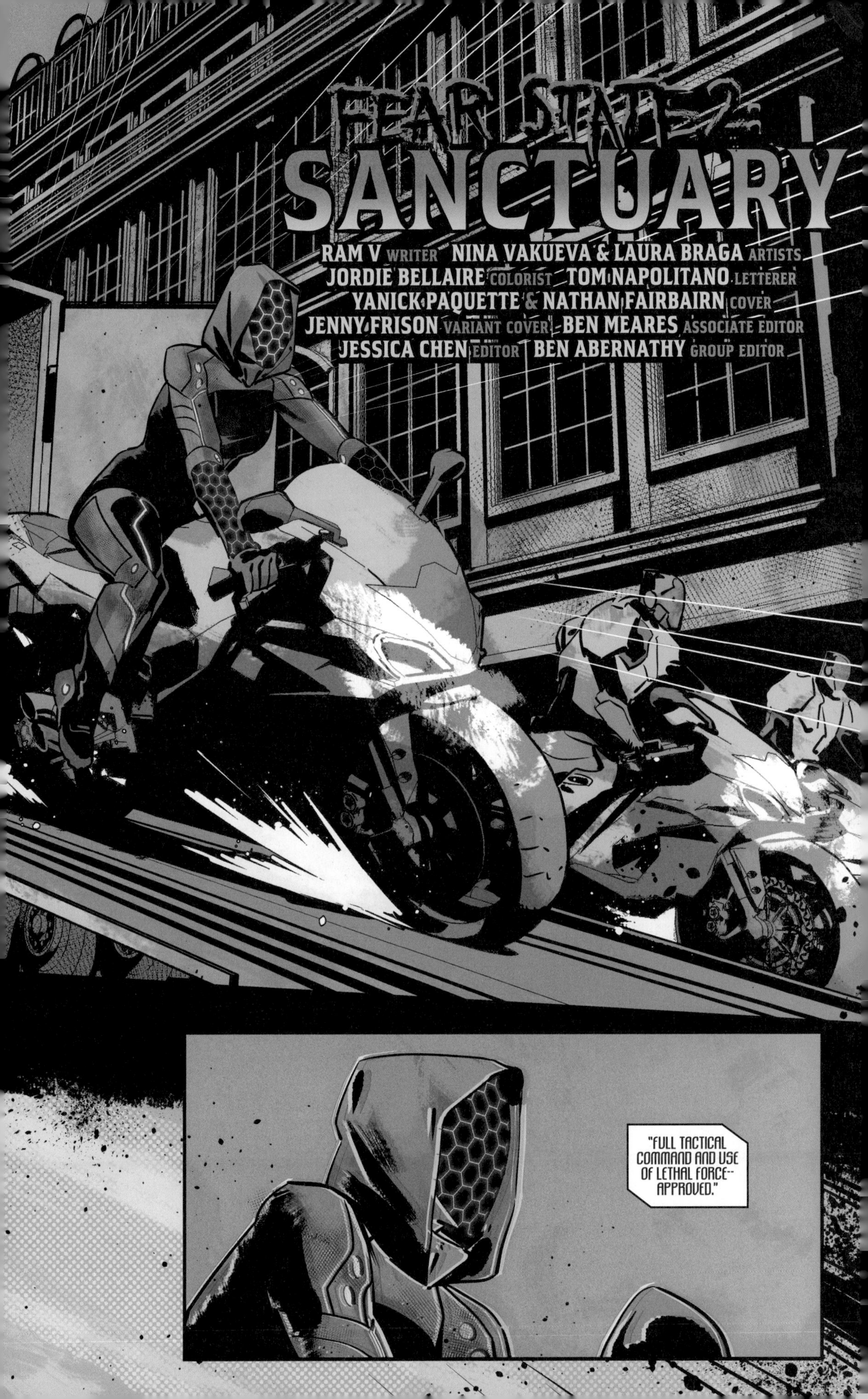

FEAR STATE 2:
SANCTUARY
RAM V WRITER NINA VAKUEVA & LAURA BRAGA ARTISTS
JORDIE BELLAIRE COLORIST TOM NAPOLITANO LETTERER
YANICK PAQUETTE & NATHAN FAIRBAIRN COVER
JENNY FRISON VARIANT COVER BEN MEARES ASSOCIATE EDITOR
JESSICA CHEN EDITOR BEN ABERNATHY GROUP EDITOR
"FULL TACTICAL COMMAND AND USE OF LETHAL FORCE-- APPROVED."

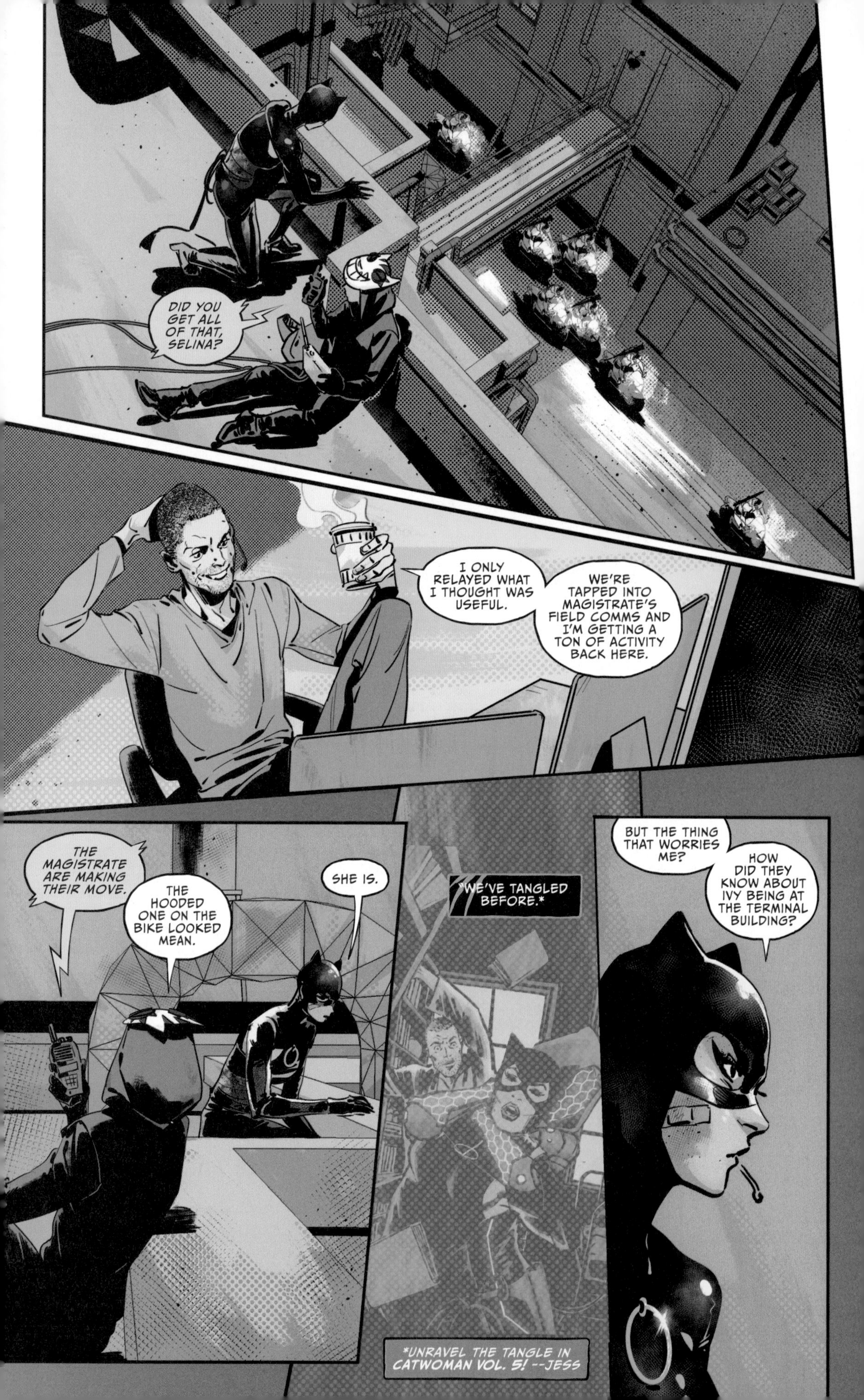
DID YOU GET ALL OF THAT, SELINA?
I ONLY RELAYED WHAT I THOUGHT WAS USEFUL.
WE'RE TAPPED INTO MAGISTRATE'S FIELD COMMS AND I'M GETTING A TON OF ACTIVITY BACK HERE.
THE MAGISTRATE ARE MAKING THEIR MOVE.
THE HOODED ONE ON THE BIKE LOOKED MEAN.
SHE IS.
WE'VE TANGLED BEFORE.
*UNRAVEL THE TANGLE IN CATWOMAN VOL. 5! --JESS
BUT THE THING THAT WORRIES ME?
HOW DID THEY KNOW ABOUT IVY BEING AT THE TERMINAL BUILDING?

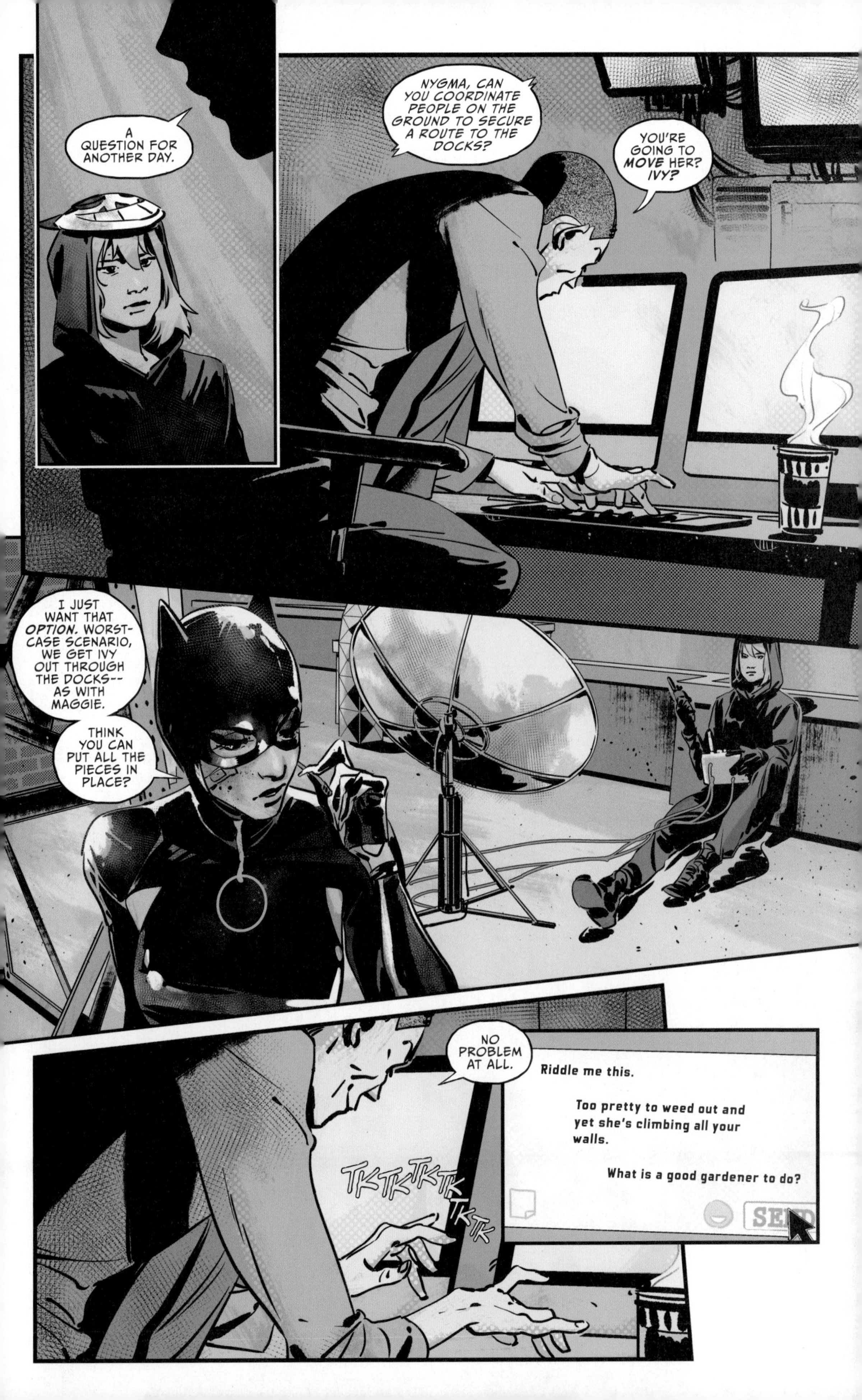
A QUESTION FOR ANOTHER DAY.
NYGMA, CAN YOU COORDINATE PEOPLE ON THE GROUND TO SECURE A ROUTE TO THE DOCKS?
YOU'RE GOING TO MOVE HER? IVY?
I JUST WANT THAT OPTION. WORST-CASE SCENARIO, WE GET IVY OUT THROUGH THE DOCKS-- AS WITH MAGGIE.
THINK YOU CAN PUT ALL THE PIECES IN PLACE?
NO PROBLEM AT ALL.
TKTKTKTK TKTK
Riddle me this.
Too pretty to weed out and yet she's climbing all your walls.
What is a good gardener to do?
SEND

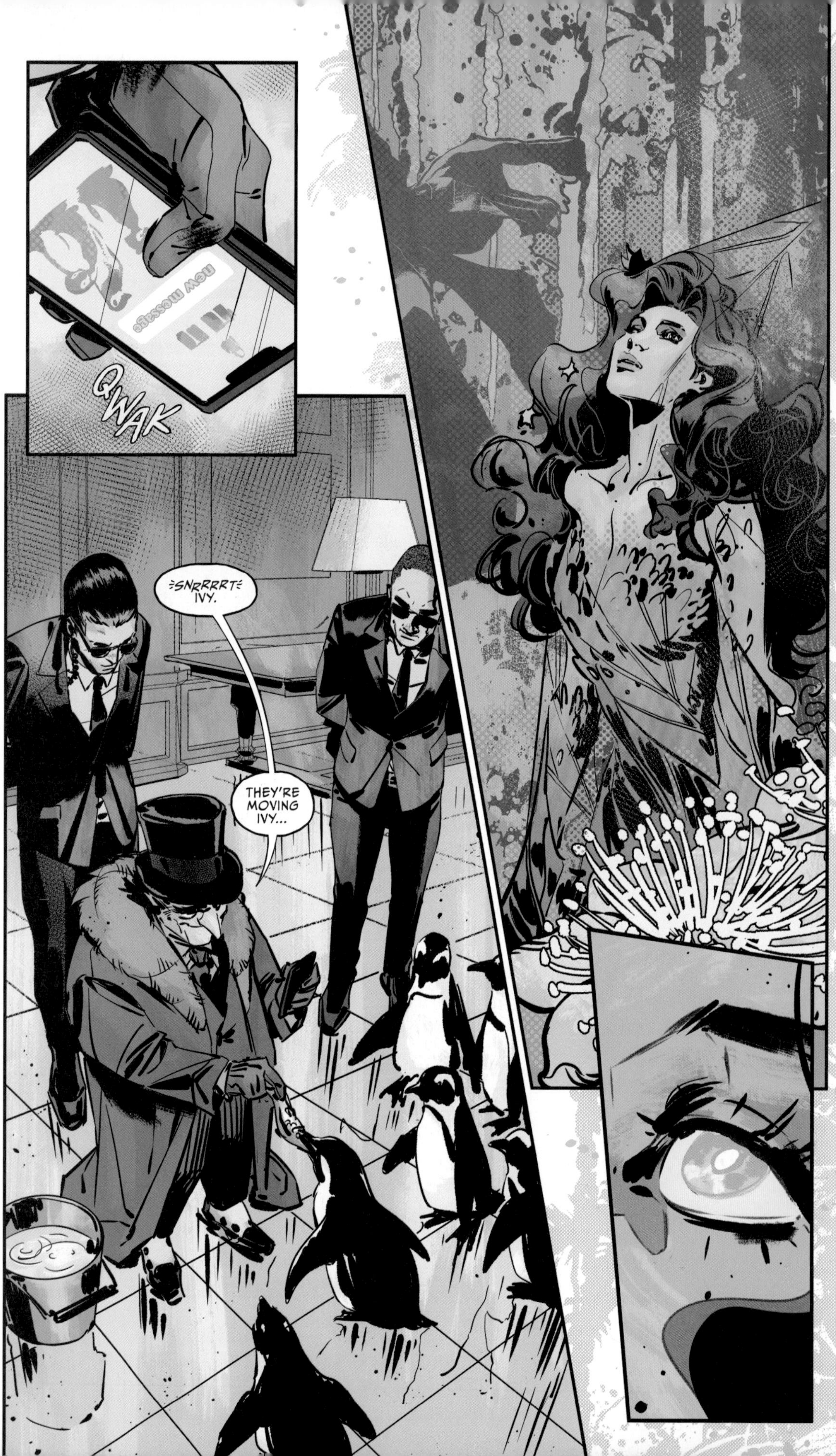
new message
QWAK
SNRRRRT
IVY.
THEY'RE MOVING IVY...

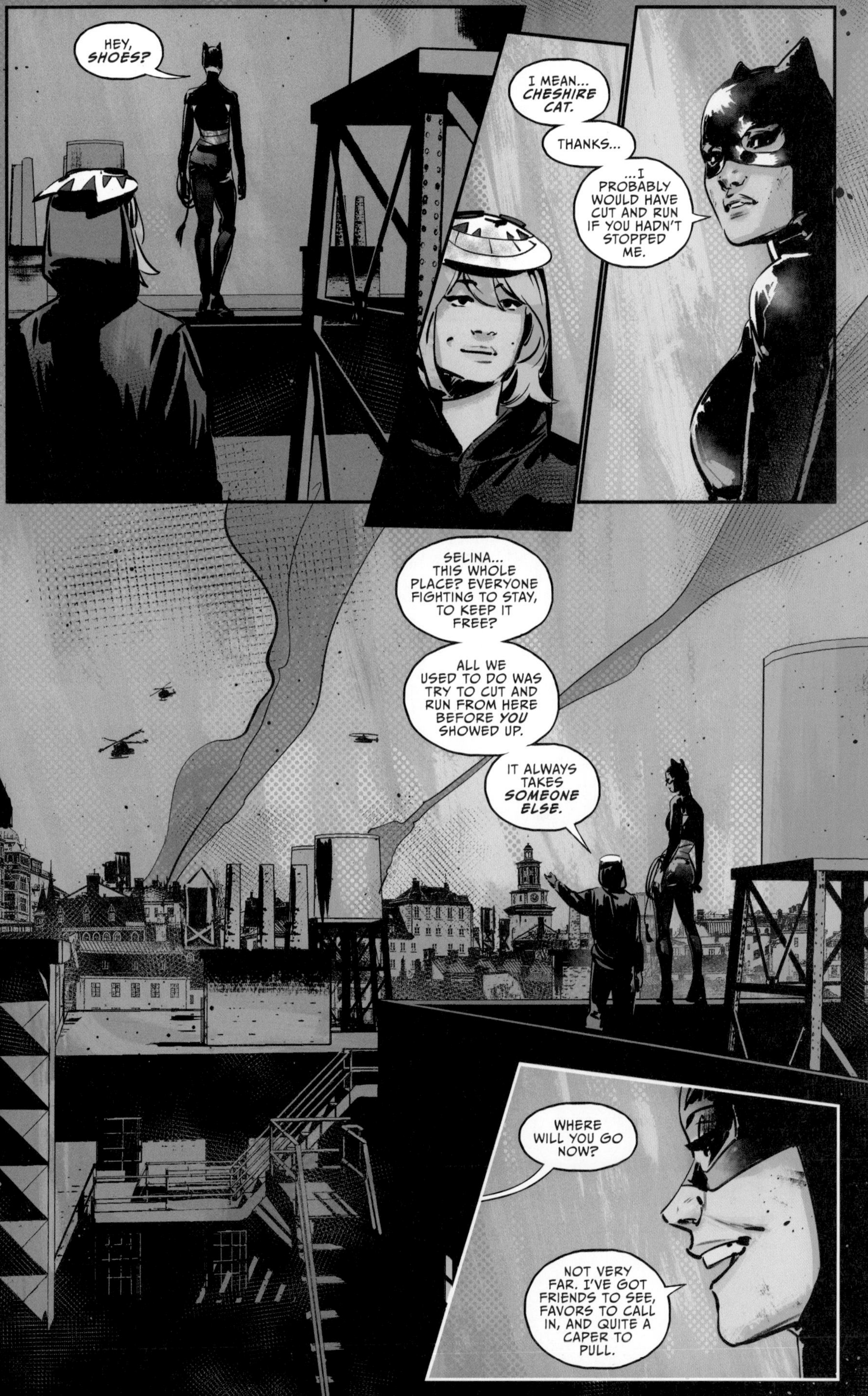
HEY, SHOES?
I MEAN... CHESHIRE CAT.
THANKS...
...I PROBABLY WOULD HAVE CUT AND RUN IF YOU HADN'T STOPPED ME.
SELINA... THIS WHOLE PLACE? EVERYONE FIGHTING TO STAY, TO KEEP IT FREE?
ALL WE USED TO DO WAS TRY TO CUT AND RUN FROM HERE BEFORE YOU SHOWED UP.
IT ALWAYS TAKES SOMEONE ELSE.
WHERE WILL YOU GO NOW?
NOT VERY FAR. I'VE GOT FRIENDS TO SEE, FAVORS TO CALL IN, AND QUITE A CAPER TO PULL.

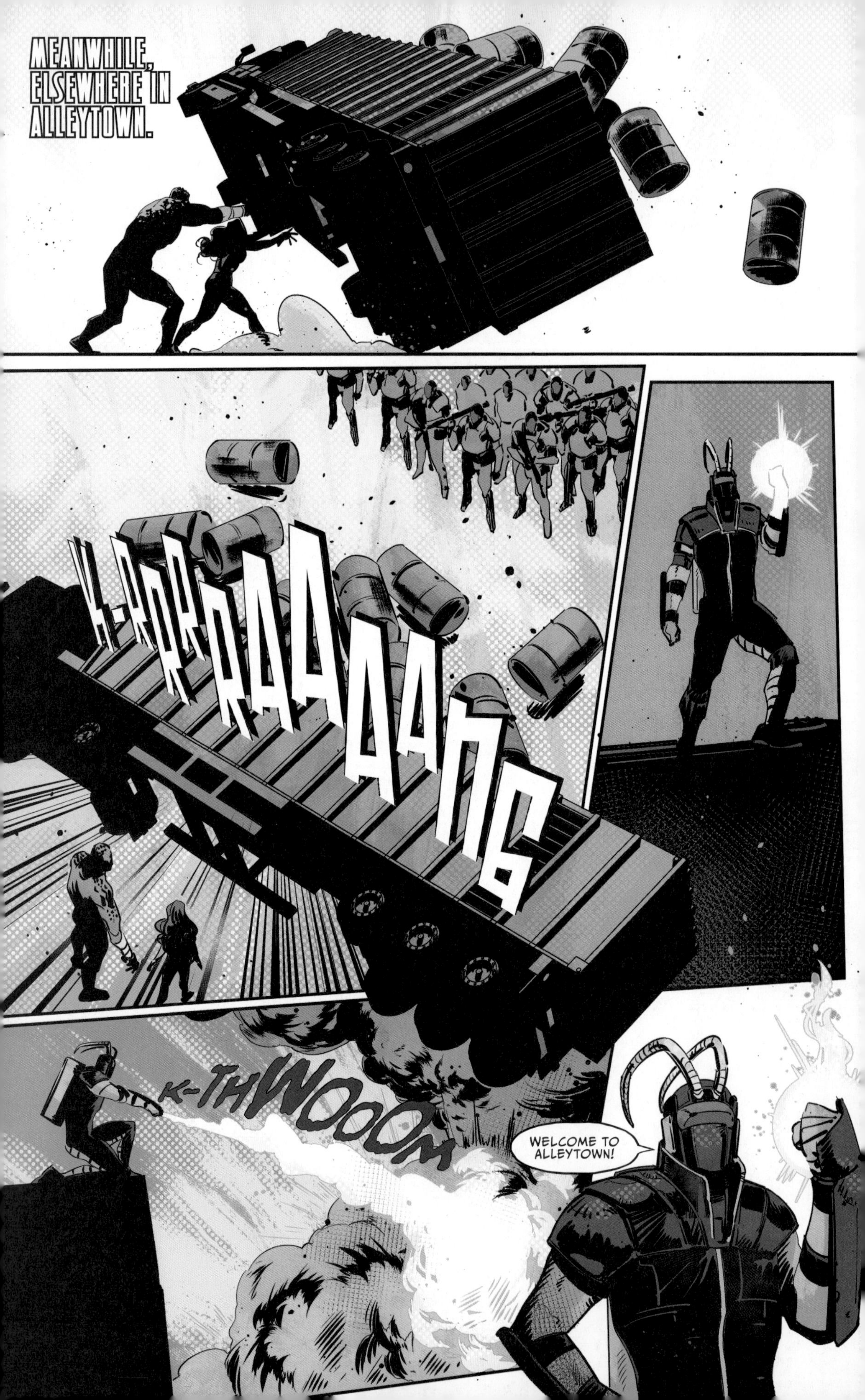
MEANWHILE, ELSEWHERE IN ALLEYTOWN.
K-RRRRAAAANG
K-THWOOOM
WELCOME TO ALLEYTOWN!

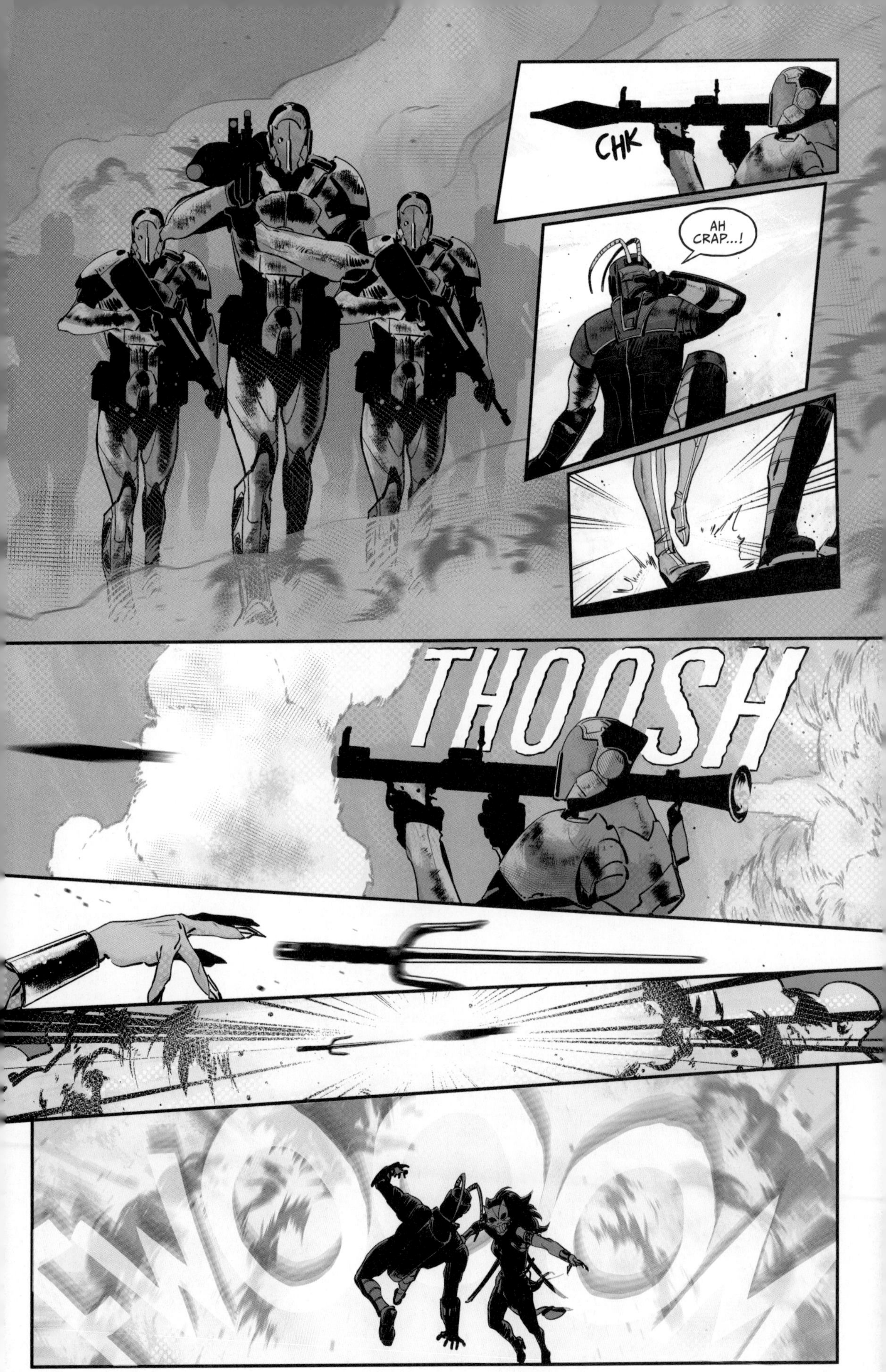
CHK
AH CRAP...!
THOOSH

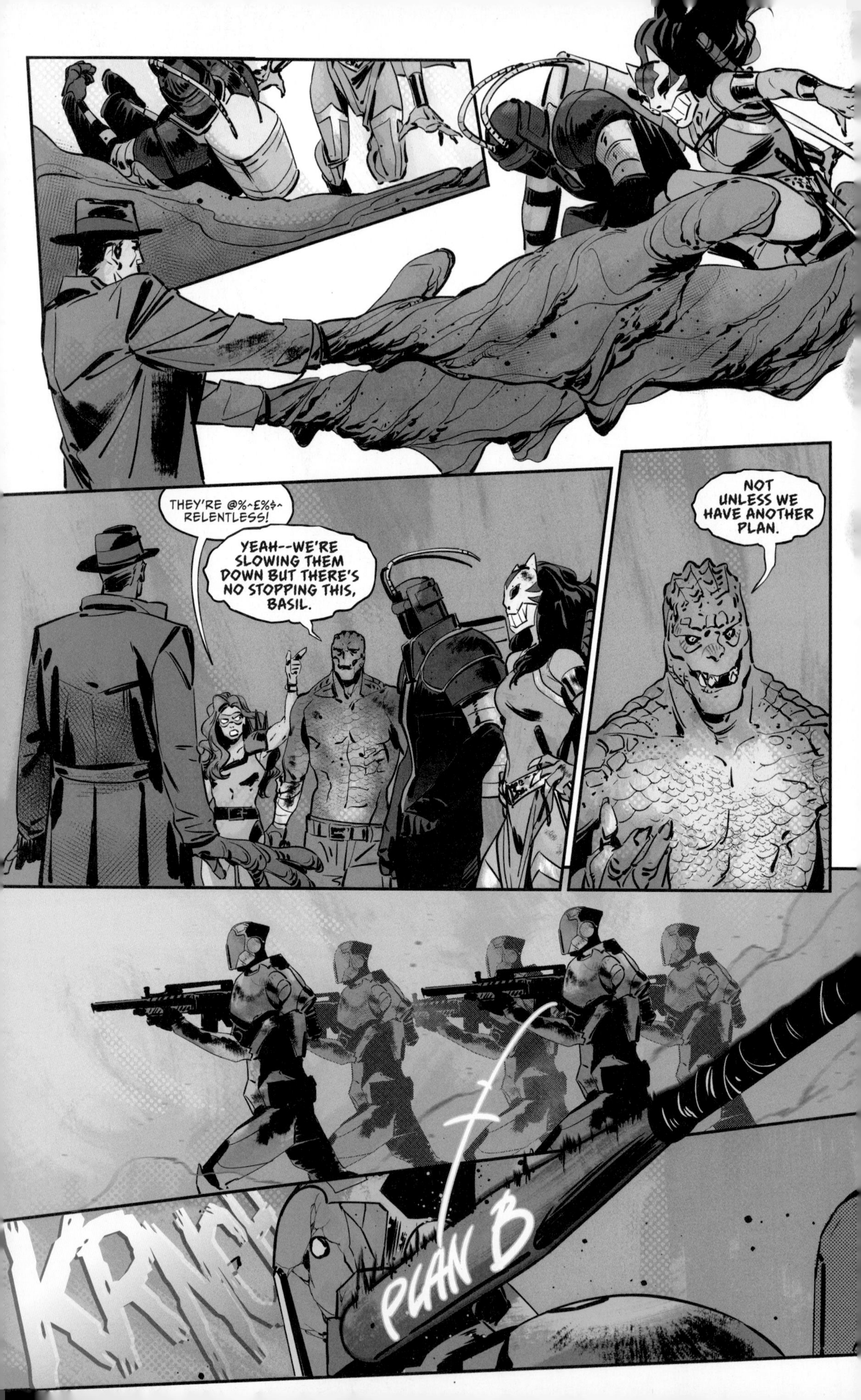
THEY'RE @%^£%$^ RELENTLESS!
YEAH--WE'RE SLOWING THEM DOWN BUT THERE'S NO STOPPING THIS, BASIL.
NOT UNLESS WE HAVE ANOTHER PLAN.
KRNCH
PLAN B

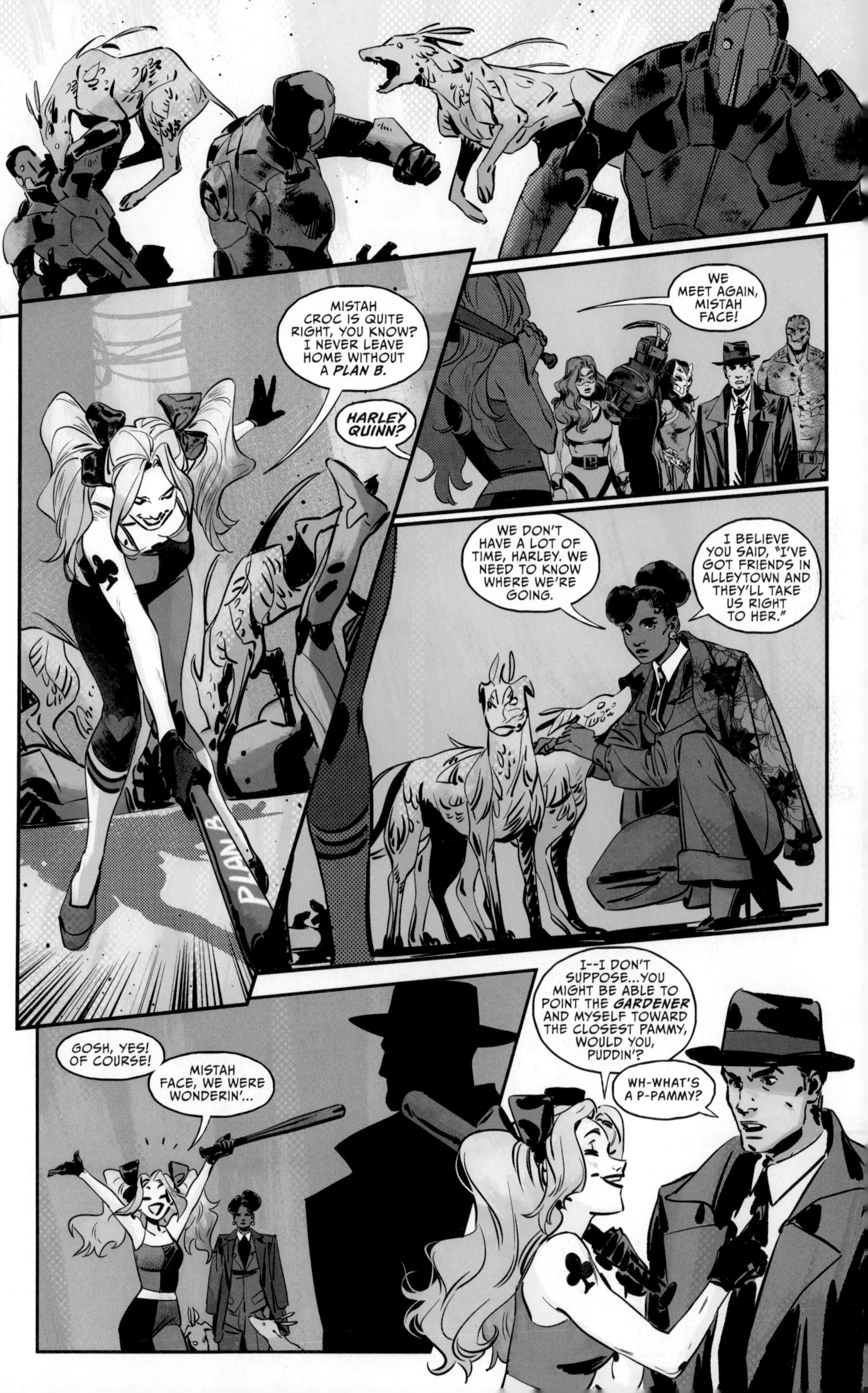
MISTAH CROC IS QUITE RIGHT, YOU KNOW? I NEVER LEAVE HOME WITHOUT A *PLAN B.*
PLAN B
HARLEY QUINN?
WE MEET AGAIN, MISTAH FACE!
WE DON'T HAVE A LOT OF TIME, HARLEY. WE NEED TO KNOW WHERE WE'RE GOING.
I BELIEVE YOU SAID, "I'VE GOT FRIENDS IN ALLEYTOWN AND THEY'LL TAKE US RIGHT TO HER."
GOSH, YES! OF COURSE!
MISTAH FACE, WE WERE WONDERIN'...
I--I DON'T SUPPOSE...YOU MIGHT BE ABLE TO POINT THE *GARDENER* AND MYSELF TOWARD THE CLOSEST PAMMY, WOULD YOU, PUDDIN'?
WH-WHAT'S A P-PAMMY?

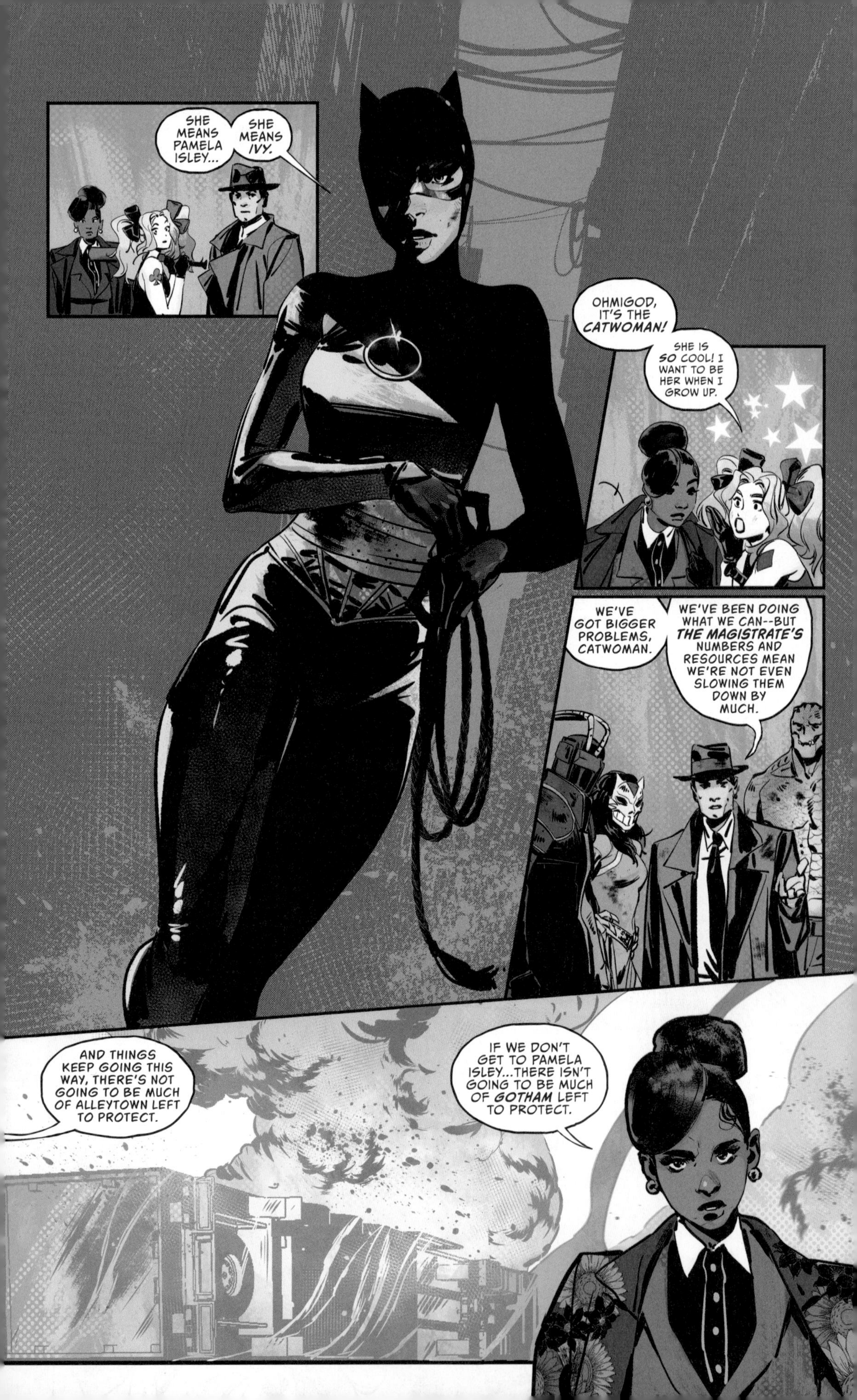
SHE MEANS PAMELA ISLEY...
SHE MEANS *IVY.*
OHMIGOD, IT'S THE *CATWOMAN!*
SHE IS *SO* COOL! I WANT TO BE HER WHEN I GROW UP.
WE'VE GOT BIGGER PROBLEMS, CATWOMAN.
WE'VE BEEN DOING WHAT WE CAN--BUT *THE MAGISTRATE'S* NUMBERS AND RESOURCES MEAN WE'RE NOT EVEN SLOWING THEM DOWN BY MUCH.
AND THINGS KEEP GOING THIS WAY, THERE'S NOT GOING TO BE MUCH OF ALLEYTOWN LEFT TO PROTECT.
IF WE DON'T GET TO PAMELA ISLEY...THERE ISN'T GOING TO BE MUCH OF *GOTHAM* LEFT TO PROTECT.

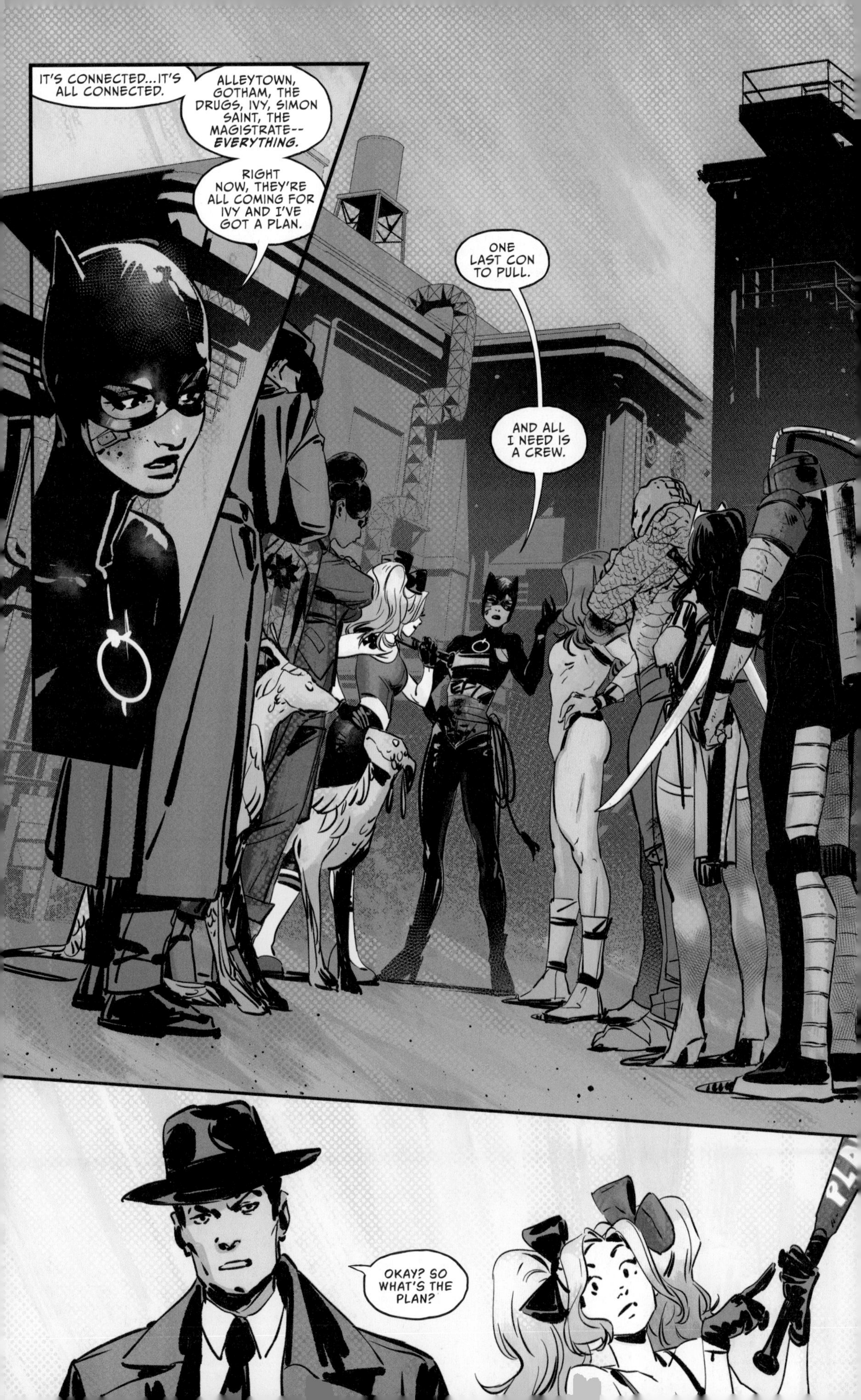
IT'S CONNECTED...IT'S ALL CONNECTED.
ALLEYTOWN, GOTHAM, THE DRUGS, IVY, SIMON SAINT, THE MAGISTRATE-- *EVERYTHING.*
RIGHT NOW, THEY'RE ALL COMING FOR IVY AND I'VE GOT A PLAN.
ONE LAST CON TO PULL.
AND ALL I NEED IS A CREW.
OKAY? SO WHAT'S THE PLAN?

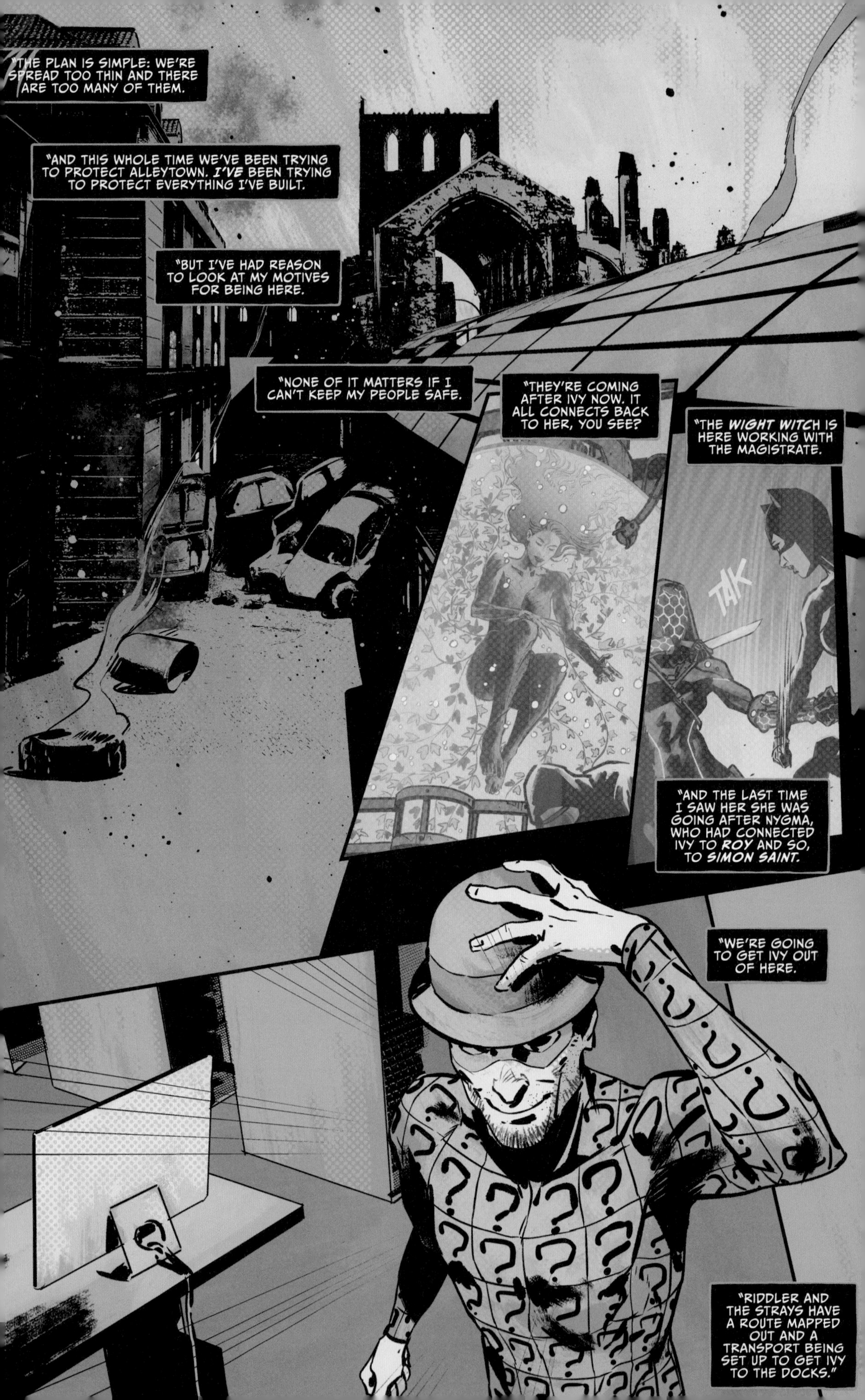
"THE PLAN IS SIMPLE: WE'RE SPREAD TOO THIN AND THERE ARE TOO MANY OF THEM.
"AND THIS WHOLE TIME WE'VE BEEN TRYING TO PROTECT ALLEYTOWN. I'VE BEEN TRYING TO PROTECT EVERYTHING I'VE BUILT.
"BUT I'VE HAD REASON TO LOOK AT MY MOTIVES FOR BEING HERE.
"NONE OF IT MATTERS IF I CAN'T KEEP MY PEOPLE SAFE.
"THEY'RE COMING AFTER IVY NOW. IT ALL CONNECTS BACK TO HER, YOU SEE?
"THE WIGHT WITCH IS HERE WORKING WITH THE MAGISTRATE.
TAK
"AND THE LAST TIME I SAW HER SHE WAS GOING AFTER NYGMA, WHO HAD CONNECTED IVY TO ROY AND SO, TO SIMON SAINT.
"WE'RE GOING TO GET IVY OUT OF HERE.
"RIDDLER AND THE STRAYS HAVE A ROUTE MAPPED OUT AND A TRANSPORT BEING SET UP TO GET IVY TO THE DOCKS."

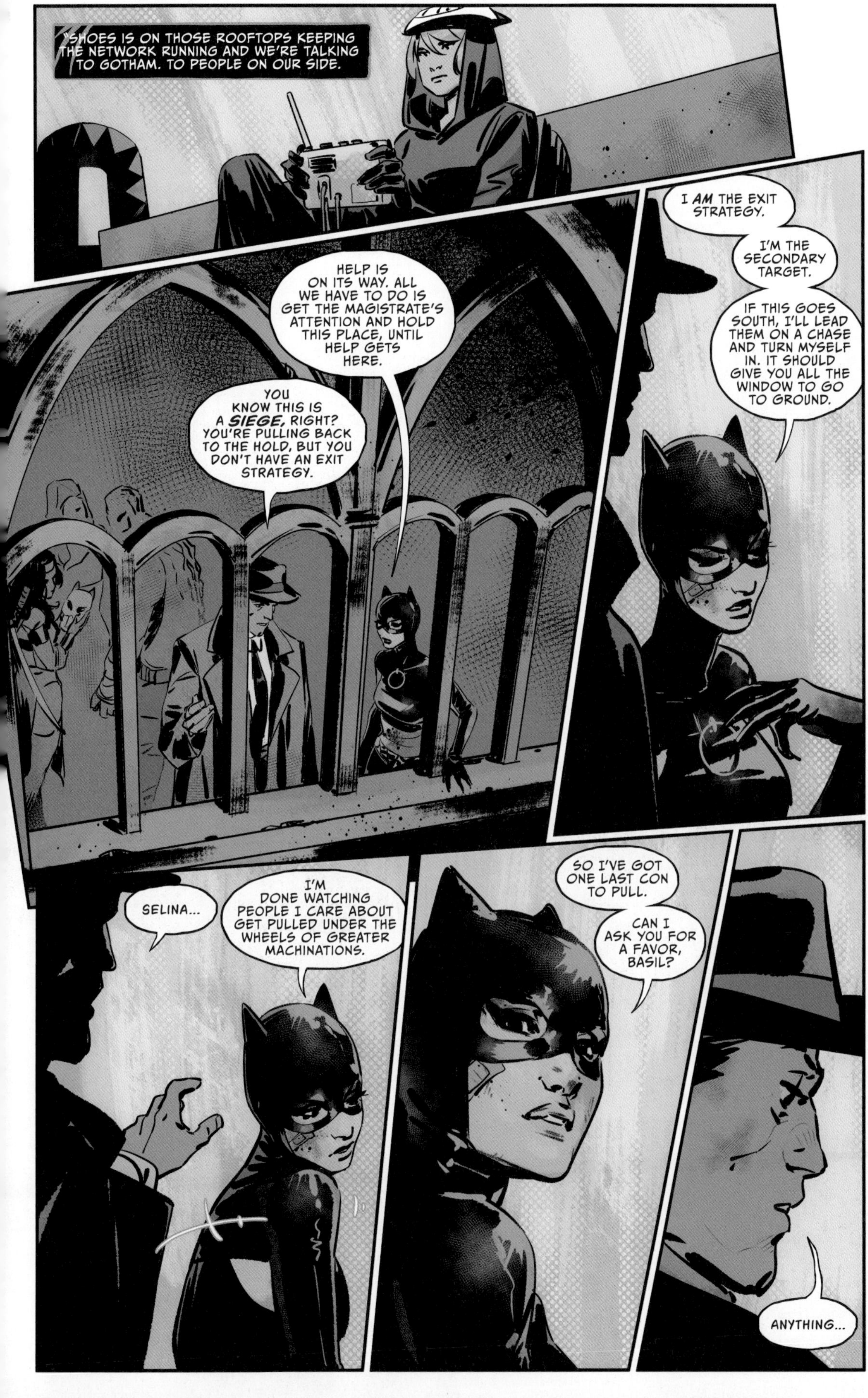
"SHOES IS ON THOSE ROOFTOPS KEEPING THE NETWORK RUNNING AND WE'RE TALKING TO GOTHAM. TO PEOPLE ON OUR SIDE.
HELP IS ON ITS WAY. ALL WE HAVE TO DO IS GET THE MAGISTRATE'S ATTENTION AND HOLD THIS PLACE, UNTIL HELP GETS HERE.
YOU KNOW THIS IS A *SIEGE,* RIGHT? YOU'RE PULLING BACK TO THE HOLD, BUT YOU DON'T HAVE AN EXIT STRATEGY.
I *AM* THE EXIT STRATEGY.
I'M THE SECONDARY TARGET.
IF THIS GOES SOUTH, I'LL LEAD THEM ON A CHASE AND TURN MYSELF IN. IT SHOULD GIVE YOU ALL THE WINDOW TO GO TO GROUND.
SELINA...
I'M DONE WATCHING PEOPLE I CARE ABOUT GET PULLED UNDER THE WHEELS OF GREATER MACHINATIONS.
SO I'VE GOT ONE LAST CON TO PULL.
CAN I ASK YOU FOR A FAVOR, BASIL?
ANYTHING...

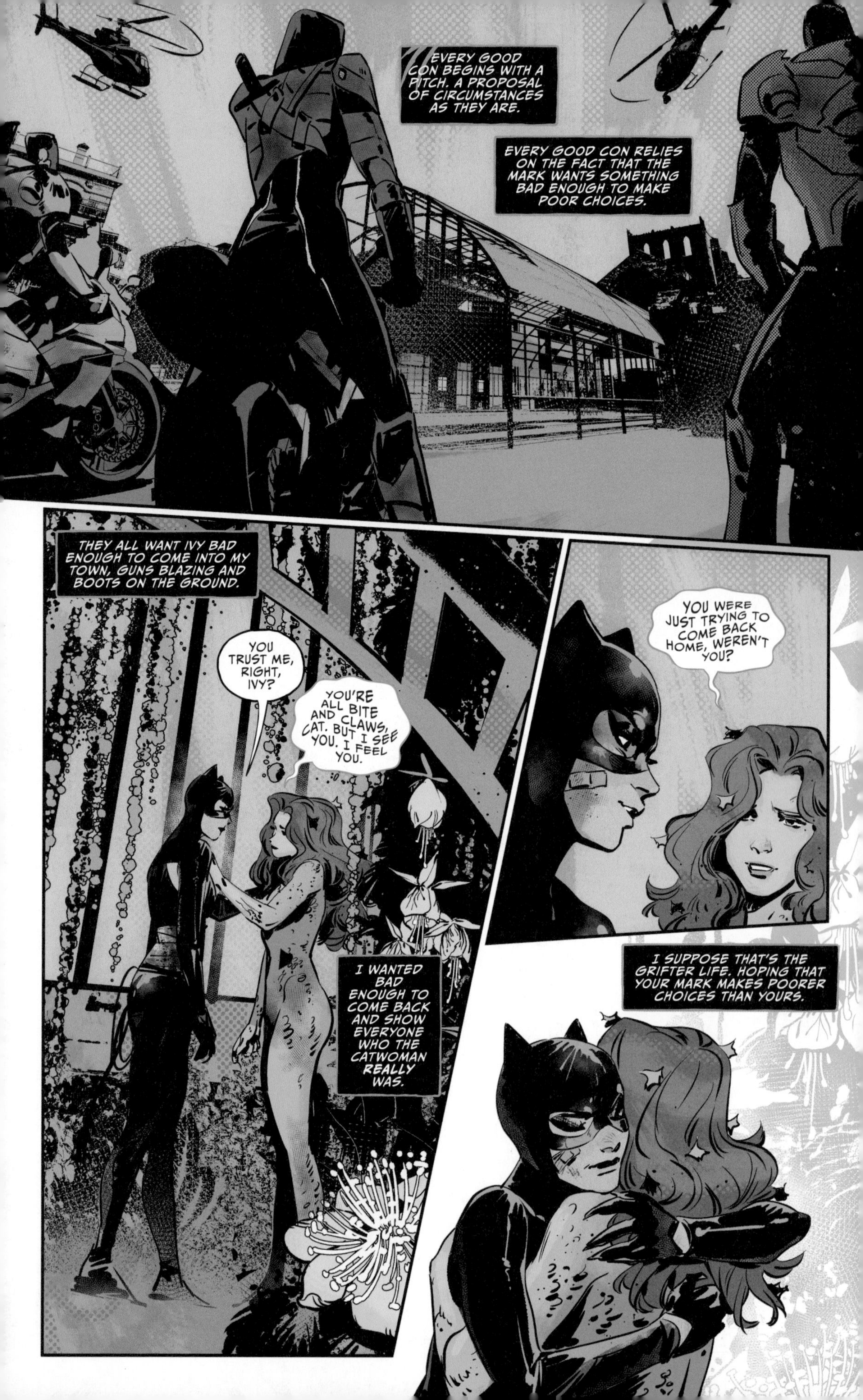
EVERY GOOD CON BEGINS WITH A PITCH. A PROPOSAL OF CIRCUMSTANCES AS THEY ARE.
EVERY GOOD CON RELIES ON THE FACT THAT THE MARK WANTS SOMETHING BAD ENOUGH TO MAKE POOR CHOICES.
THEY ALL WANT IVY BAD ENOUGH TO COME INTO MY TOWN, GUNS BLAZING AND BOOTS ON THE GROUND.
YOU TRUST ME, RIGHT, IVY?
YOU'RE ALL BITE AND CLAWS, CAT. BUT I SEE YOU. I FEEL YOU.
I WANTED BAD ENOUGH TO COME BACK AND SHOW EVERYONE WHO THE CATWOMAN REALLY WAS.
YOU WERE JUST TRYING TO COME BACK HOME, WEREN'T YOU?
I SUPPOSE THAT'S THE GRIFTER LIFE. HOPING THAT YOUR MARK MAKES POORER CHOICES THAN YOURS.

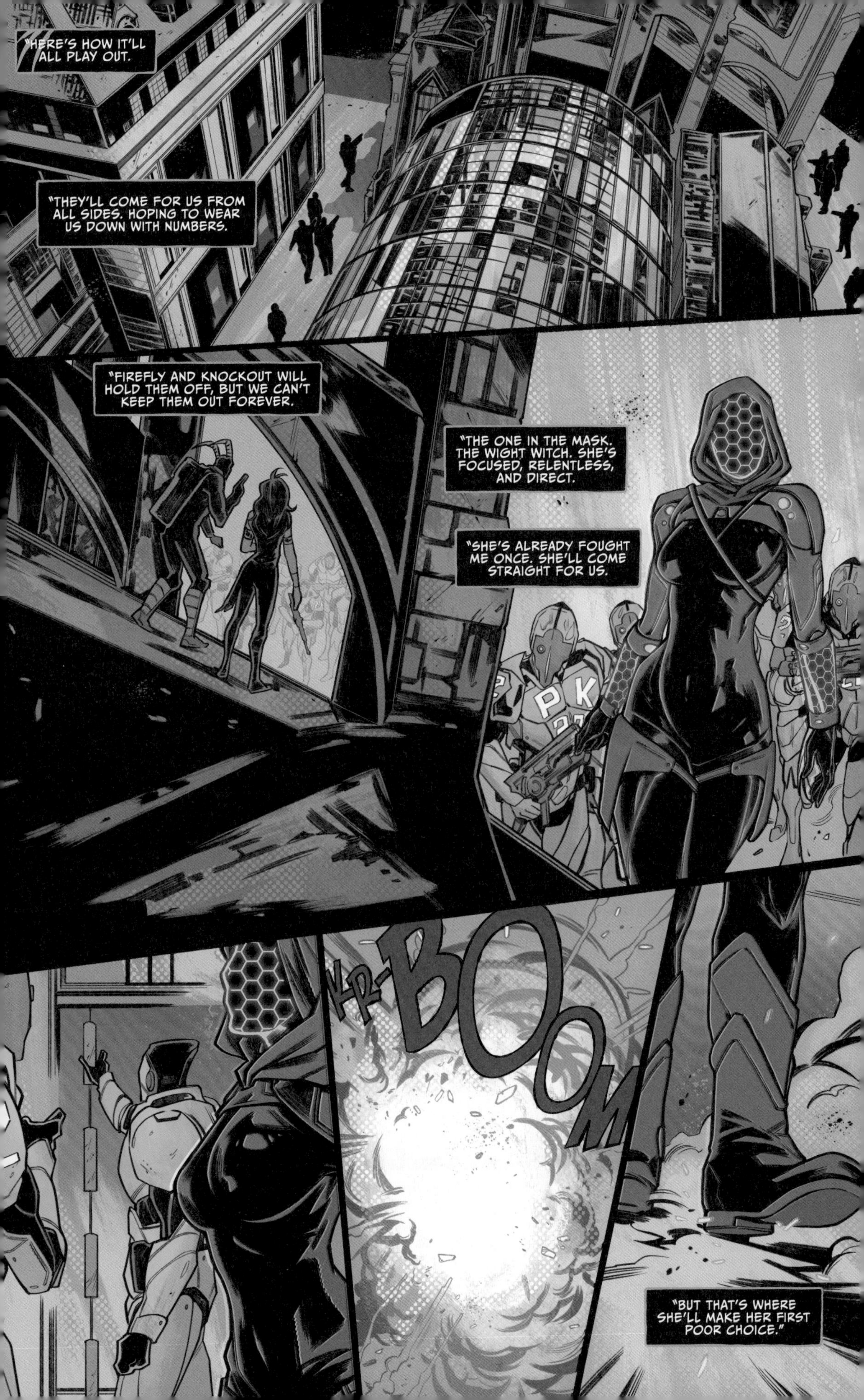
"HERE'S HOW IT'LL ALL PLAY OUT.
"THEY'LL COME FOR US FROM ALL SIDES. HOPING TO WEAR US DOWN WITH NUMBERS.
"FIREFLY AND KNOCKOUT WILL HOLD THEM OFF, BUT WE CAN'T KEEP THEM OUT FOREVER.
"THE ONE IN THE MASK. THE WIGHT WITCH. SHE'S FOCUSED, RELENTLESS, AND DIRECT.
"SHE'S ALREADY FOUGHT ME ONCE. SHE'LL COME STRAIGHT FOR US.
PK
KR-BOOOM
"BUT THAT'S WHERE SHE'LL MAKE HER FIRST POOR CHOICE."

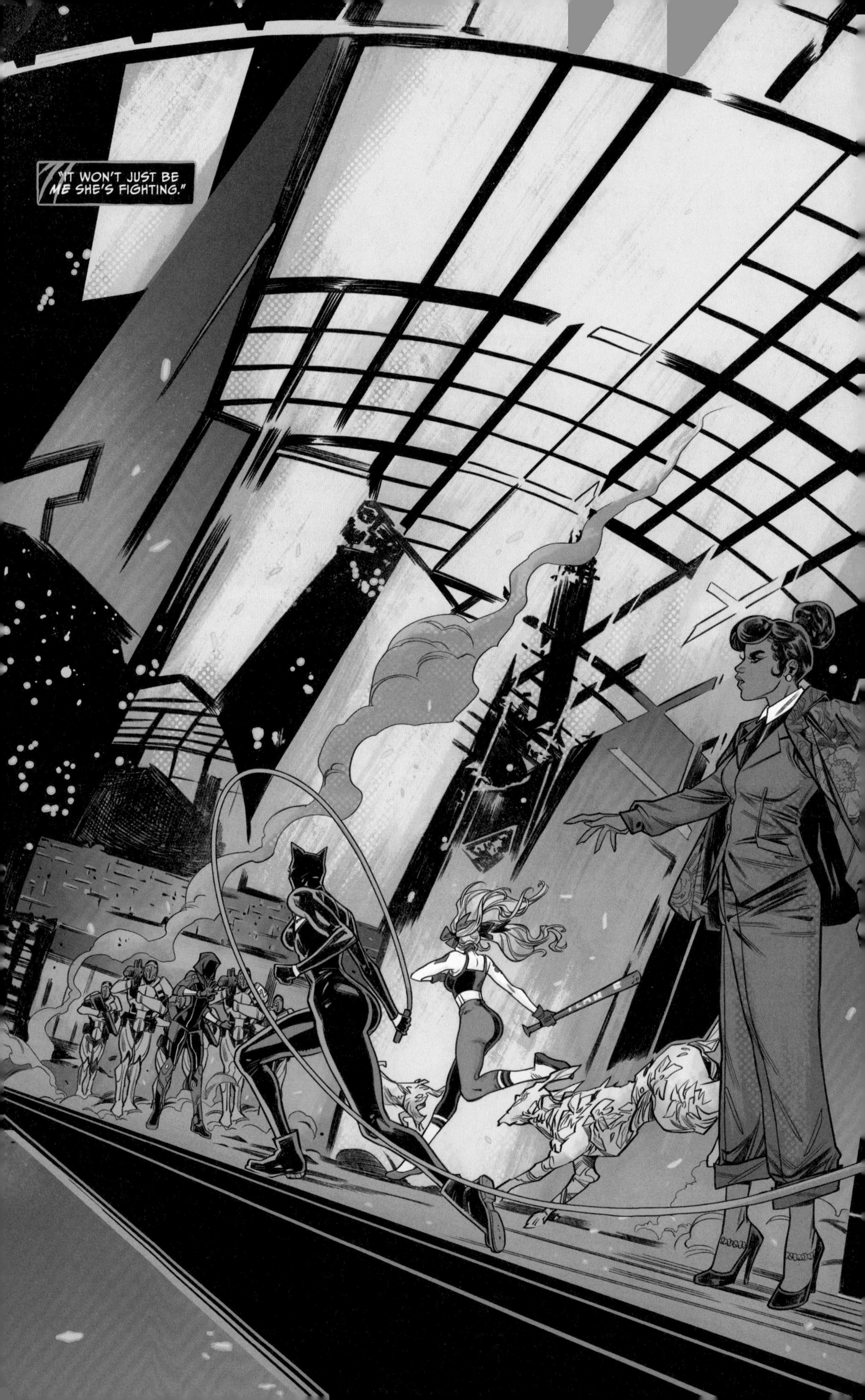
"IT WON'T JUST BE ME SHE'S FIGHTING."

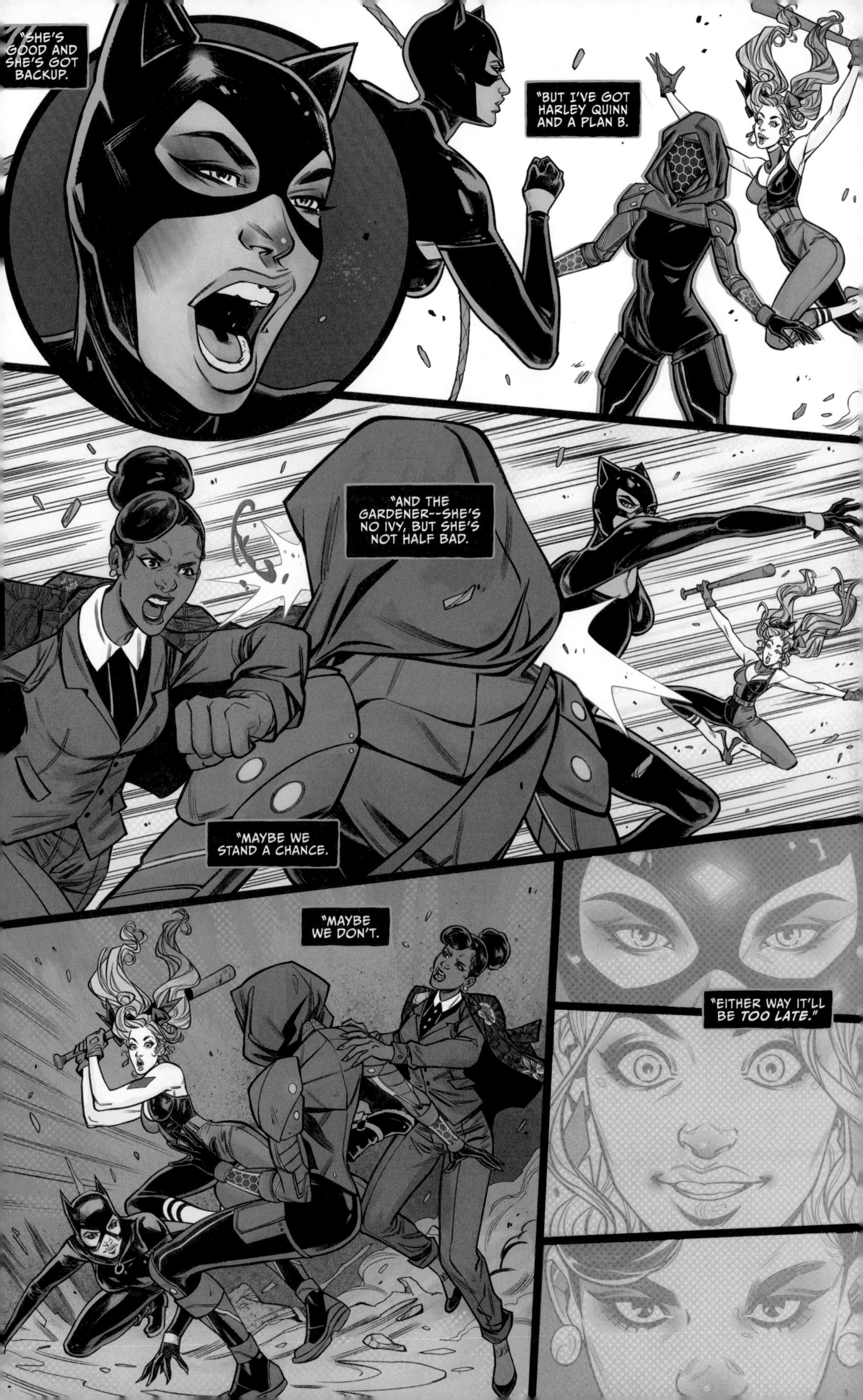
"SHE'S GOOD AND SHE'S GOT BACKUP.
"BUT I'VE GOT HARLEY QUINN AND A PLAN B.
"AND THE GARDENER--SHE'S NO IVY, BUT SHE'S NOT HALF BAD.
"MAYBE WE STAND A CHANCE.
"MAYBE WE DON'T.
"EITHER WAY IT'LL BE *TOO LATE.*"

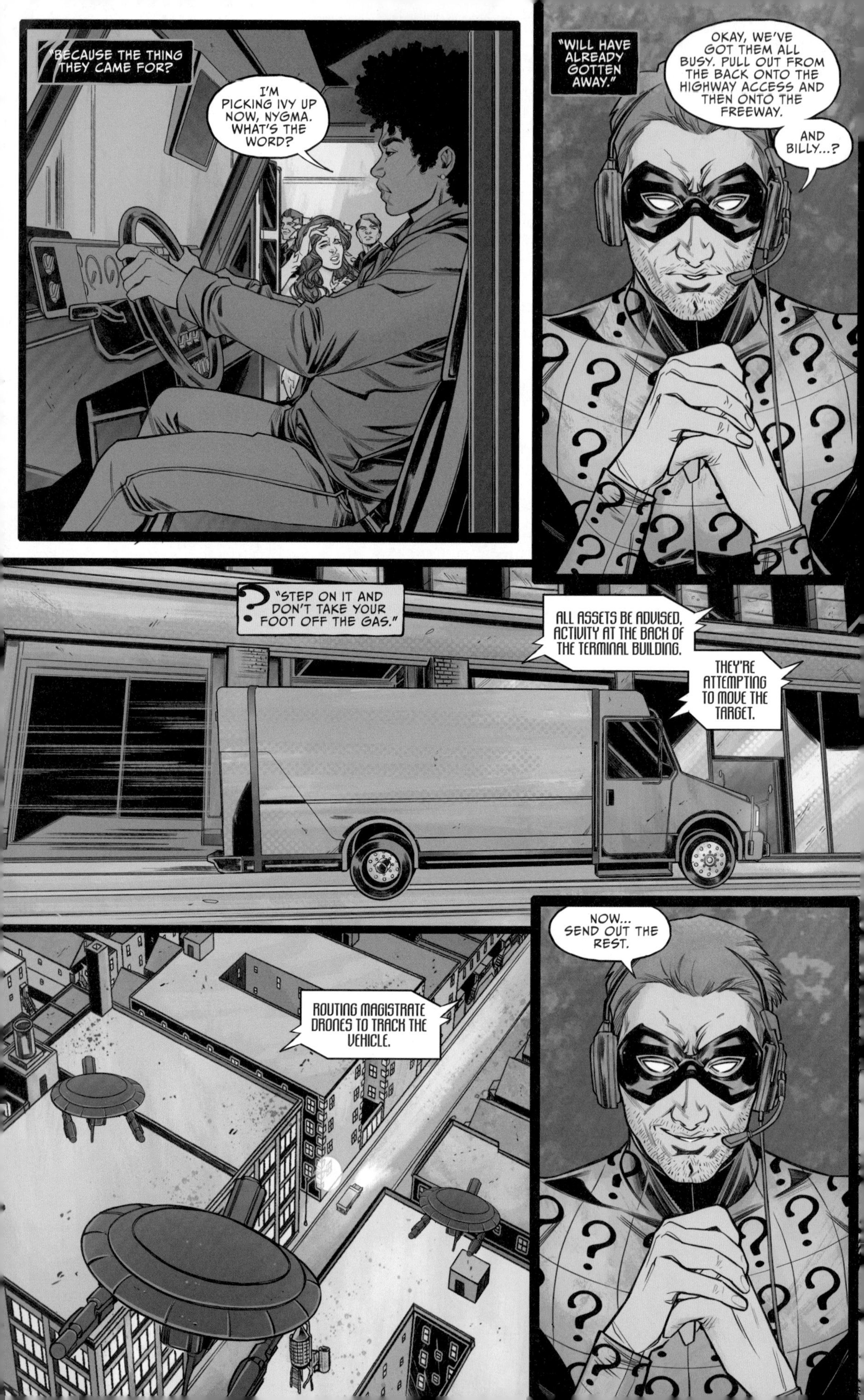
"BECAUSE THE THING THEY CAME FOR?
I'M PICKING IVY UP NOW, NYGMA. WHAT'S THE WORD?
"WILL HAVE ALREADY GOTTEN AWAY."
OKAY, WE'VE GOT THEM ALL BUSY. PULL OUT FROM THE BACK ONTO THE HIGHWAY ACCESS AND THEN ONTO THE FREEWAY.
AND BILLY...?
"STEP ON IT AND DON'T TAKE YOUR FOOT OFF THE GAS."
ALL ASSETS BE ADVISED, ACTIVITY AT THE BACK OF THE TERMINAL BUILDING.
THEY'RE ATTEMPTING TO MOVE THE TARGET.
ROUTING MAGISTRATE DRONES TO TRACK THE VEHICLE.
NOW... SEND OUT THE REST.

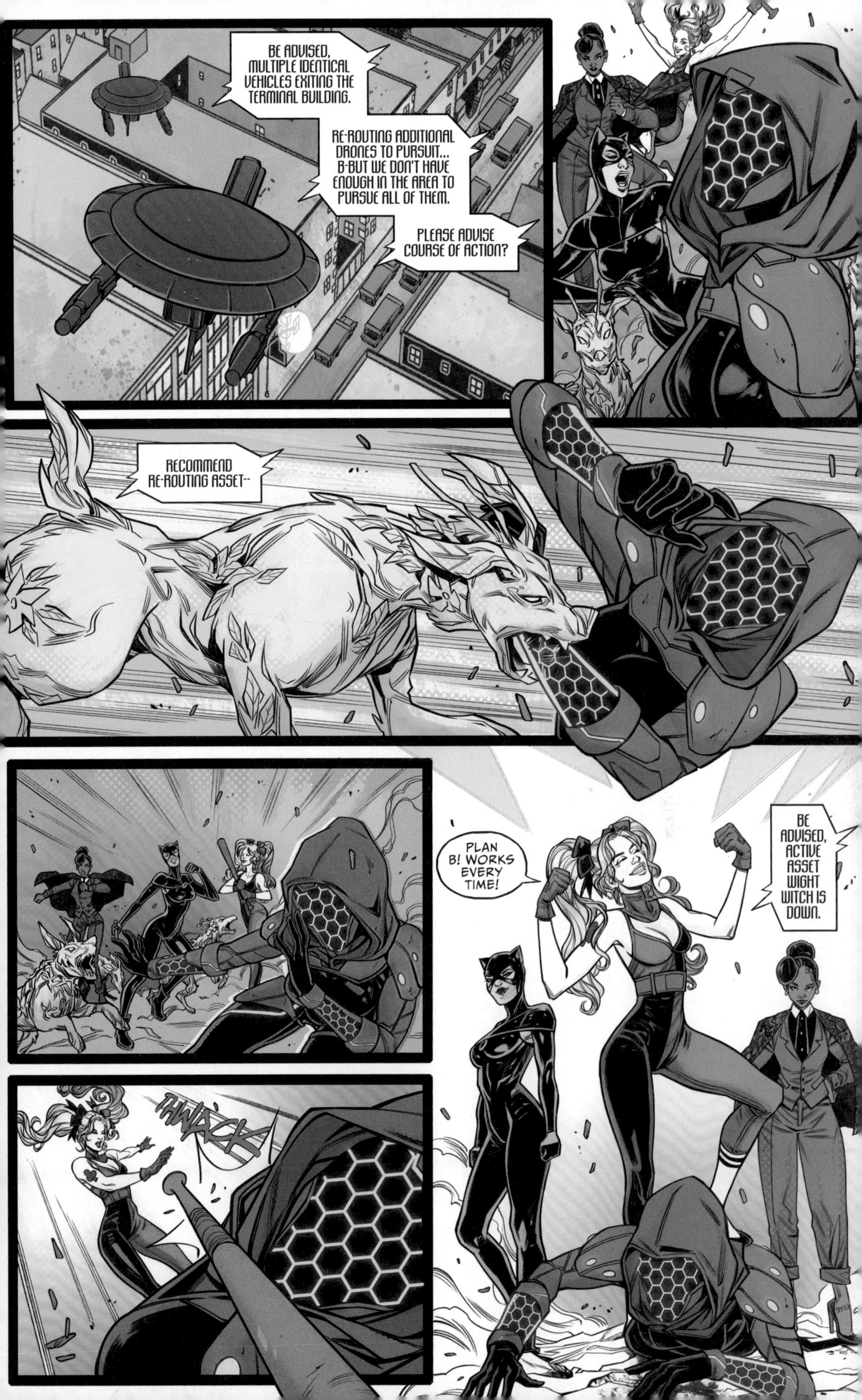
BE ADVISED, MULTIPLE IDENTICAL VEHICLES EXITING THE TERMINAL BUILDING.
RE-ROUTING ADDITIONAL DRONES TO PURSUIT... B-BUT WE DON'T HAVE ENOUGH IN THE AREA TO PURSUE ALL OF THEM.
PLEASE ADVISE COURSE OF ACTION?
RECOMMEND RE-ROUTING ASSET--
THWACK
PLAN B! WORKS EVERY TIME!
BE ADVISED, ACTIVE ASSET WIGHT WITCH IS DOWN.

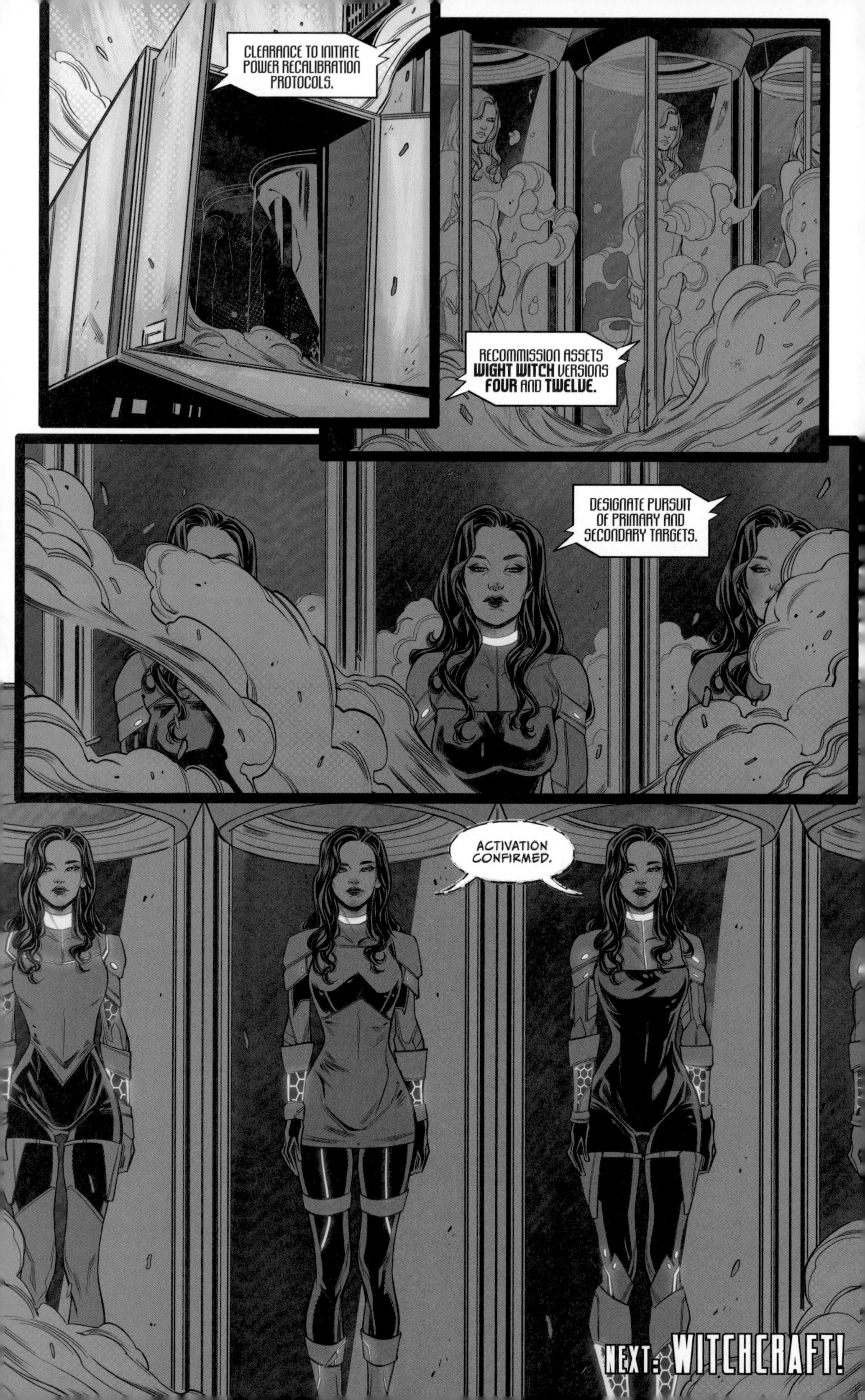
CLEARANCE TO INITIATE POWER RECALIBRATION PROTOCOLS.
RECOMMISSION ASSETS **WIGHT WITCH** VERSIONS **FOUR** AND **TWELVE.**
DESIGNATE PURSUIT OF PRIMARY AND SECONDARY TARGETS.
ACTIVATION CONFIRMED.
NEXT: WITCHCRAFT!

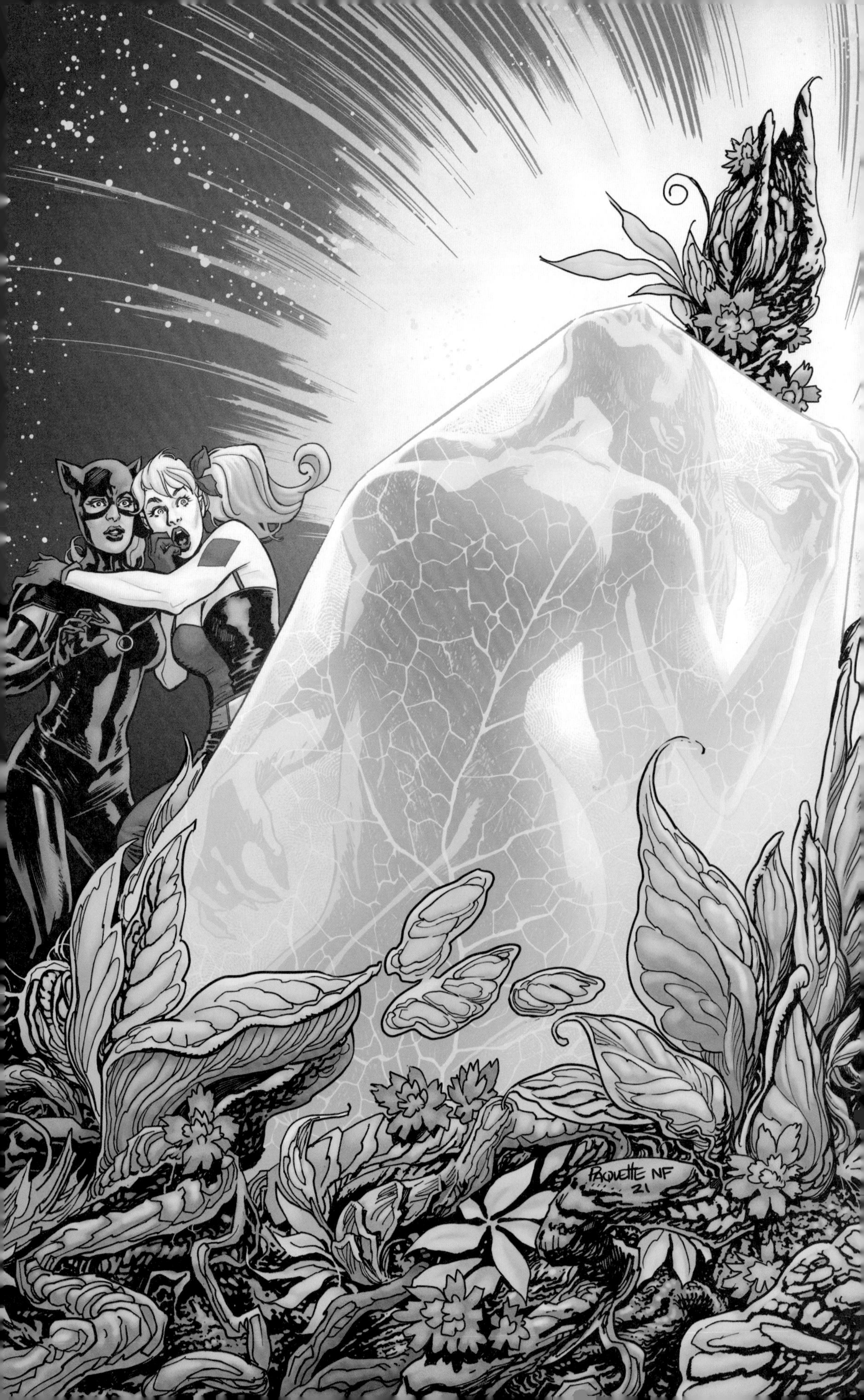
PAQUETTE NF
21

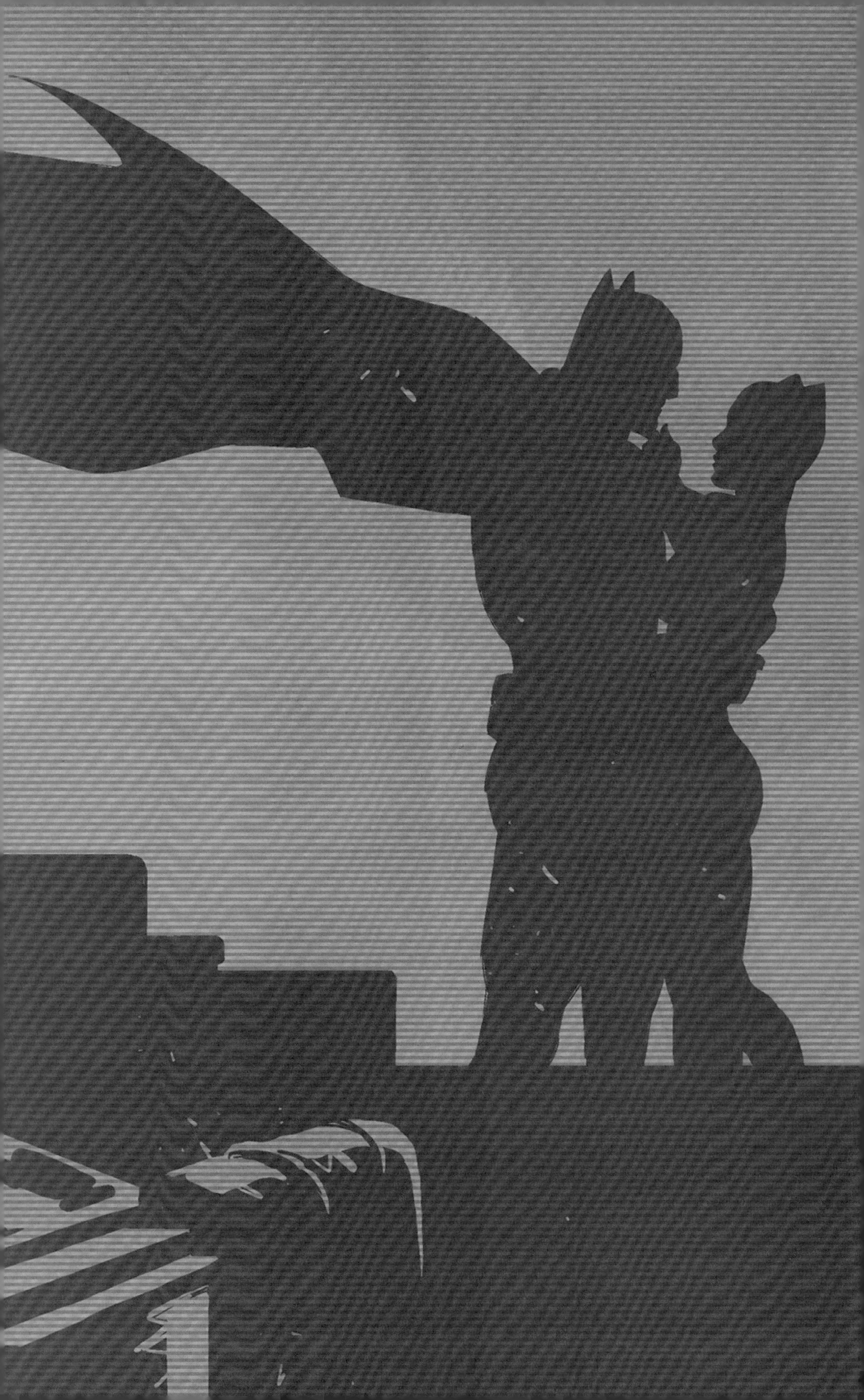

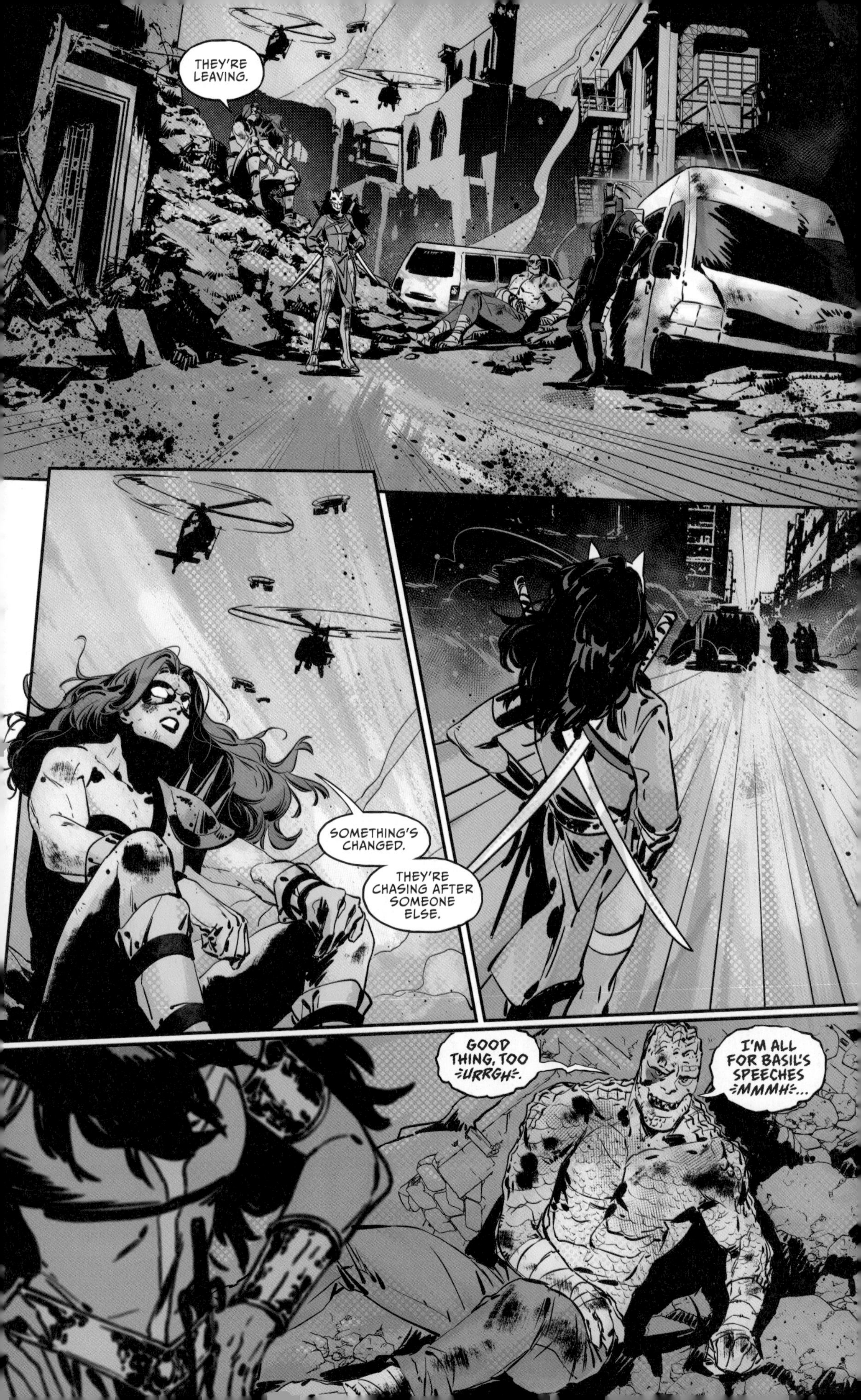
THEY'RE LEAVING.
SOMETHING'S CHANGED.
THEY'RE CHASING AFTER SOMEONE ELSE.
GOOD THING, TOO -URRGH-.
I'M ALL FOR BASIL'S SPEECHES -MMMH-...

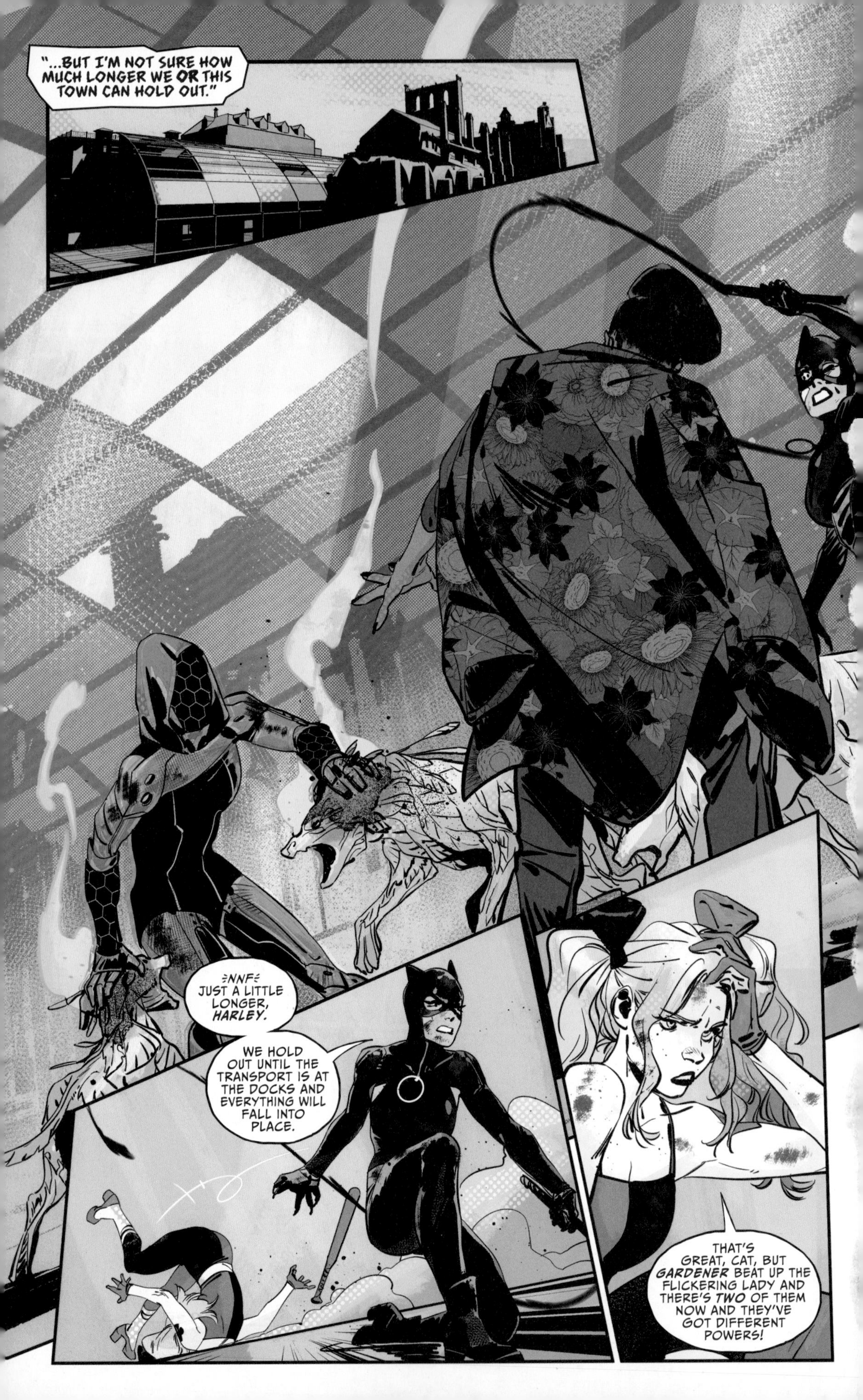
"...BUT I'M NOT SURE HOW MUCH LONGER WE OR THIS TOWN CAN HOLD OUT."
NNF JUST A LITTLE LONGER, HARLEY.
WE HOLD OUT UNTIL THE TRANSPORT IS AT THE DOCKS AND EVERYTHING WILL FALL INTO PLACE.
THAT'S GREAT, CAT, BUT GARDENER BEAT UP THE FLICKERING LADY AND THERE'S TWO OF THEM NOW AND THEY'VE GOT DIFFERENT POWERS!

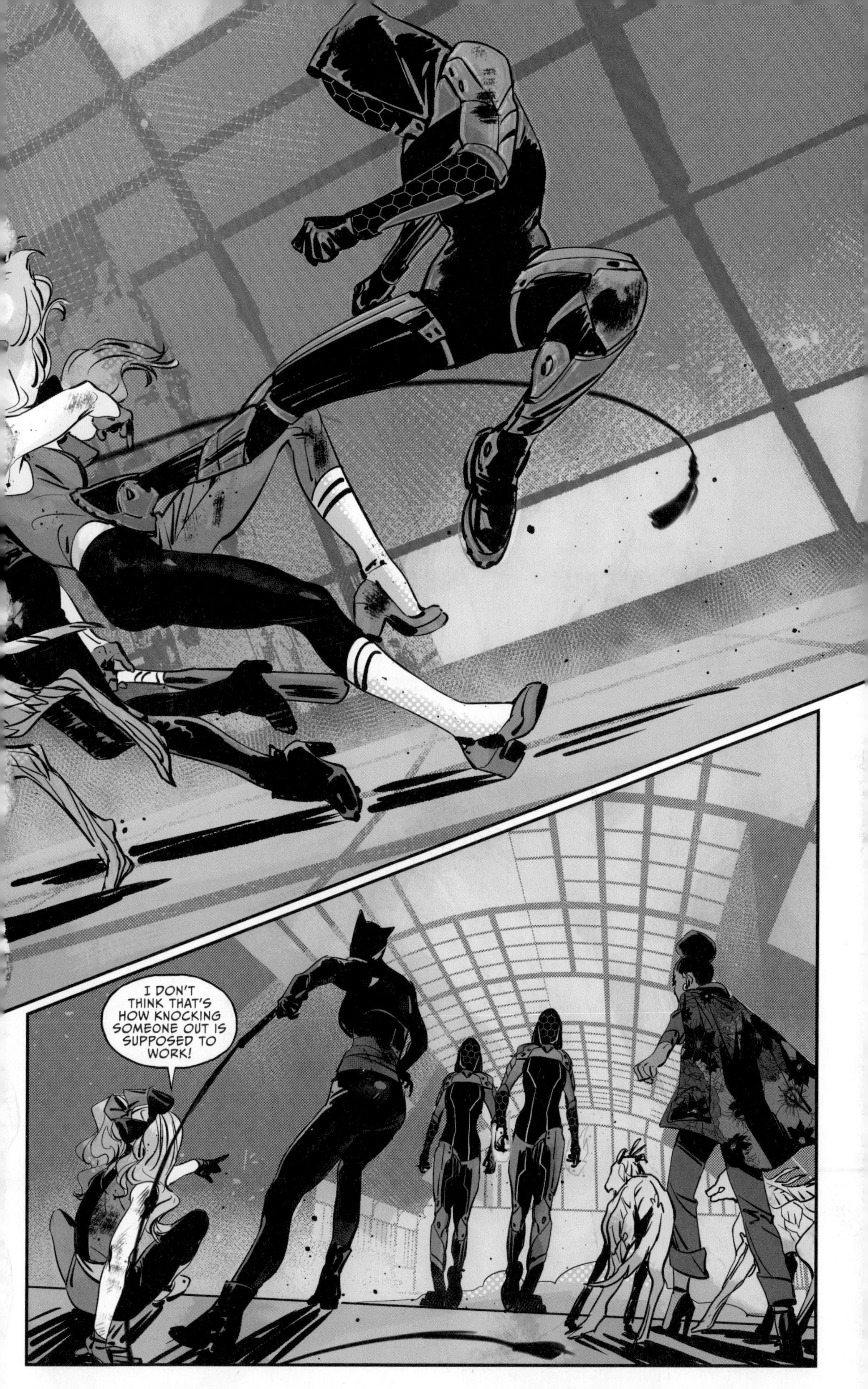
I DON'T THINK THAT'S HOW KNOCKING SOMEONE OUT IS SUPPOSED TO WORK!

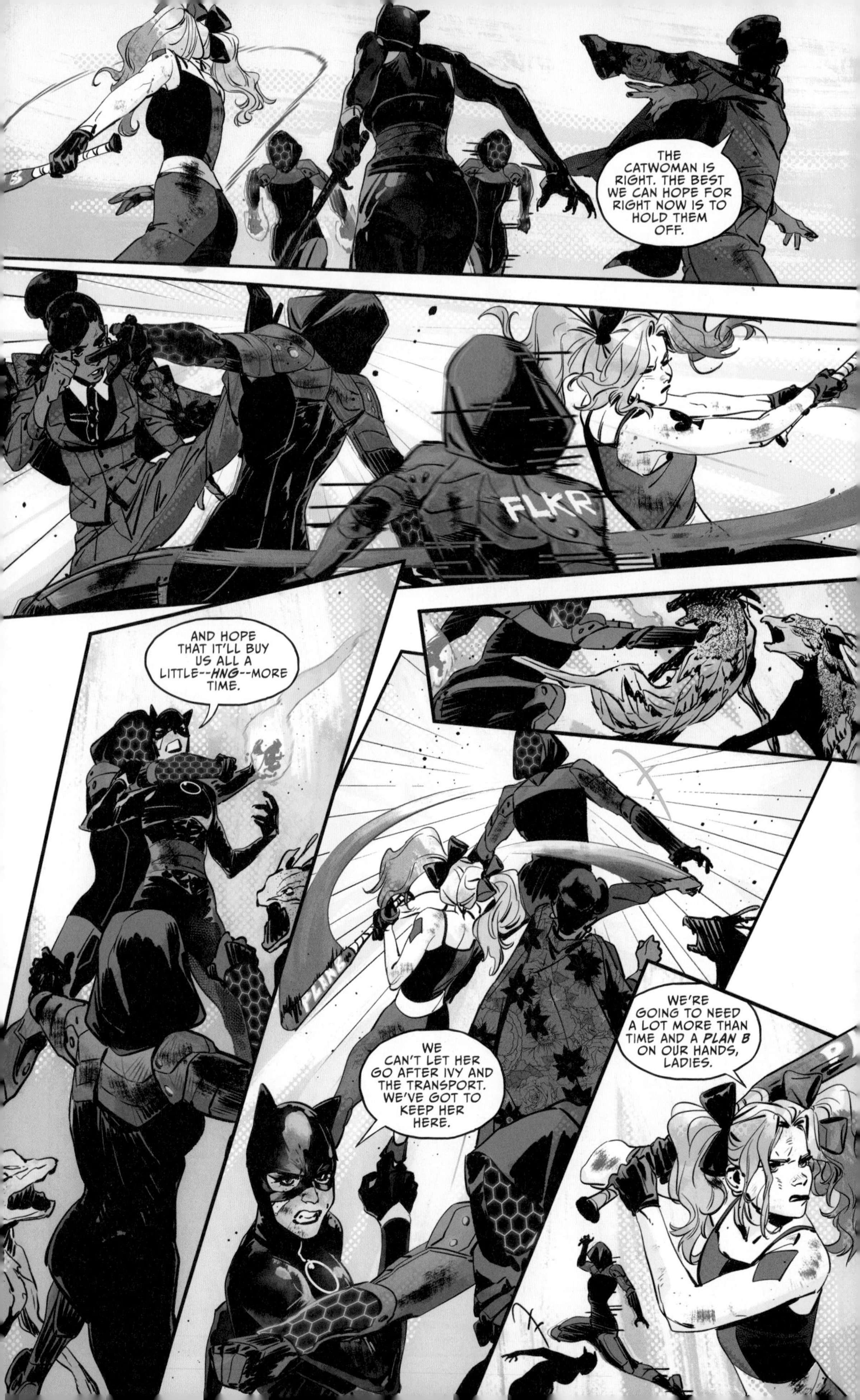
THE CATWOMAN IS RIGHT. THE BEST WE CAN HOPE FOR RIGHT NOW IS TO HOLD THEM OFF.
FLKR
AND HOPE THAT IT'LL BUY US ALL A LITTLE--*HNG*--MORE TIME.
PLINK
WE CAN'T LET HER GO AFTER IVY AND THE TRANSPORT. WE'VE GOT TO KEEP HER HERE.
WE'RE GOING TO NEED A LOT MORE THAN TIME AND A *PLAN B* ON OUR HANDS, LADIES.

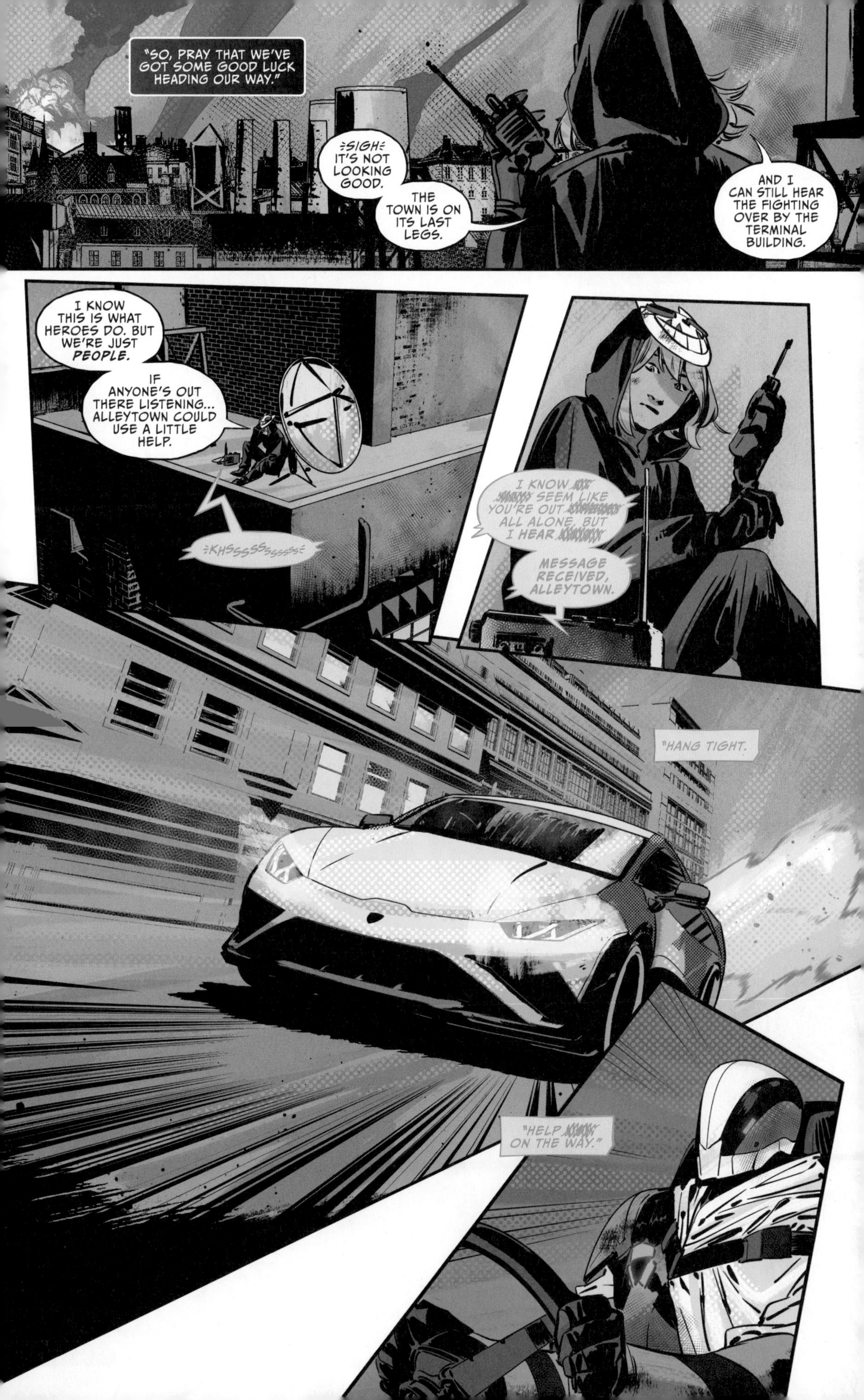
"SO, PRAY THAT WE'VE GOT SOME GOOD LUCK HEADING OUR WAY."
SIGH IT'S NOT LOOKING GOOD.
THE TOWN IS ON ITS LAST LEGS.
AND I CAN STILL HEAR THE FIGHTING OVER BY THE TERMINAL BUILDING.
I KNOW THIS IS WHAT HEROES DO. BUT WE'RE JUST *PEOPLE*.
IF ANYONE'S OUT THERE LISTENING... ALLEYTOWN COULD USE A LITTLE HELP.
KHSSSSSSSSSSS
I KNOW SEEM LIKE YOU'RE OUT ALL ALONE, BUT I HEAR
MESSAGE RECEIVED, ALLEYTOWN.
"HANG TIGHT.
"HELP ON THE WAY."

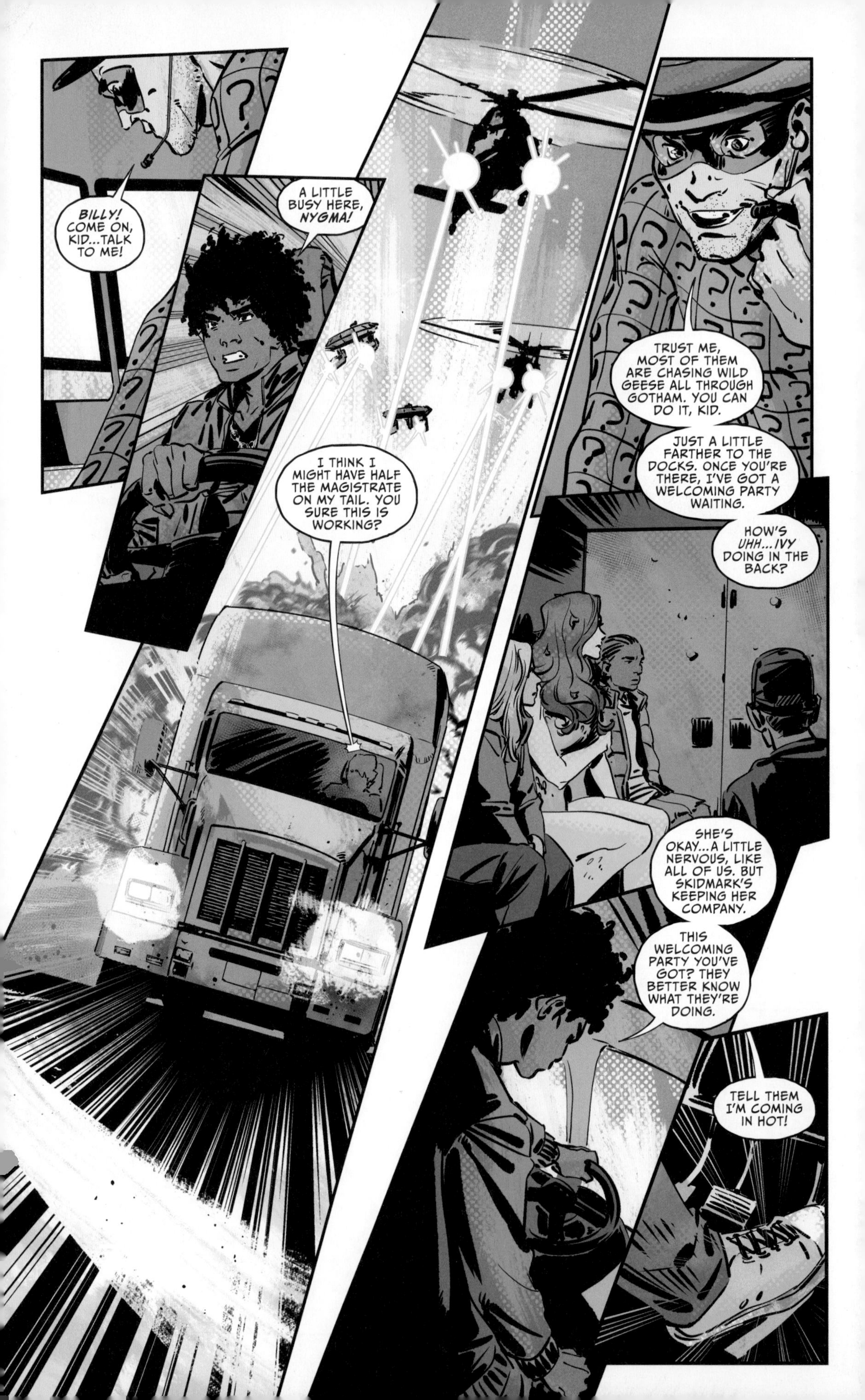
BILLY! COME ON, KID...TALK TO ME!
A LITTLE BUSY HERE, NYGMA!
I THINK I MIGHT HAVE HALF THE MAGISTRATE ON MY TAIL. YOU SURE THIS IS WORKING?
TRUST ME, MOST OF THEM ARE CHASING WILD GEESE ALL THROUGH GOTHAM. YOU CAN DO IT, KID.
JUST A LITTLE FARTHER TO THE DOCKS. ONCE YOU'RE THERE, I'VE GOT A WELCOMING PARTY WAITING.
HOW'S UHH...IVY DOING IN THE BACK?
SHE'S OKAY...A LITTLE NERVOUS, LIKE ALL OF US. BUT SKIDMARK'S KEEPING HER COMPANY.
THIS WELCOMING PARTY YOU'VE GOT? THEY BETTER KNOW WHAT THEY'RE DOING.
TELL THEM I'M COMING IN HOT!

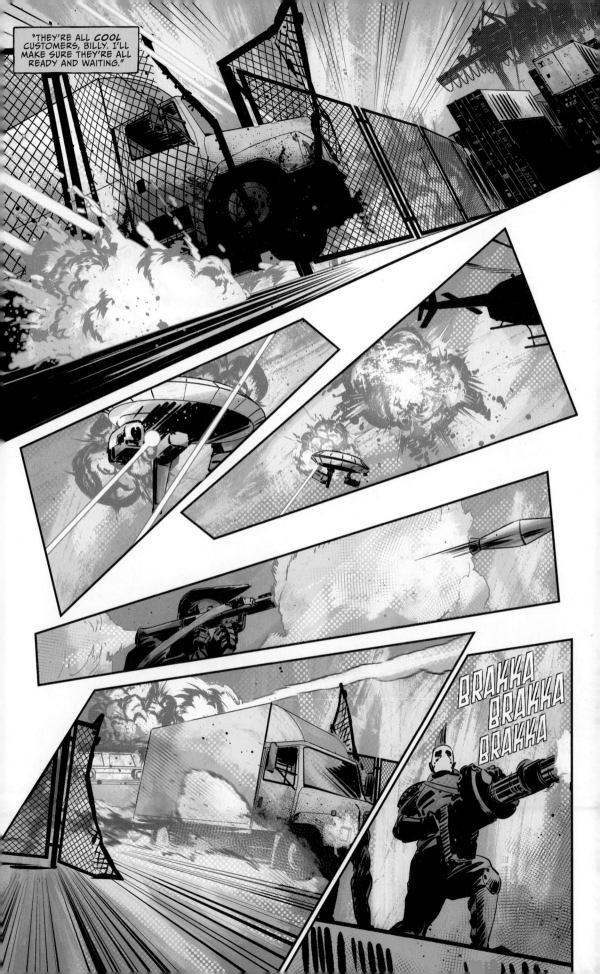

"THEY'RE ALL *COOL*
CUSTOMERS, BILLY. I'LL
MAKE SURE THEY'RE ALL
READY AND WAITING."

BRAKKA
BRAKKA
BRAKKA

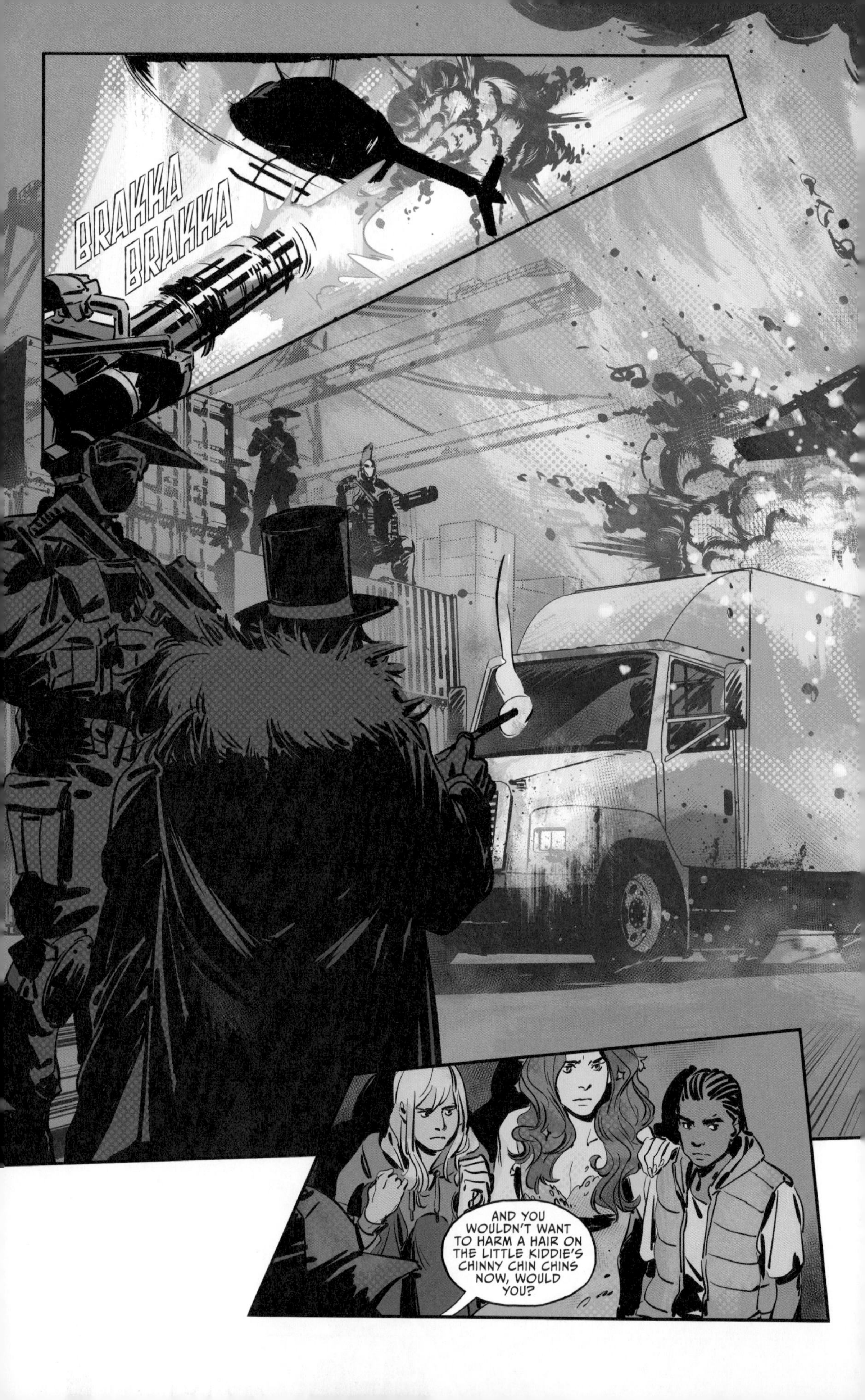
BRAKKA BRAKKA
AND YOU WOULDN'T WANT TO HARM A HAIR ON THE LITTLE KIDDIE'S CHINNY CHIN CHINS NOW, WOULD YOU?

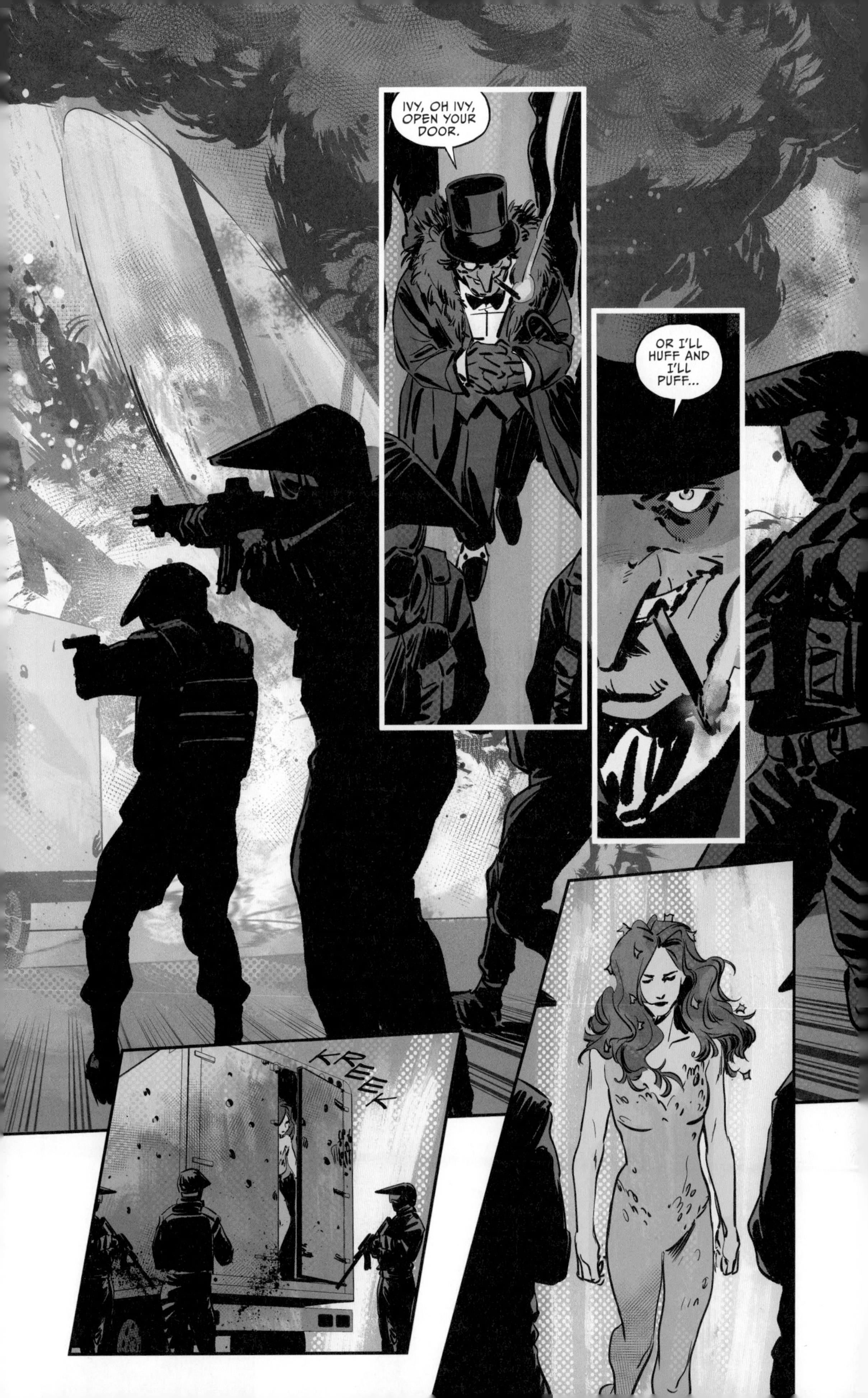
IVY, OH IVY, OPEN YOUR DOOR.
OR I'LL HUFF AND I'LL PUFF...
KREEK

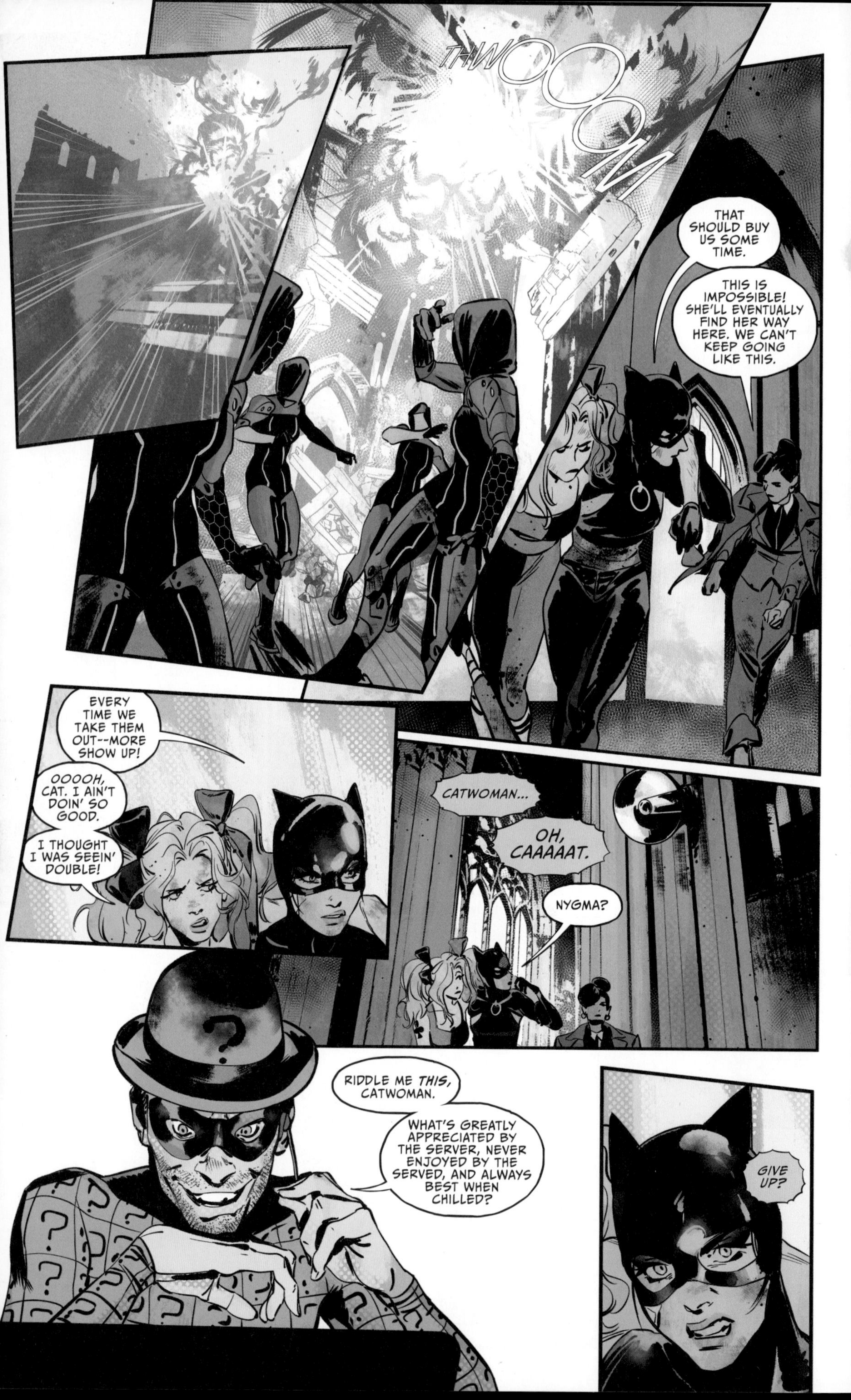
THWOOOM
THAT SHOULD BUY US SOME TIME.
THIS IS IMPOSSIBLE! SHE'LL EVENTUALLY FIND HER WAY HERE. WE CAN'T KEEP GOING LIKE THIS.
EVERY TIME WE TAKE THEM OUT--MORE SHOW UP!
OOOOH, CAT. I AIN'T DOIN' SO GOOD.
I THOUGHT I WAS SEEIN' DOUBLE!
CATWOMAN...
OH, CAAAAAT.
NYGMA?
RIDDLE ME THIS, CATWOMAN.
WHAT'S GREATLY APPRECIATED BY THE SERVER, NEVER ENJOYED BY THE SERVED, AND ALWAYS BEST WHEN CHILLED?
GIVE UP?

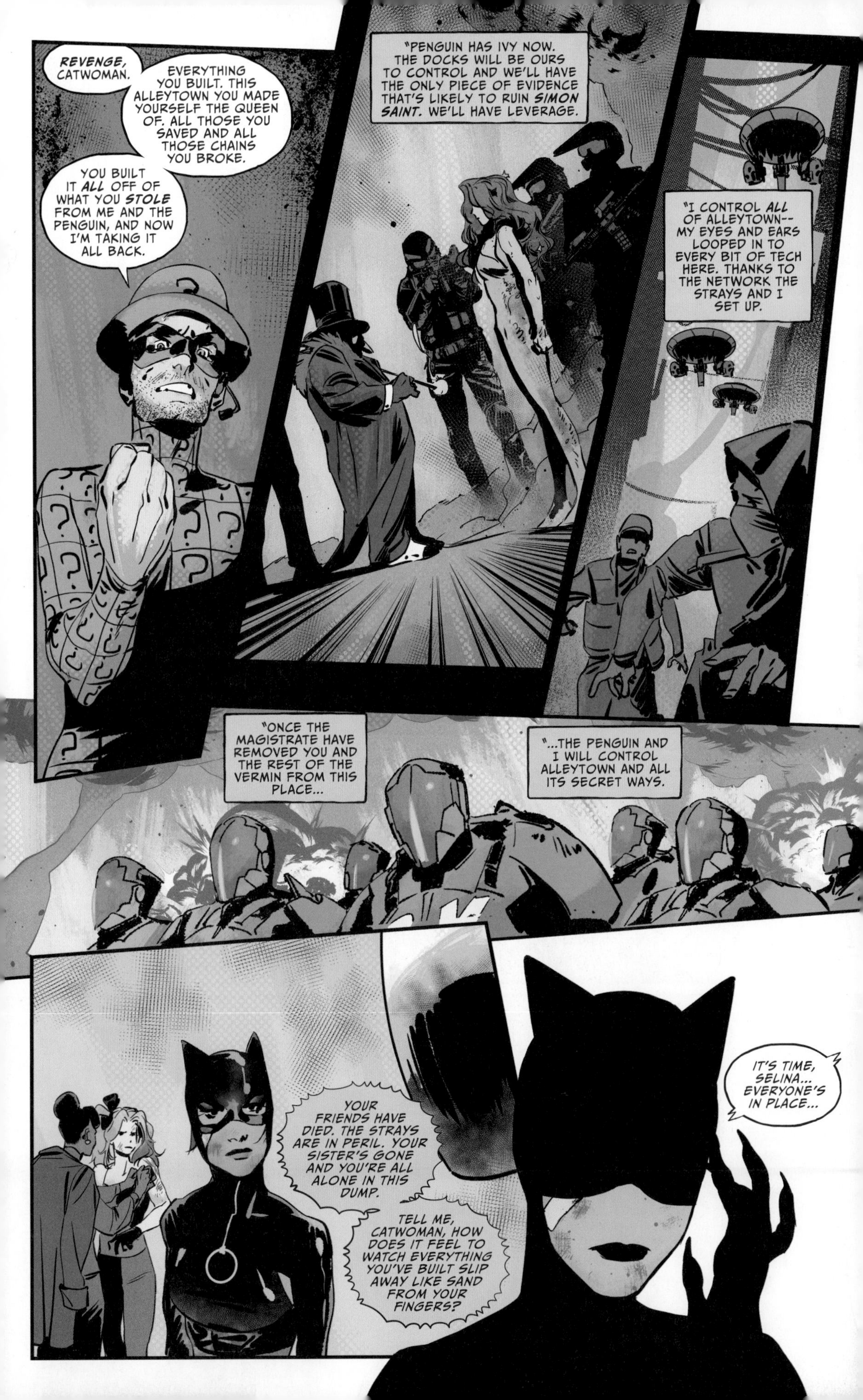
REVENGE, CATWOMAN.
EVERYTHING YOU BUILT. THIS ALLEYTOWN YOU MADE YOURSELF THE QUEEN OF. ALL THOSE YOU SAVED AND ALL THOSE CHAINS YOU BROKE.
YOU BUILT IT ALL OFF OF WHAT YOU STOLE FROM ME AND THE PENGUIN, AND NOW I'M TAKING IT ALL BACK.
"PENGUIN HAS IVY NOW. THE DOCKS WILL BE OURS TO CONTROL AND WE'LL HAVE THE ONLY PIECE OF EVIDENCE THAT'S LIKELY TO RUIN SIMON SAINT. WE'LL HAVE LEVERAGE.
"I CONTROL ALL OF ALLEYTOWN-- MY EYES AND EARS LOOPED IN TO EVERY BIT OF TECH HERE. THANKS TO THE NETWORK THE STRAYS AND I SET UP.
"ONCE THE MAGISTRATE HAVE REMOVED YOU AND THE REST OF THE VERMIN FROM THIS PLACE...
"...THE PENGUIN AND I WILL CONTROL ALLEYTOWN AND ALL ITS SECRET WAYS.
YOUR FRIENDS HAVE DIED. THE STRAYS ARE IN PERIL. YOUR SISTER'S GONE AND YOU'RE ALL ALONE IN THIS DUMP.
TELL ME, CATWOMAN, HOW DOES IT FEEL TO WATCH EVERYTHING YOU'VE BUILT SLIP AWAY LIKE SAND FROM YOUR FINGERS?
IT'S TIME, SELINA... EVERYONE'S IN PLACE...

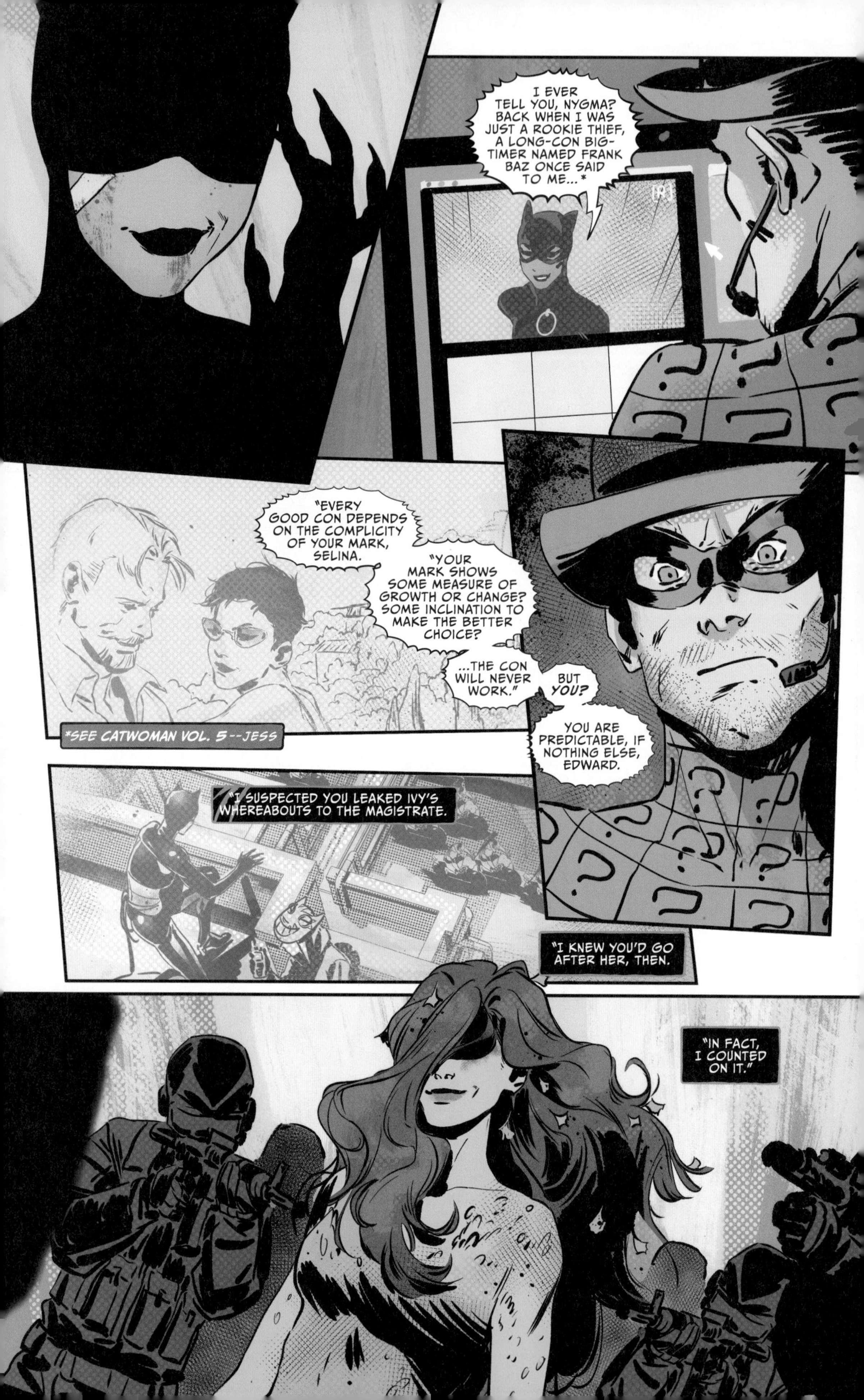

I EVER TELL YOU, NYGMA? BACK WHEN I WAS JUST A ROOKIE THIEF, A LONG-CON BIG-TIMER NAMED FRANK BAZ ONCE SAID TO ME...*
"EVERY GOOD CON DEPENDS ON THE COMPLICITY OF YOUR MARK, SELINA.
"YOUR MARK SHOWS SOME MEASURE OF GROWTH OR CHANGE? SOME INCLINATION TO MAKE THE BETTER CHOICE?
...THE CON WILL NEVER WORK."
*SEE CATWOMAN VOL. 5--JESS
BUT YOU?
YOU ARE PREDICTABLE, IF NOTHING ELSE, EDWARD.
"I SUSPECTED YOU LEAKED IVY'S WHEREABOUTS TO THE MAGISTRATE.
"I KNEW YOU'D GO AFTER HER, THEN.
"IN FACT, I COUNTED ON IT."

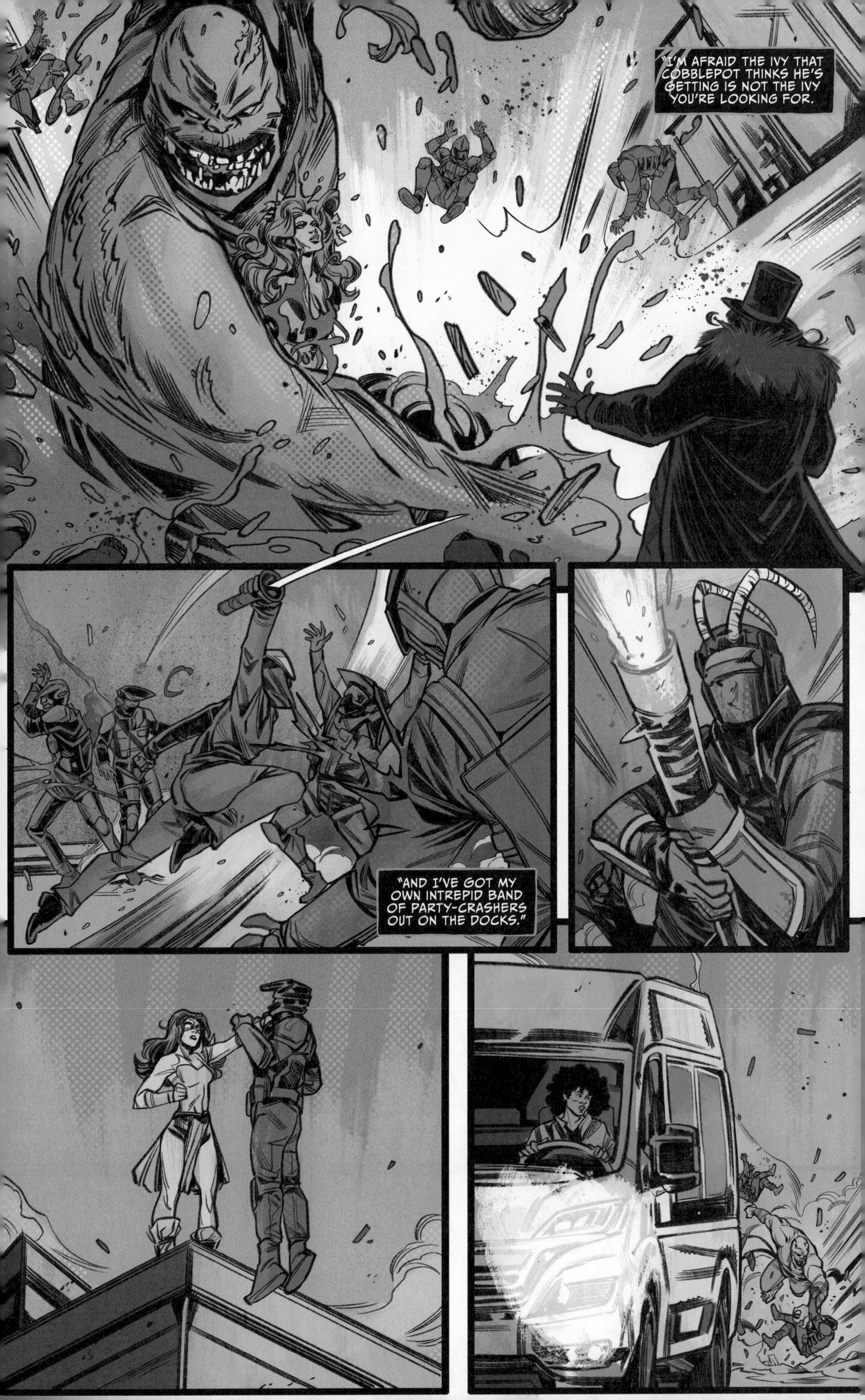
"I'M AFRAID THE IVY THAT COBBLEPOT THINKS HE'S GETTING IS NOT THE IVY YOU'RE LOOKING FOR.
"AND I'VE GOT MY OWN INTREPID BAND OF PARTY-CRASHERS OUT ON THE DOCKS."

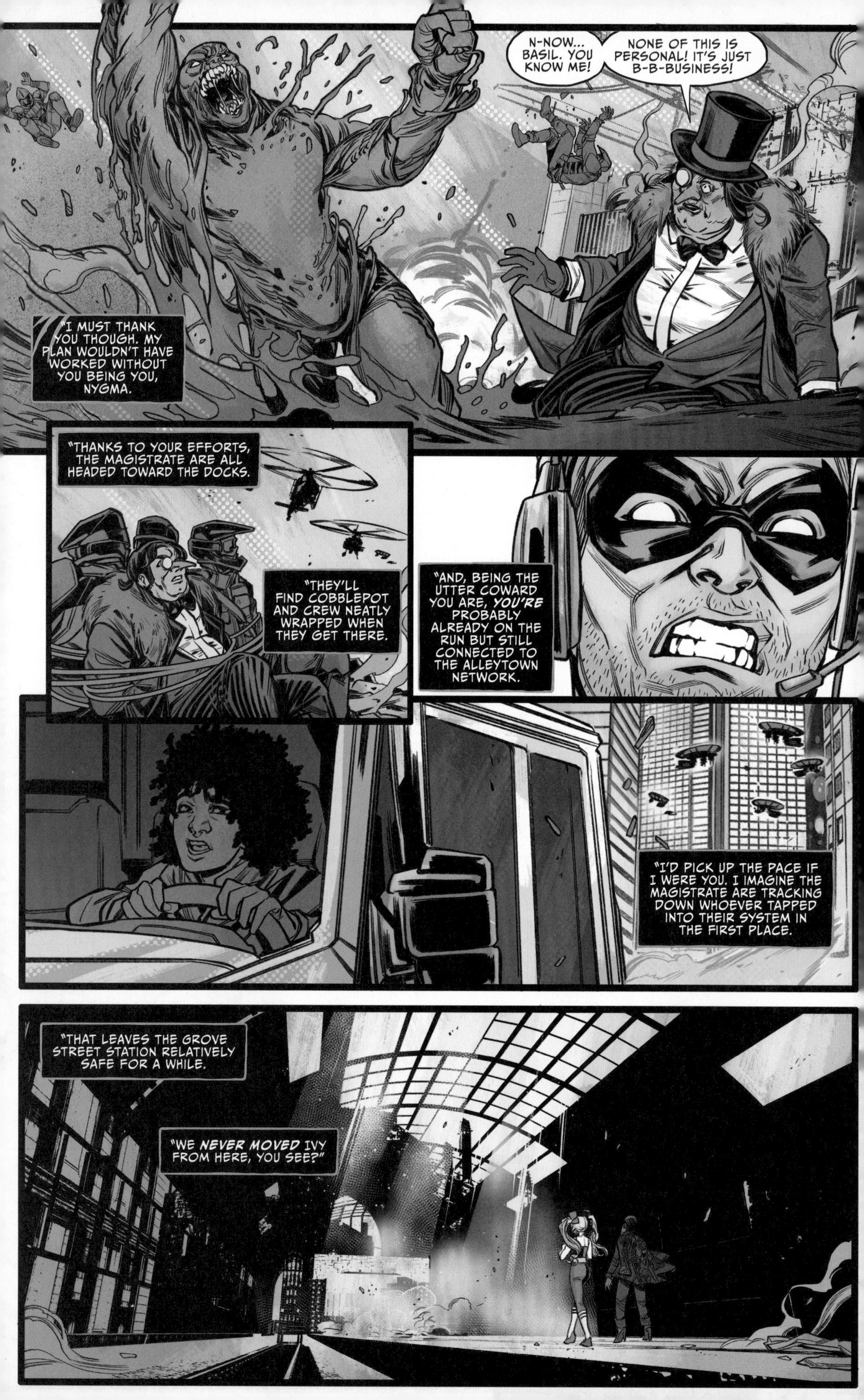
N-NOW... BASIL. YOU KNOW ME!
NONE OF THIS IS PERSONAL! IT'S JUST B-B-BUSINESS!
"I MUST THANK YOU THOUGH. MY PLAN WOULDN'T HAVE WORKED WITHOUT YOU BEING YOU, NYGMA.
"THANKS TO YOUR EFFORTS, THE MAGISTRATE ARE ALL HEADED TOWARD THE DOCKS.
"THEY'LL FIND COBBLEPOT AND CREW NEATLY WRAPPED WHEN THEY GET THERE.
"AND, BEING THE UTTER COWARD YOU ARE, YOU'RE PROBABLY ALREADY ON THE RUN BUT STILL CONNECTED TO THE ALLEYTOWN NETWORK.
"I'D PICK UP THE PACE IF I WERE YOU. I IMAGINE THE MAGISTRATE ARE TRACKING DOWN WHOEVER TAPPED INTO THEIR SYSTEM IN THE FIRST PLACE.
"THAT LEAVES THE GROVE STREET STATION RELATIVELY SAFE FOR A WHILE.
"WE NEVER MOVED IVY FROM HERE, YOU SEE?"

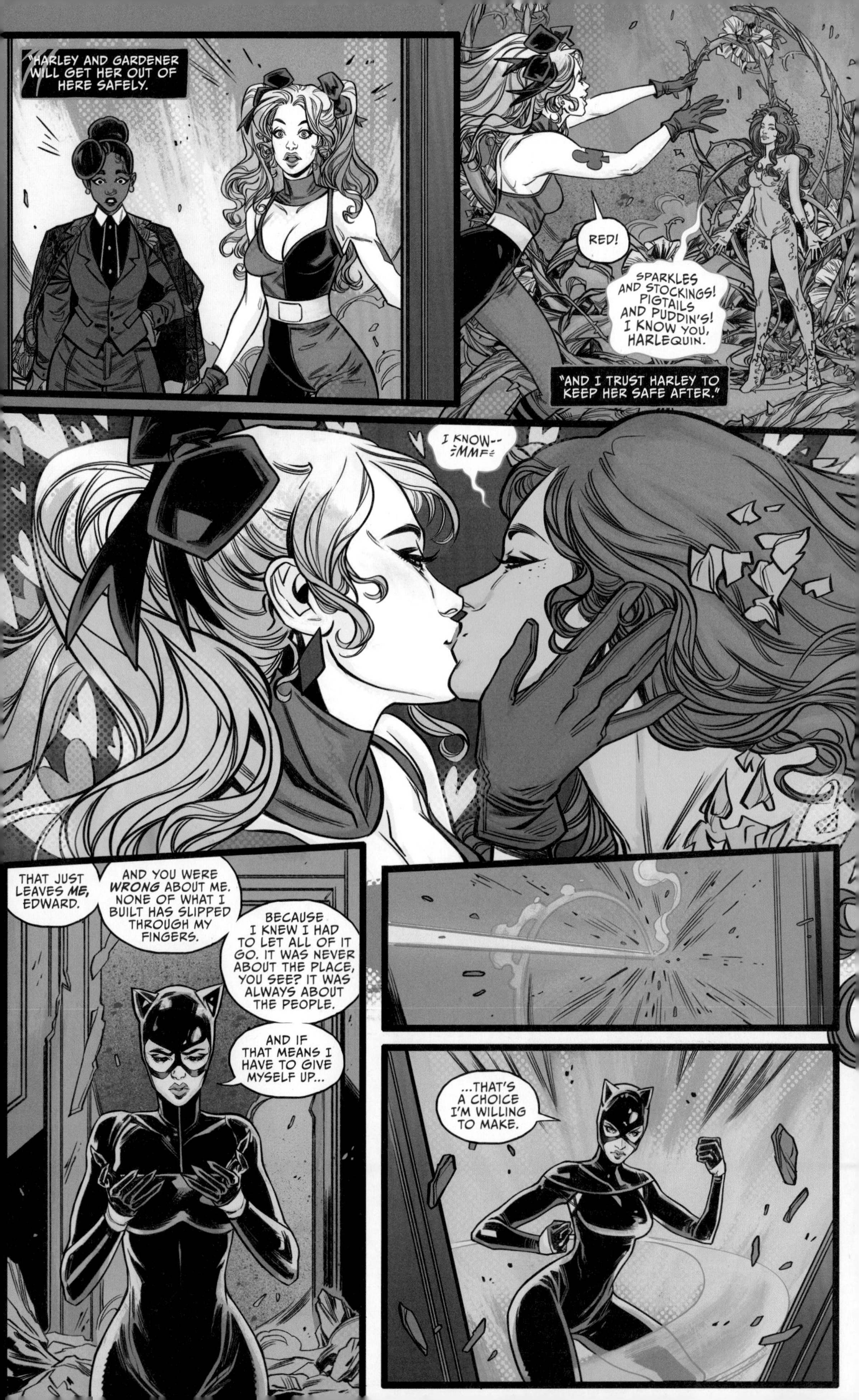
"HARLEY AND GARDENER WILL GET HER OUT OF HERE SAFELY.
RED!
SPARKLES AND STOCKINGS! PIGTAILS AND PUDDIN'S! I KNOW YOU, HARLEQUIN.
"AND I TRUST HARLEY TO KEEP HER SAFE AFTER."
I KNOW-- MMF
THAT JUST LEAVES ME, EDWARD.
AND YOU WERE WRONG ABOUT ME. NONE OF WHAT I BUILT HAS SLIPPED THROUGH MY FINGERS.
BECAUSE I KNEW I HAD TO LET ALL OF IT GO. IT WAS NEVER ABOUT THE PLACE, YOU SEE? IT WAS ALWAYS ABOUT THE PEOPLE.
AND IF THAT MEANS I HAVE TO GIVE MYSELF UP...
...THAT'S A CHOICE I'M WILLING TO MAKE.

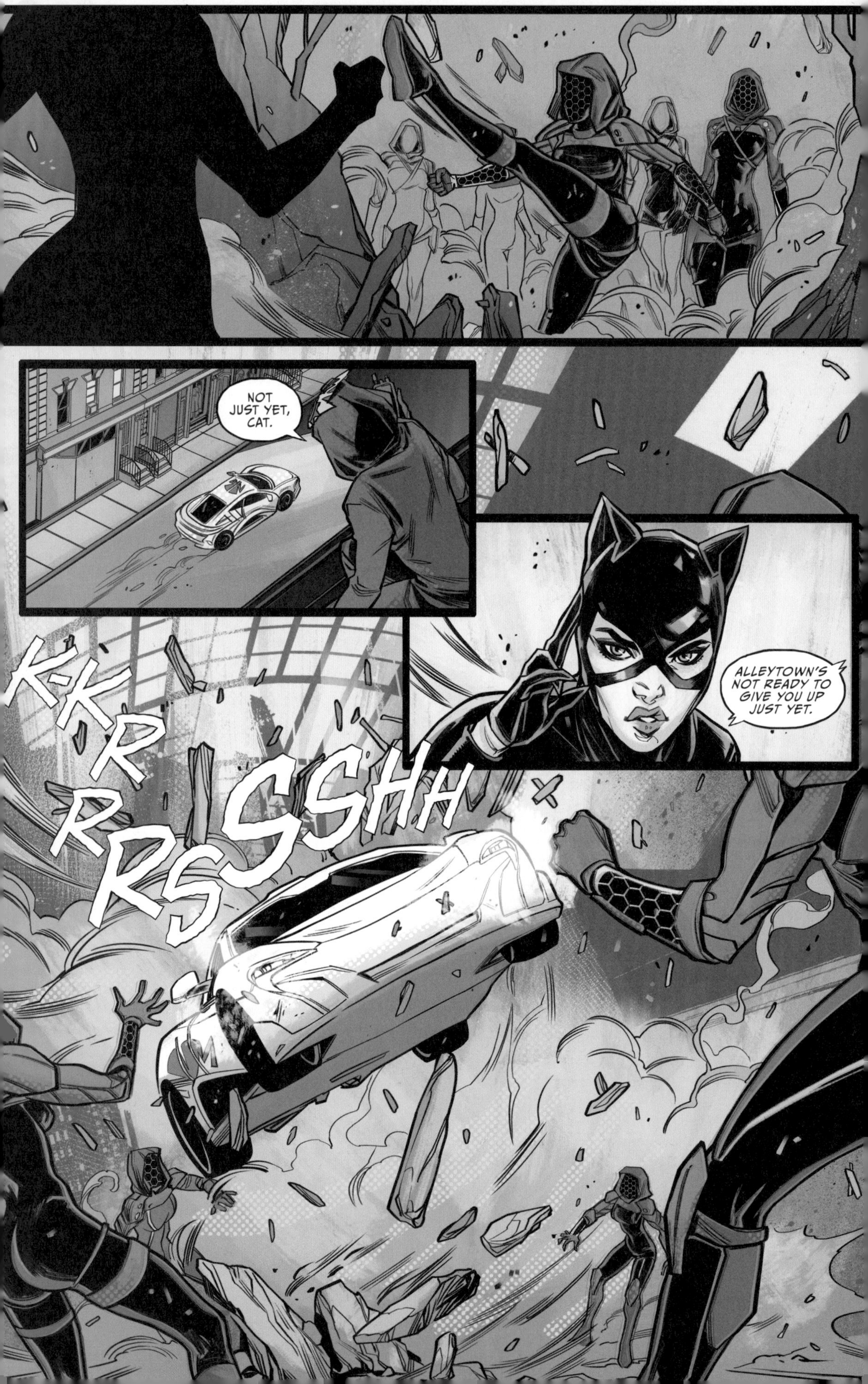
NOT JUST YET, CAT.
ALLEYTOWN'S NOT READY TO GIVE YOU UP JUST YET.
K-KRRRSSSHH

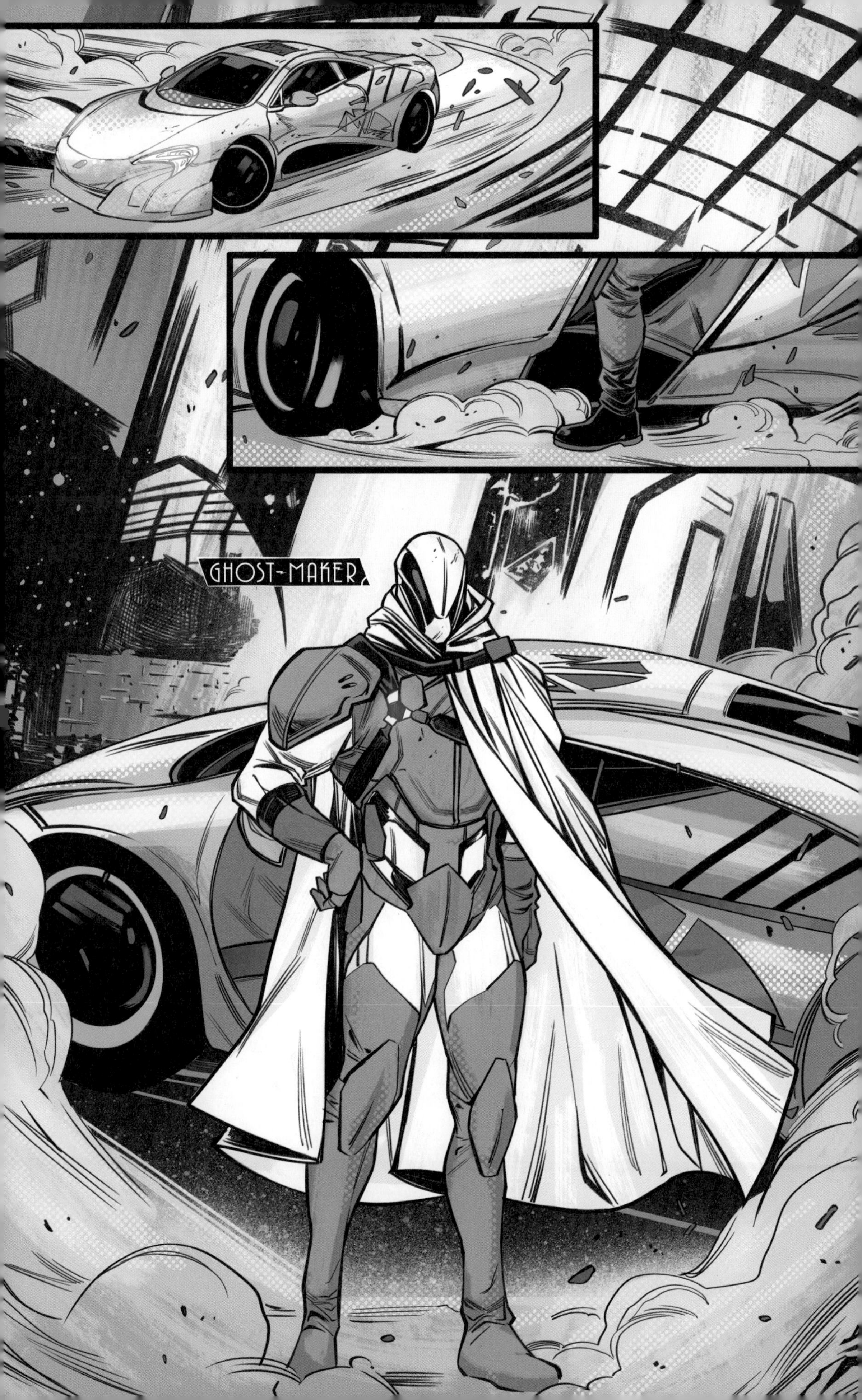
GHOST-MAKER

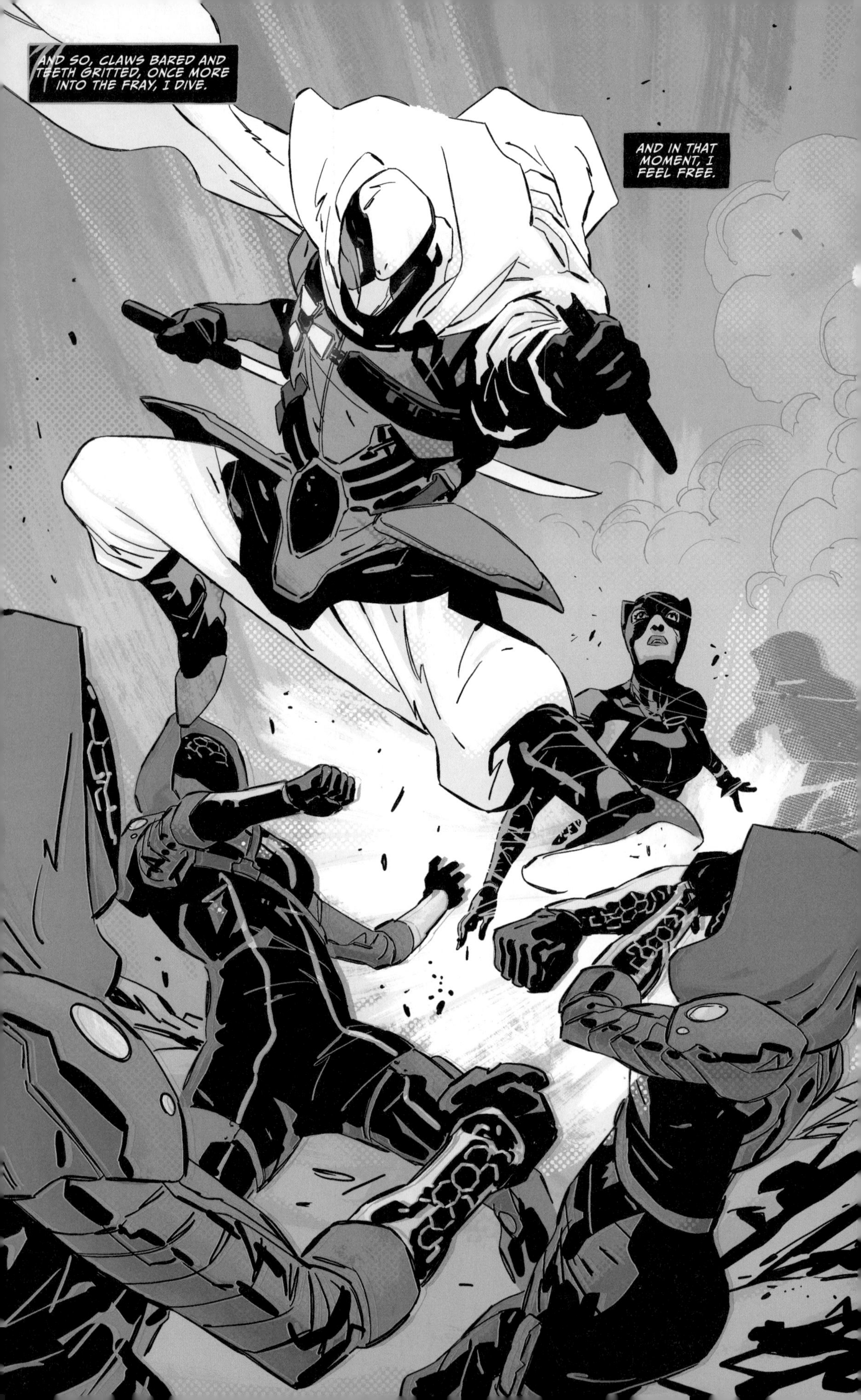
AND SO, CLAWS BARED AND TEETH GRITTED, ONCE MORE INTO THE FRAY, I DIVE.
AND IN THAT MOMENT, I FEEL FREE.

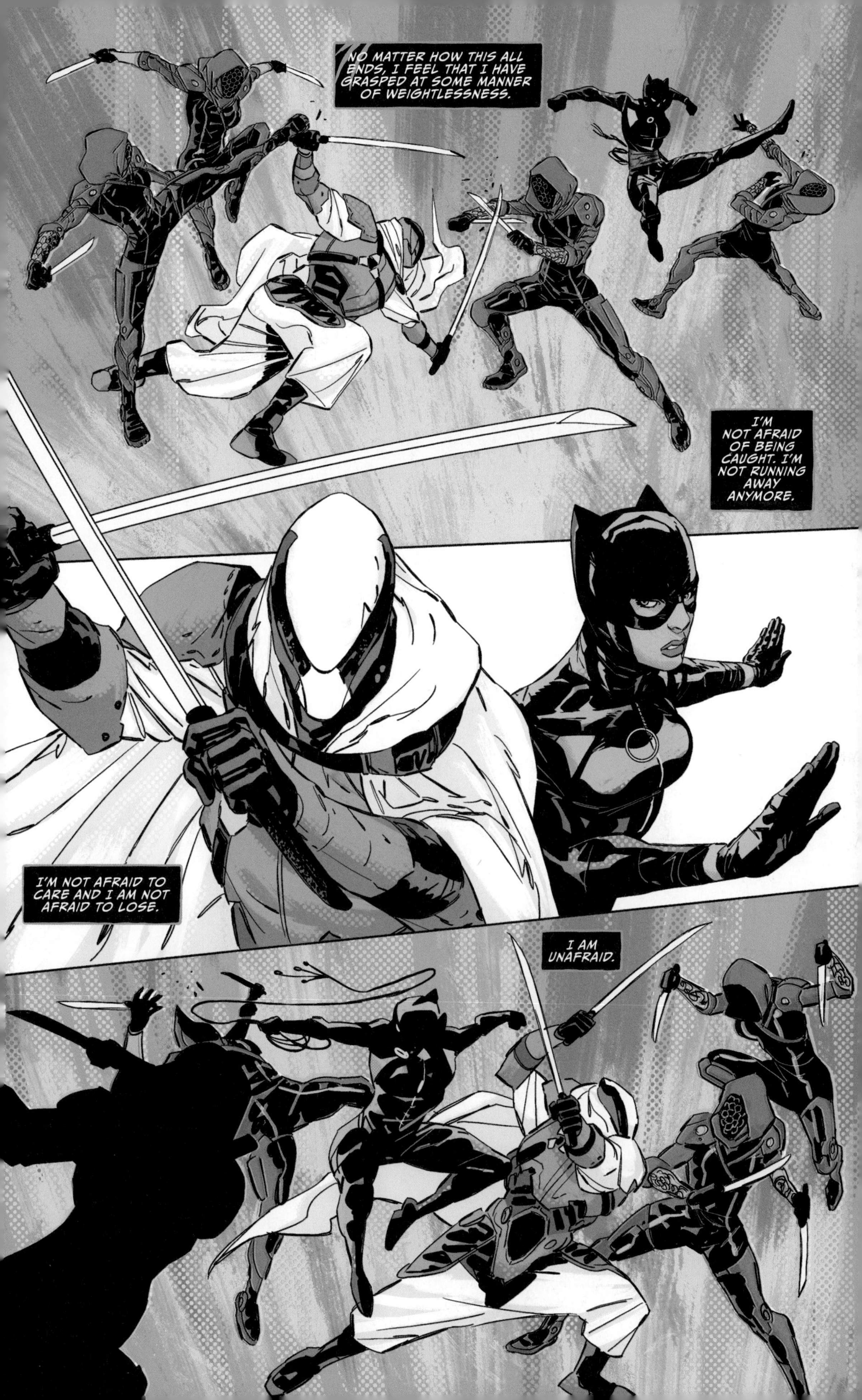
NO MATTER HOW THIS ALL ENDS, I FEEL THAT I HAVE GRASPED AT SOME MANNER OF WEIGHTLESSNESS.
I'M NOT AFRAID OF BEING CAUGHT. I'M NOT RUNNING AWAY ANYMORE.
I'M NOT AFRAID TO CARE AND I AM NOT AFRAID TO LOSE.
I AM UNAFRAID.

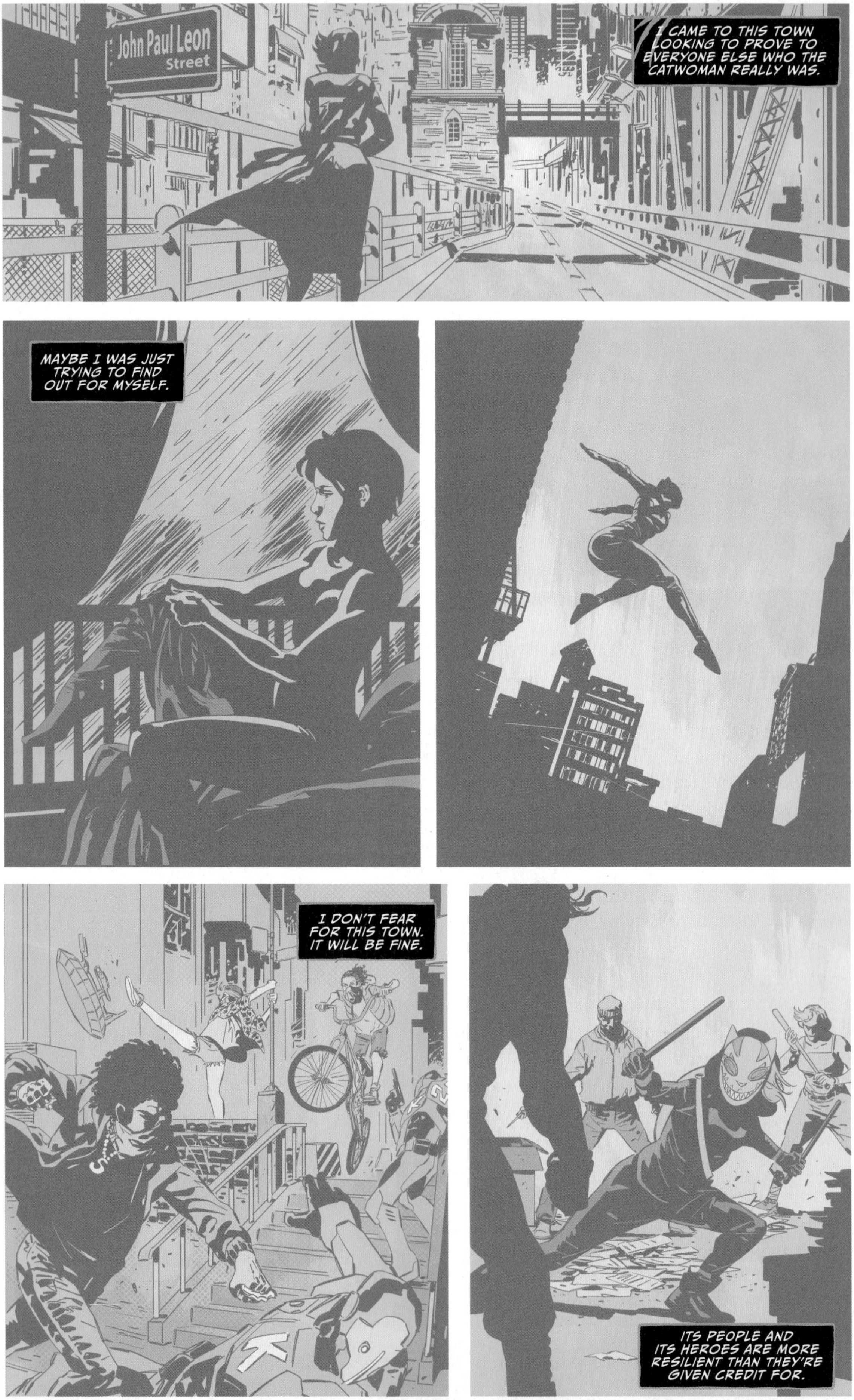
John Paul Leon Street
I CAME TO THIS TOWN LOOKING TO PROVE TO EVERYONE ELSE WHO THE CATWOMAN REALLY WAS.
MAYBE I WAS JUST TRYING TO FIND OUT FOR MYSELF.
I DON'T FEAR FOR THIS TOWN. IT WILL BE FINE.
ITS PEOPLE AND ITS HEROES ARE MORE RESILIENT THAN THEY'RE GIVEN CREDIT FOR.

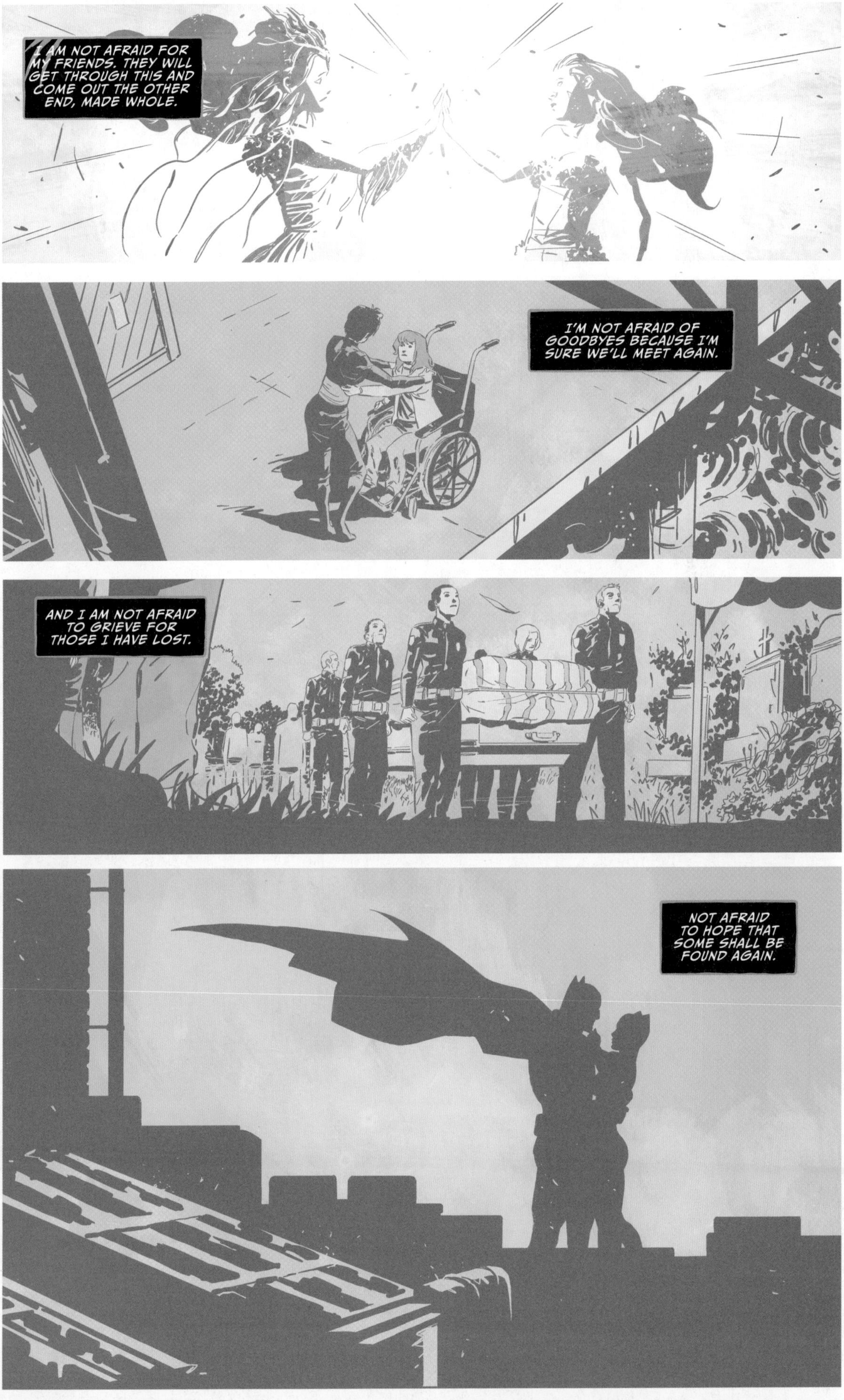
I AM NOT AFRAID FOR MY FRIENDS. THEY WILL GET THROUGH THIS AND COME OUT THE OTHER END, MADE WHOLE.
I'M NOT AFRAID OF GOODBYES BECAUSE I'M SURE WE'LL MEET AGAIN.
AND I AM NOT AFRAID TO GRIEVE FOR THOSE I HAVE LOST.
NOT AFRAID TO HOPE THAT SOME SHALL BE FOUND AGAIN.

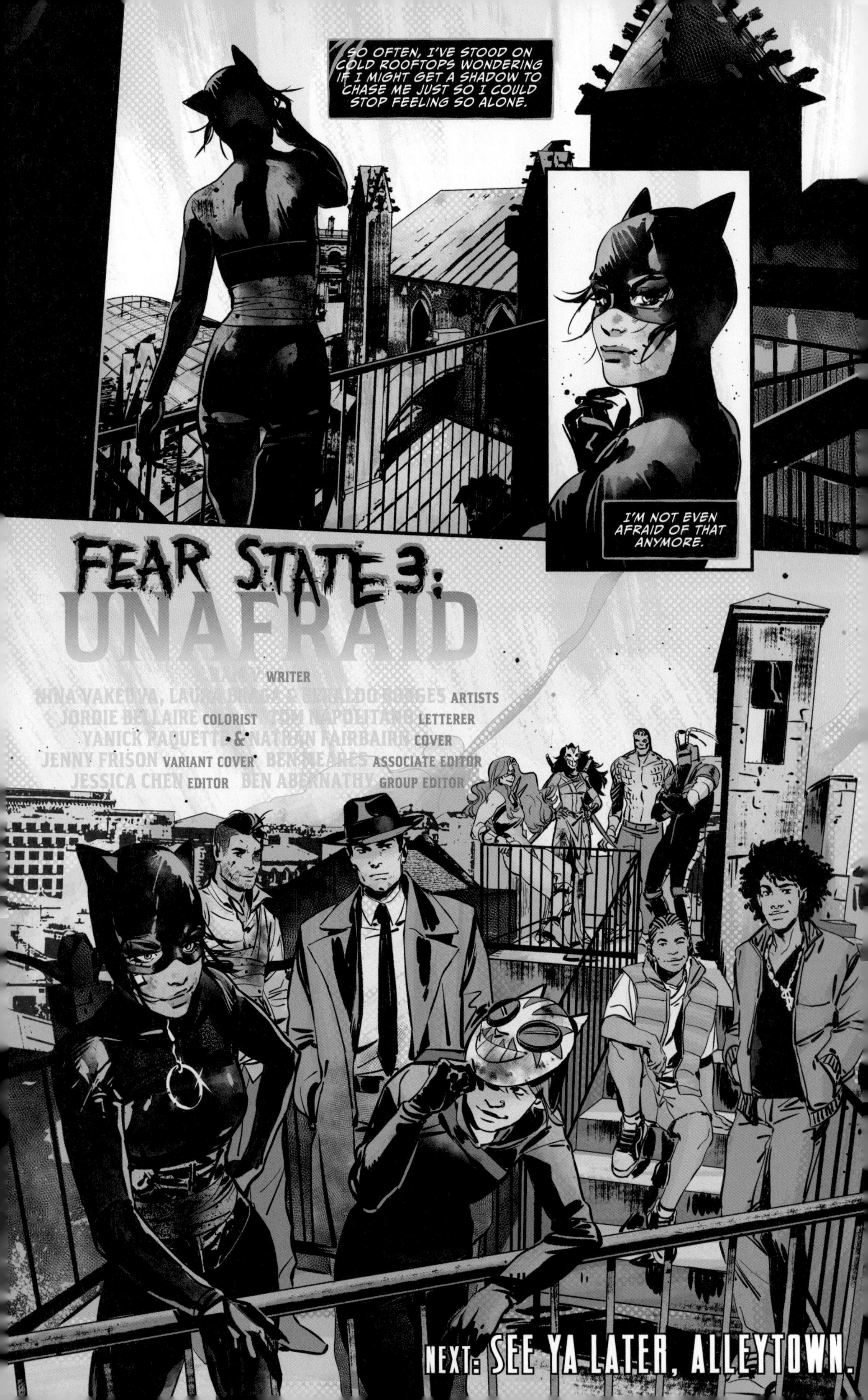
SO OFTEN, I'VE STOOD ON COLD ROOFTOPS WONDERING IF I MIGHT GET A SHADOW TO CHASE ME JUST SO I COULD STOP FEELING SO ALONE.
I'M NOT EVEN AFRAID OF THAT ANYMORE.
FEAR STATE 3:
UNAFRAID
WRITER
NINA VAKUEVA, LAURA BRAGA & GERALDO BORGES ARTISTS
JORDIE BELLAIRE COLORIST TOM NAPOLITANO LETTERER
YANICK PAQUETTE & NATHAN FAIRBAIRN COVER
JENNY FRISON VARIANT COVER BEN MEARES ASSOCIATE EDITOR
JESSICA CHEN EDITOR BEN ABERNATHY GROUP EDITOR
NEXT: SEE YA LATER, ALLEYTOWN.

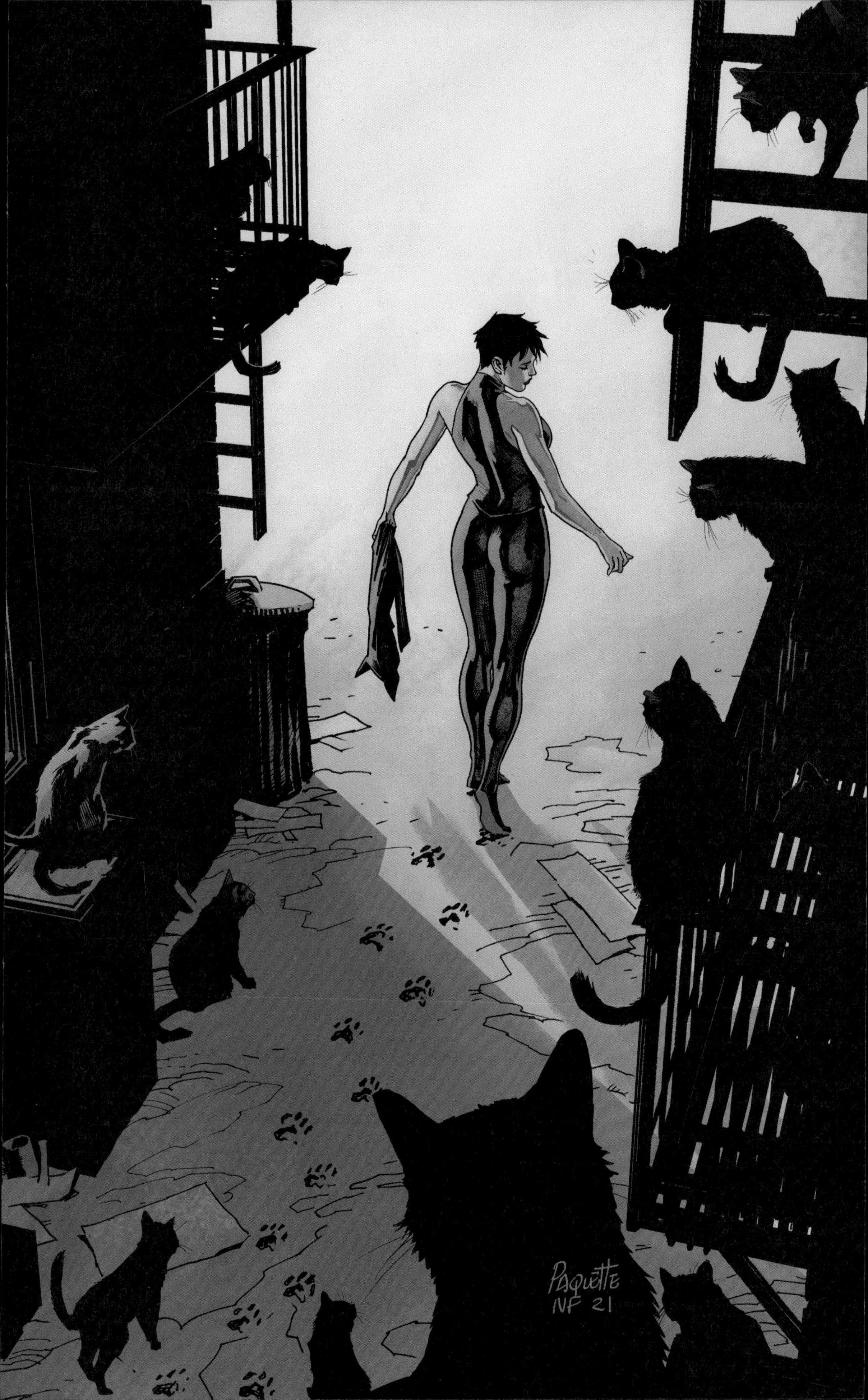
PAQUETTE
NF 21

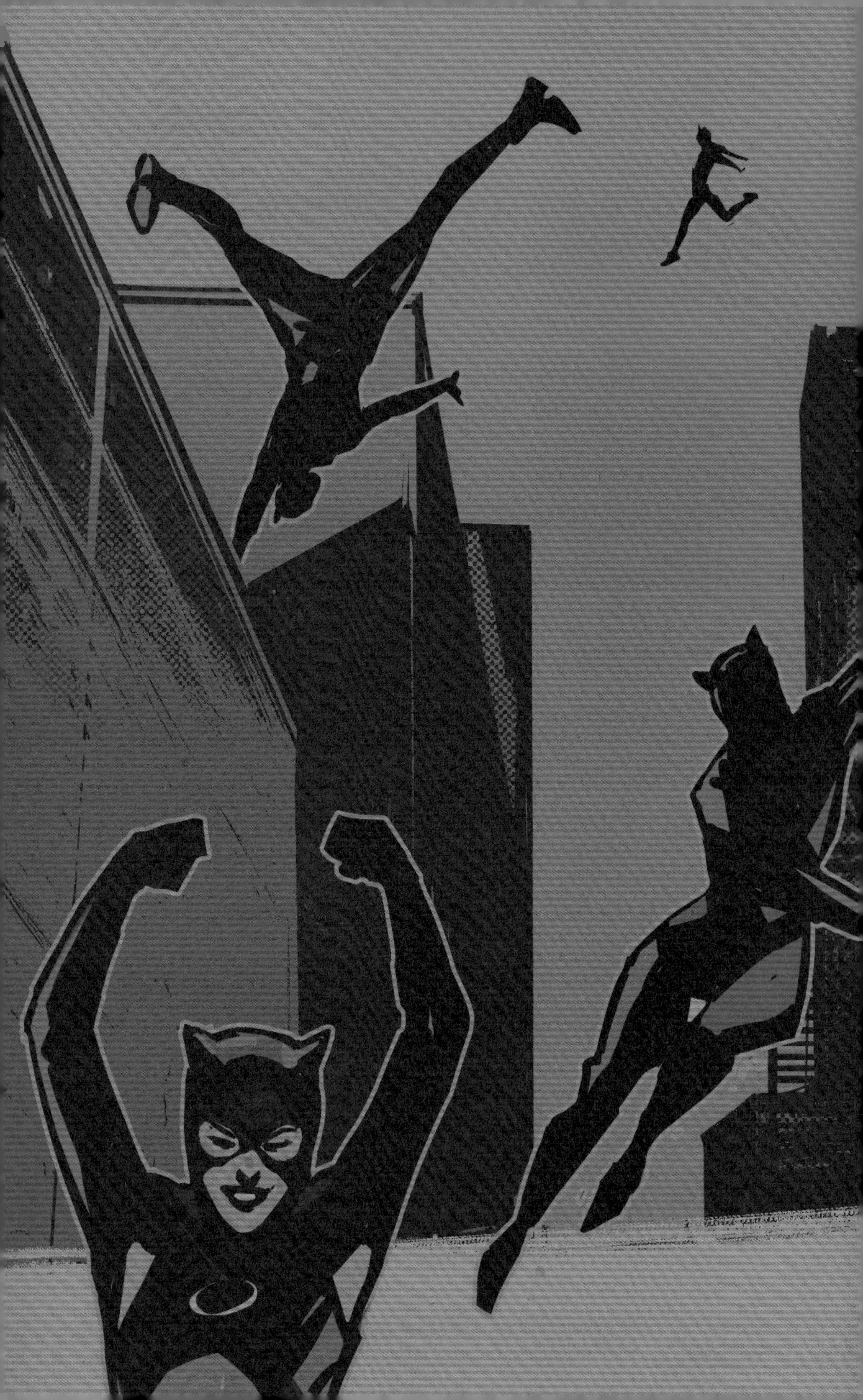

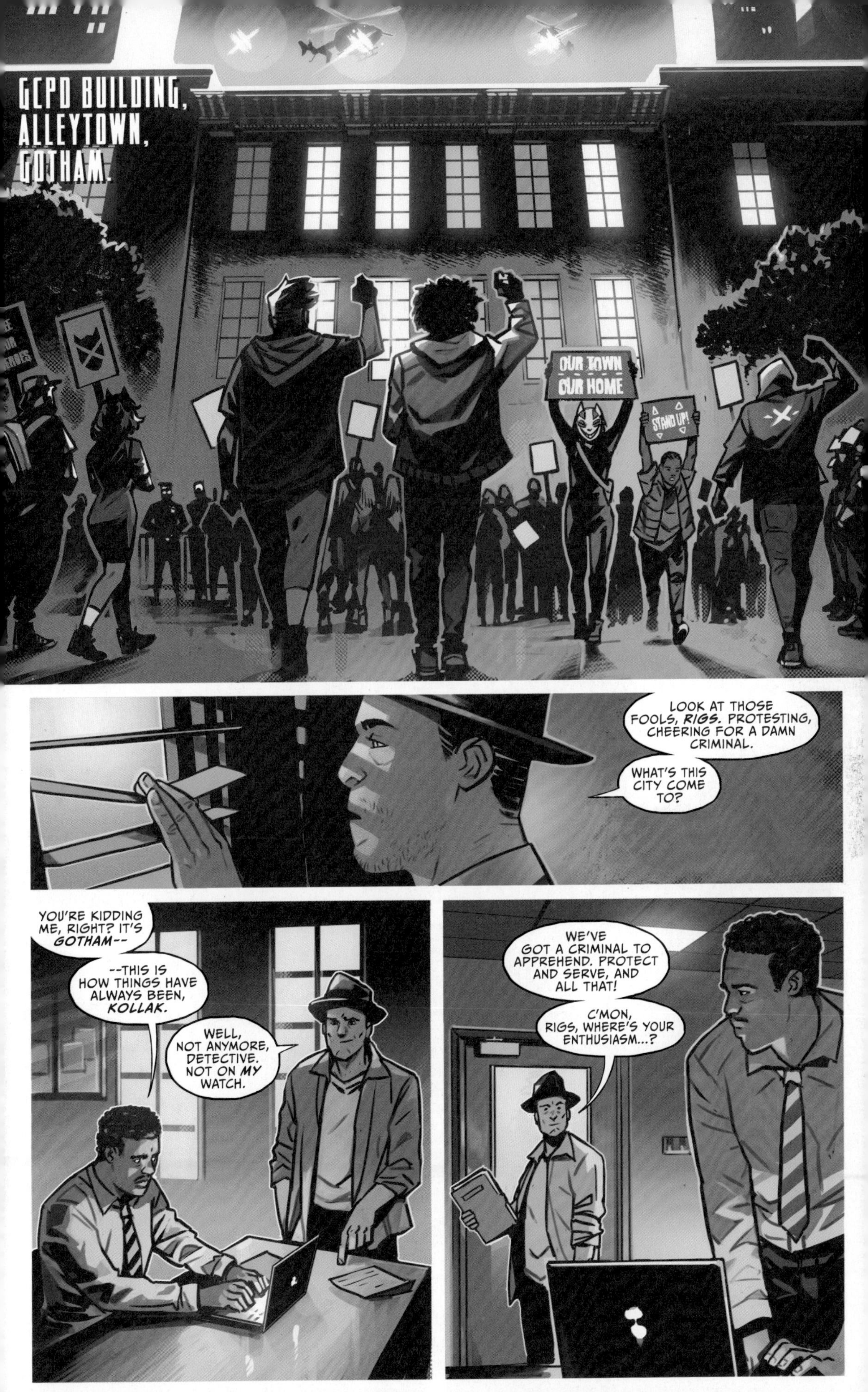
GCPD BUILDING, ALLEYTOWN, GOTHAM.
OUR TOWN OUR HOME
STAND UP!
LOOK AT THOSE FOOLS, *RIGS.* PROTESTING, CHEERING FOR A DAMN CRIMINAL.
WHAT'S THIS CITY COME TO?
YOU'RE KIDDING ME, RIGHT? IT'S *GOTHAM*--
--THIS IS HOW THINGS HAVE ALWAYS BEEN, *KOLLAK.*
WELL, NOT ANYMORE, DETECTIVE. NOT ON *MY* WATCH.
WE'VE GOT A CRIMINAL TO APPREHEND. PROTECT AND SERVE, AND ALL THAT!
C'MON, RIGS, WHERE'S YOUR ENTHUSIASM...?

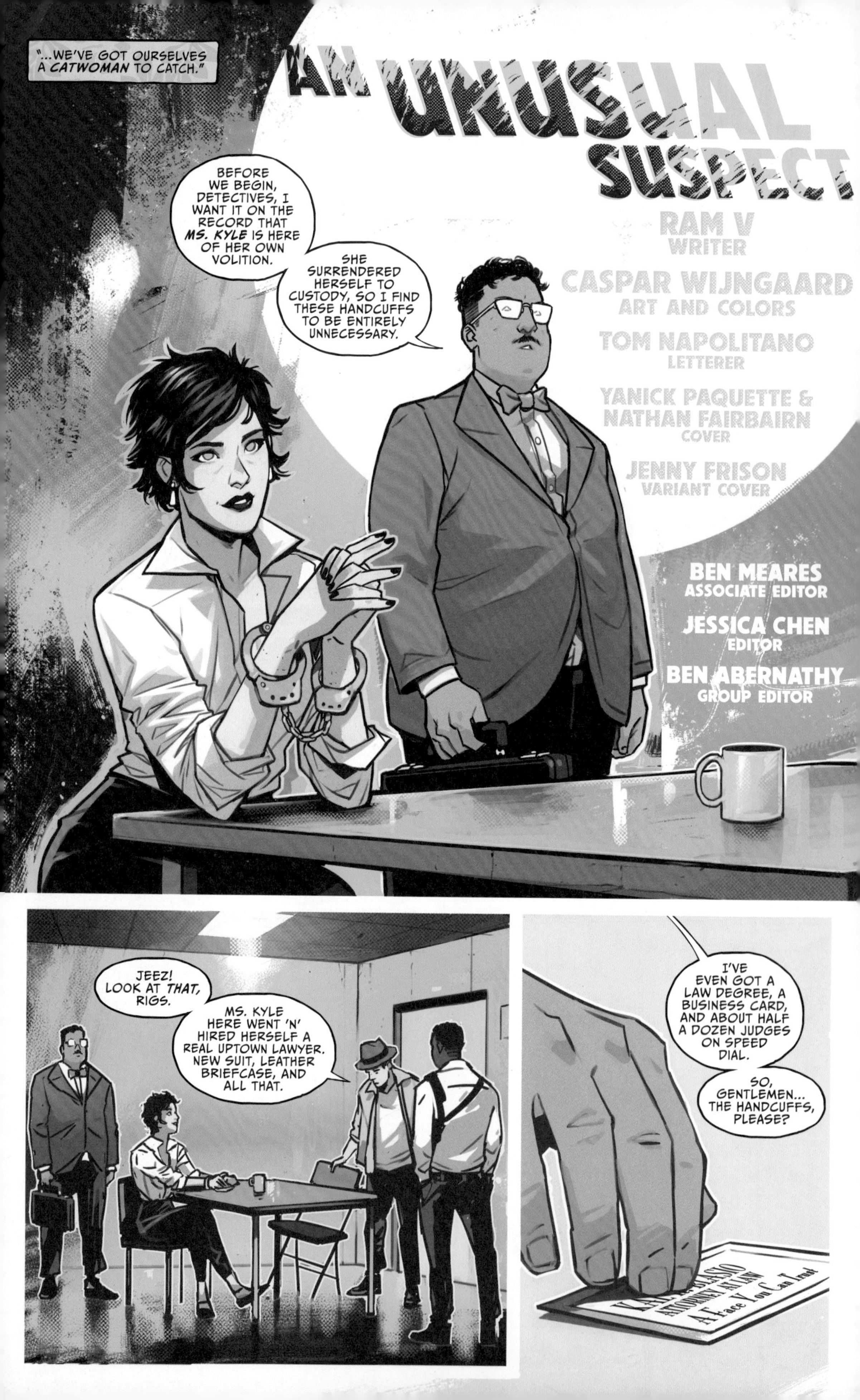

"...WE'VE GOT OURSELVES A *CATWOMAN* TO CATCH."
AN UNUSUAL SUSPECT
RAM V WRITER
CASPAR WIJNGAARD ART AND COLORS
TOM NAPOLITANO LETTERER
YANICK PAQUETTE & NATHAN FAIRBAIRN COVER
JENNY FRISON VARIANT COVER
BEN MEARES ASSOCIATE EDITOR
JESSICA CHEN EDITOR
BEN ABERNATHY GROUP EDITOR
BEFORE WE BEGIN, DETECTIVES, I WANT IT ON THE RECORD THAT *MS. KYLE* IS HERE OF HER OWN VOLITION.
SHE SURRENDERED HERSELF TO CUSTODY, SO I FIND THESE HANDCUFFS TO BE ENTIRELY UNNECESSARY.
JEEZ! LOOK AT *THAT,* RIGS.
MS. KYLE HERE WENT 'N' HIRED HERSELF A REAL UPTOWN LAWYER. NEW SUIT, LEATHER BRIEFCASE, AND ALL THAT.
I'VE EVEN GOT A LAW DEGREE, A BUSINESS CARD, AND ABOUT HALF A DOZEN JUDGES ON SPEED DIAL.
SO, GENTLEMEN... THE HANDCUFFS, PLEASE?
ATTORNEY AT LAW
A Face You Can Trust

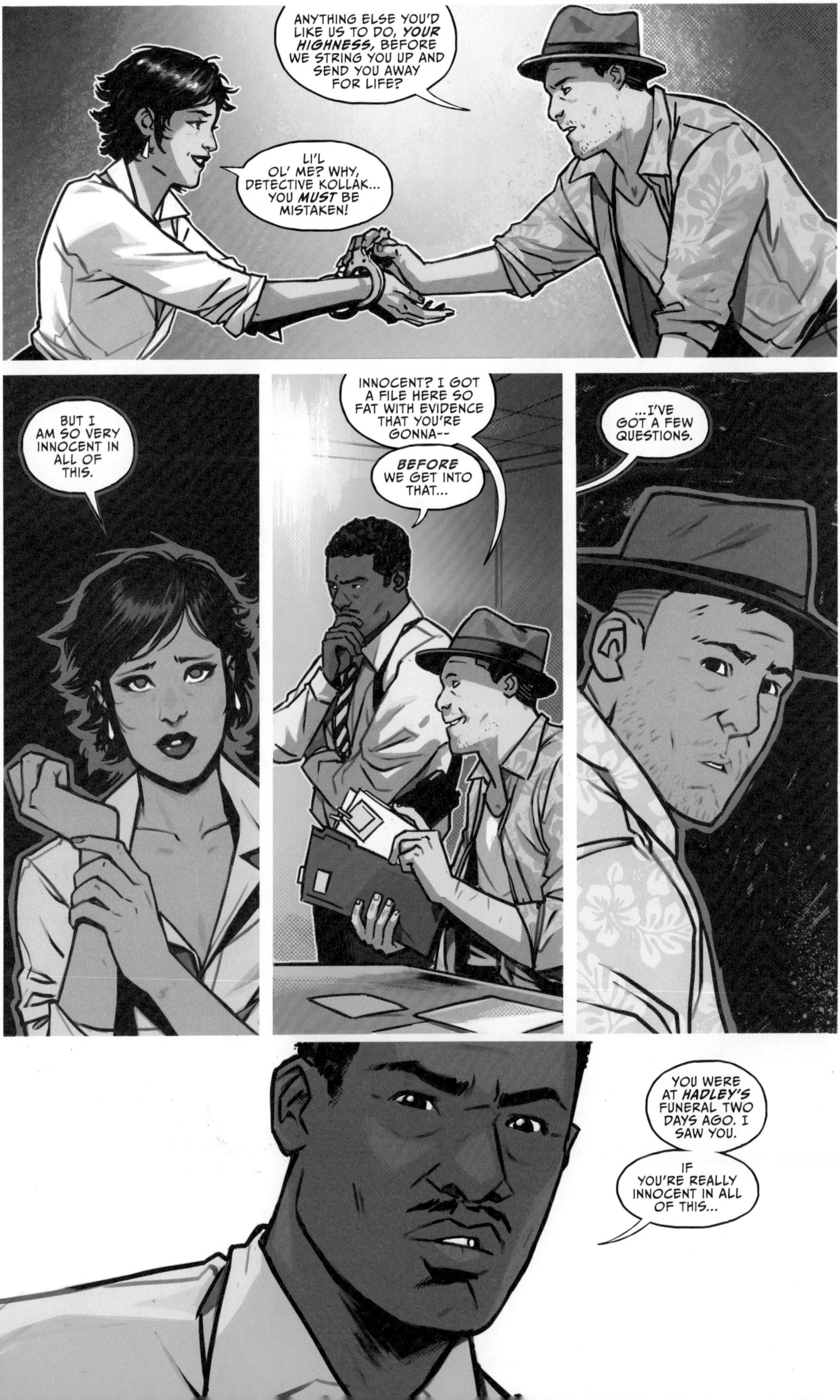
ANYTHING ELSE YOU'D LIKE US TO DO, *YOUR HIGHNESS,* BEFORE WE STRING YOU UP AND SEND YOU AWAY FOR LIFE?
LI'L OL' ME? WHY, DETECTIVE KOLLAK... YOU *MUST* BE MISTAKEN!
BUT I AM SO VERY INNOCENT IN ALL OF THIS.
INNOCENT? I GOT A FILE HERE SO FAT WITH EVIDENCE THAT YOU'RE GONNA--
BEFORE WE GET INTO THAT...
...I'VE GOT A FEW QUESTIONS.
YOU WERE AT *HADLEY'S* FUNERAL TWO DAYS AGO. I SAW YOU.
IF YOU'RE REALLY INNOCENT IN ALL OF THIS...

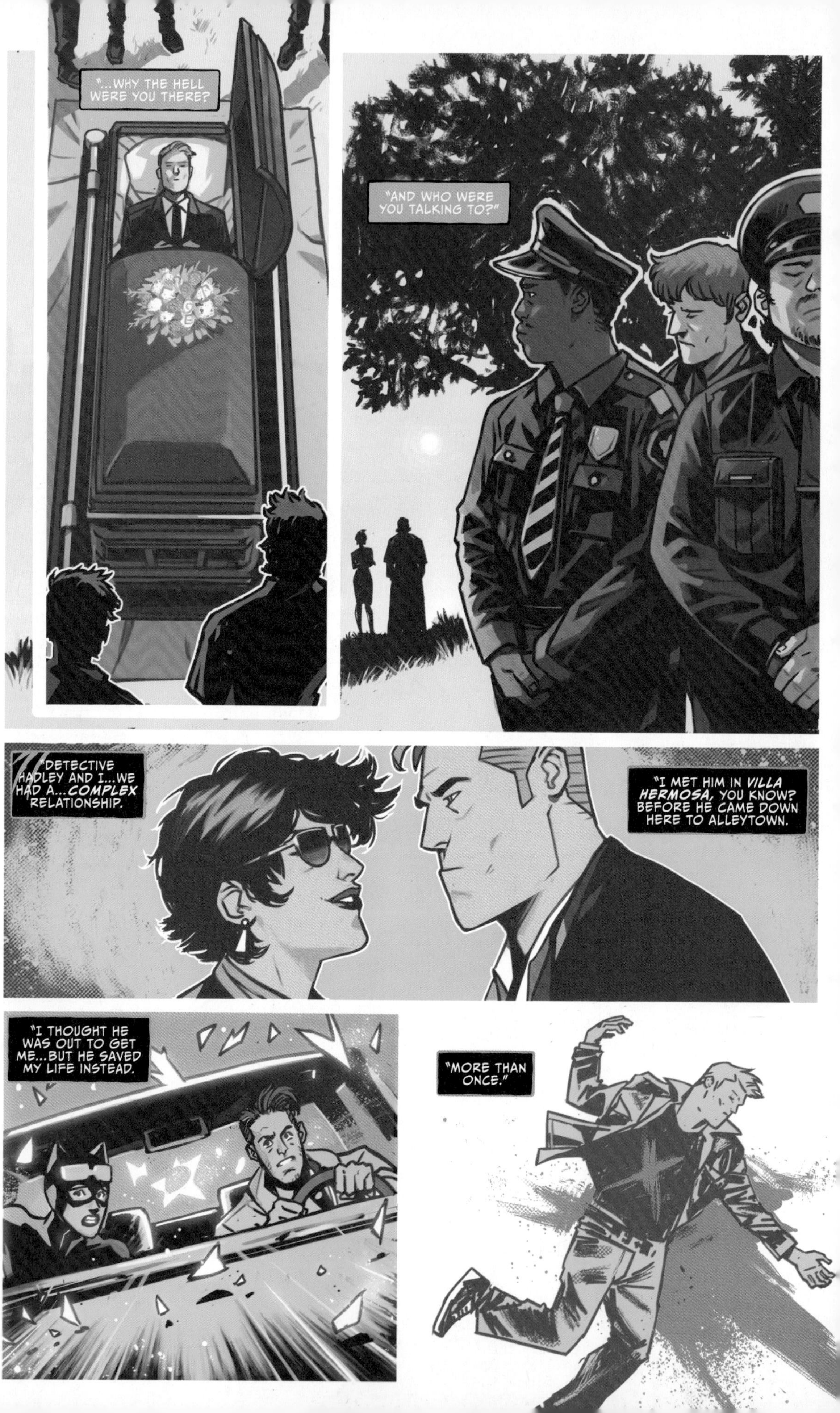
"...WHY THE HELL WERE YOU THERE?
"AND WHO WERE YOU TALKING TO?"
"DETECTIVE HADLEY AND I...WE HAD A...COMPLEX RELATIONSHIP.
"I MET HIM IN VILLA HERMOSA, YOU KNOW? BEFORE HE CAME DOWN HERE TO ALLEYTOWN.
"I THOUGHT HE WAS OUT TO GET ME...BUT HE SAVED MY LIFE INSTEAD.
"MORE THAN ONCE."

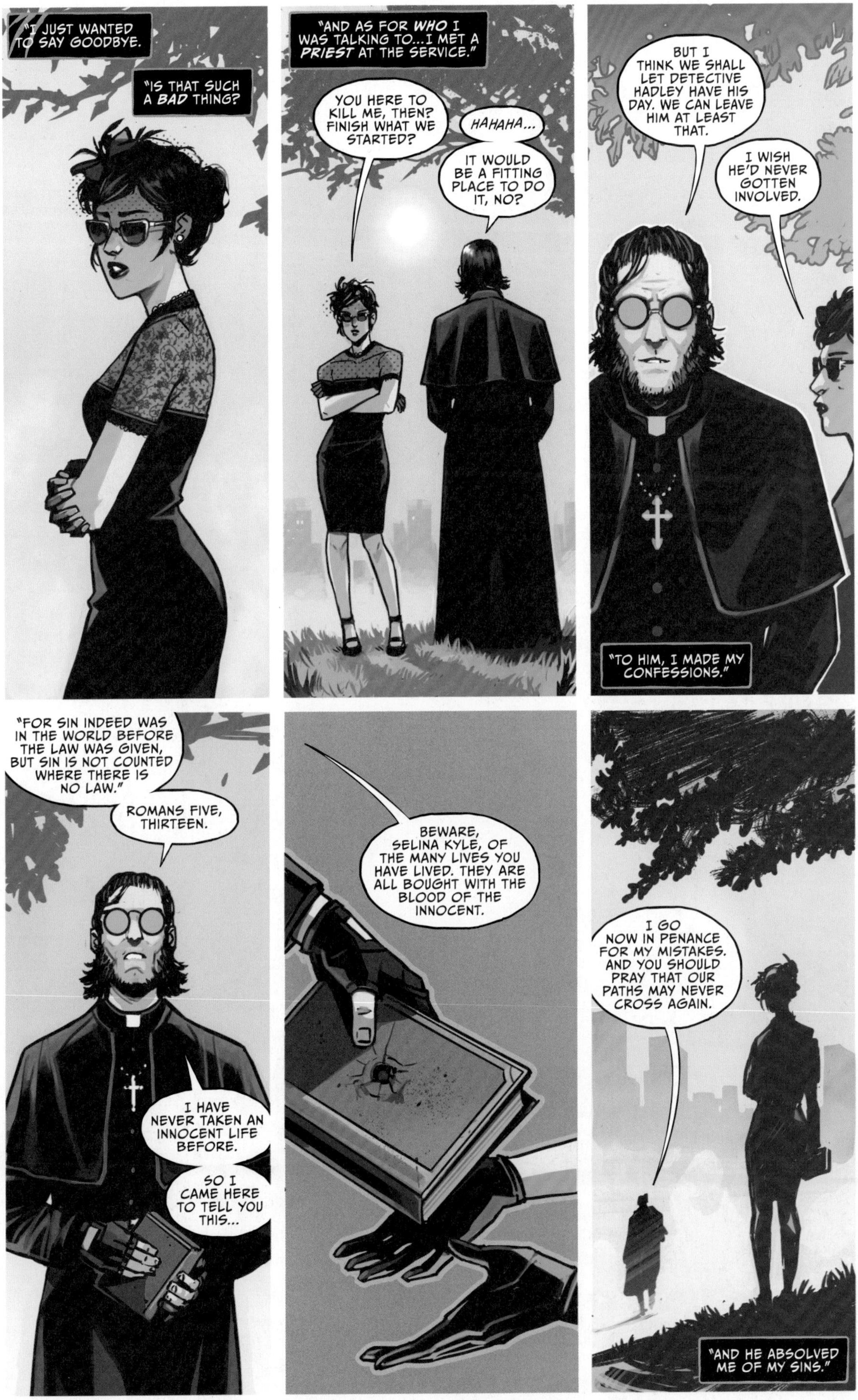
"I JUST WANTED TO SAY GOODBYE.
"IS THAT SUCH A BAD THING?
"AND AS FOR WHO I WAS TALKING TO...I MET A PRIEST AT THE SERVICE."
YOU HERE TO KILL ME, THEN? FINISH WHAT WE STARTED?
HAHAHA...
IT WOULD BE A FITTING PLACE TO DO IT, NO?
BUT I THINK WE SHALL LET DETECTIVE HADLEY HAVE HIS DAY. WE CAN LEAVE HIM AT LEAST THAT.
I WISH HE'D NEVER GOTTEN INVOLVED.
"TO HIM, I MADE MY CONFESSIONS."
"FOR SIN INDEED WAS IN THE WORLD BEFORE THE LAW WAS GIVEN, BUT SIN IS NOT COUNTED WHERE THERE IS NO LAW."
ROMANS FIVE, THIRTEEN.
I HAVE NEVER TAKEN AN INNOCENT LIFE BEFORE.
SO I CAME HERE TO TELL YOU THIS...
BEWARE, SELINA KYLE, OF THE MANY LIVES YOU HAVE LIVED. THEY ARE ALL BOUGHT WITH THE BLOOD OF THE INNOCENT.
I GO NOW IN PENANCE FOR MY MISTAKES. AND YOU SHOULD PRAY THAT OUR PATHS MAY NEVER CROSS AGAIN.
"AND HE ABSOLVED ME OF MY SINS."

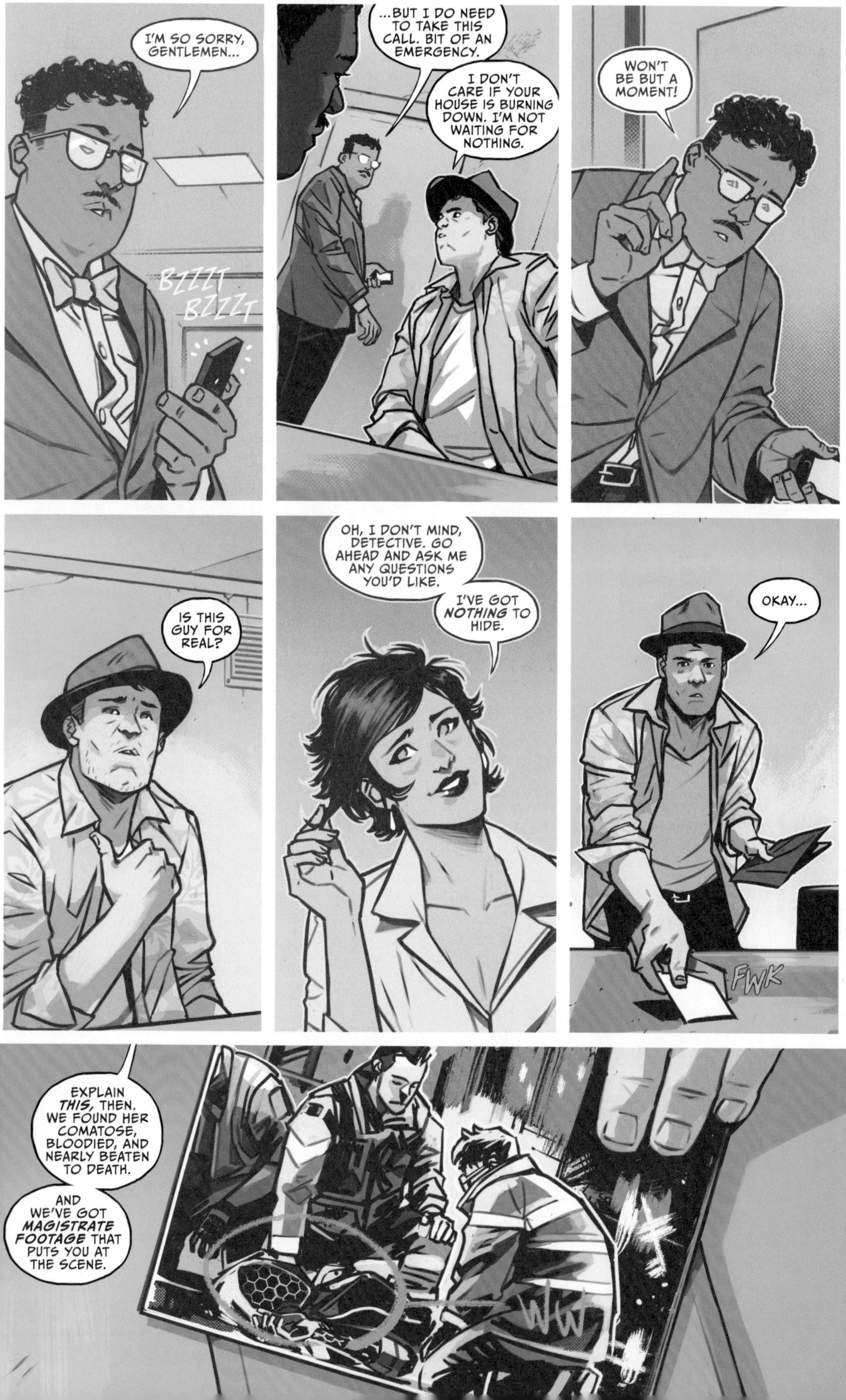
I'M SO SORRY, GENTLEMEN...
BZZZT BZZZT
...BUT I DO NEED TO TAKE THIS CALL. BIT OF AN EMERGENCY.
I DON'T CARE IF YOUR HOUSE IS BURNING DOWN. I'M NOT WAITING FOR NOTHING.
WON'T BE BUT A MOMENT!
IS THIS GUY FOR REAL?
OH, I DON'T MIND, DETECTIVE. GO AHEAD AND ASK ME ANY QUESTIONS YOU'D LIKE.
I'VE GOT NOTHING TO HIDE.
OKAY...
FWK
EXPLAIN THIS, THEN. WE FOUND HER COMATOSE, BLOODIED, AND NEARLY BEATEN TO DEATH.
AND WE'VE GOT MAGISTRATE FOOTAGE THAT PUTS YOU AT THE SCENE.

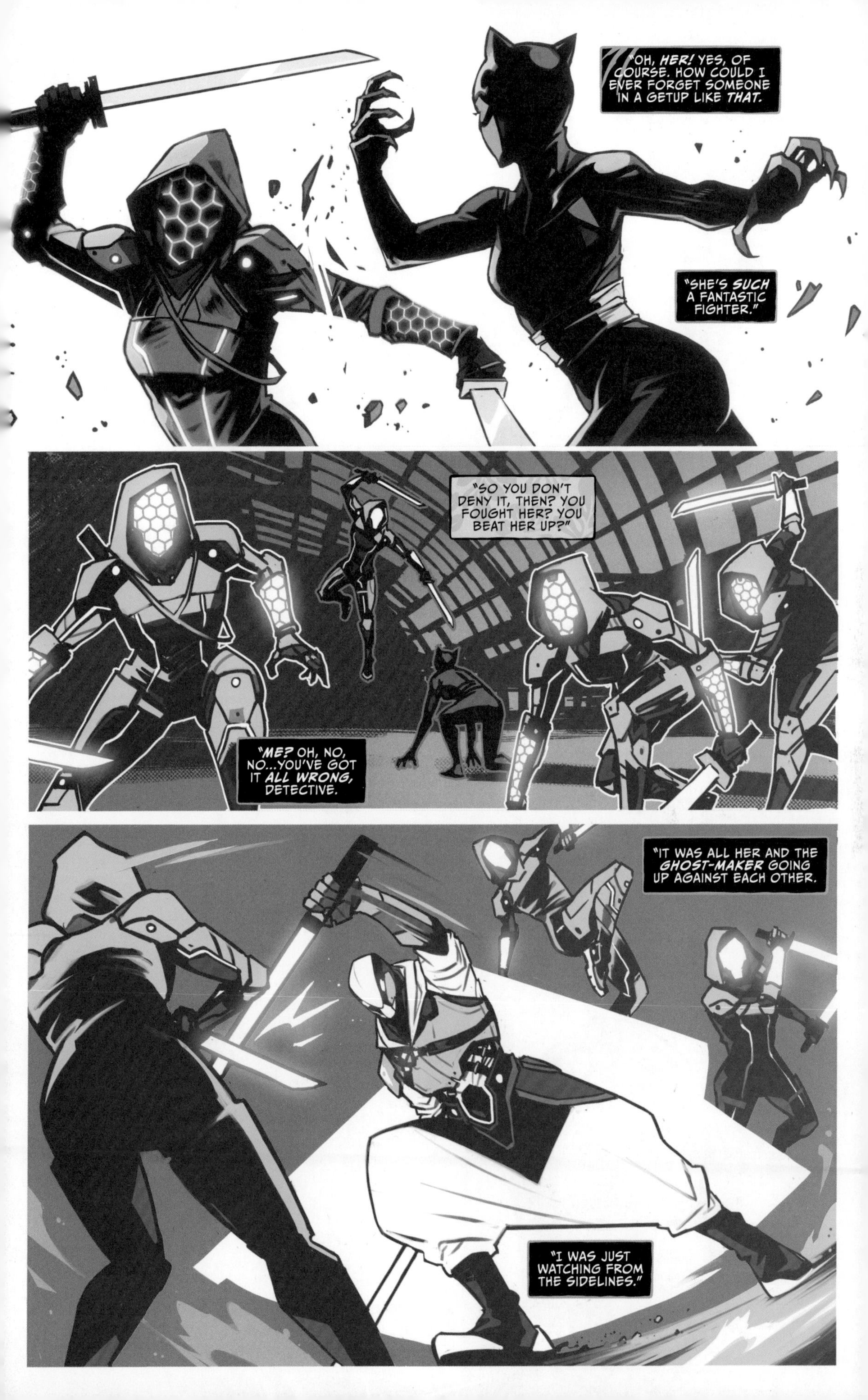
"OH, *HER!* YES, OF COURSE. HOW COULD I EVER FORGET SOMEONE IN A GETUP LIKE *THAT.*
"SHE'S *SUCH* A FANTASTIC FIGHTER."
"SO YOU DON'T DENY IT, THEN? YOU FOUGHT HER? YOU BEAT HER UP?"
"*ME?* OH, NO, NO...YOU'VE GOT IT *ALL WRONG,* DETECTIVE.
"IT WAS ALL HER AND THE *GHOST-MAKER* GOING UP AGAINST EACH OTHER.
"I WAS JUST WATCHING FROM THE SIDELINES."

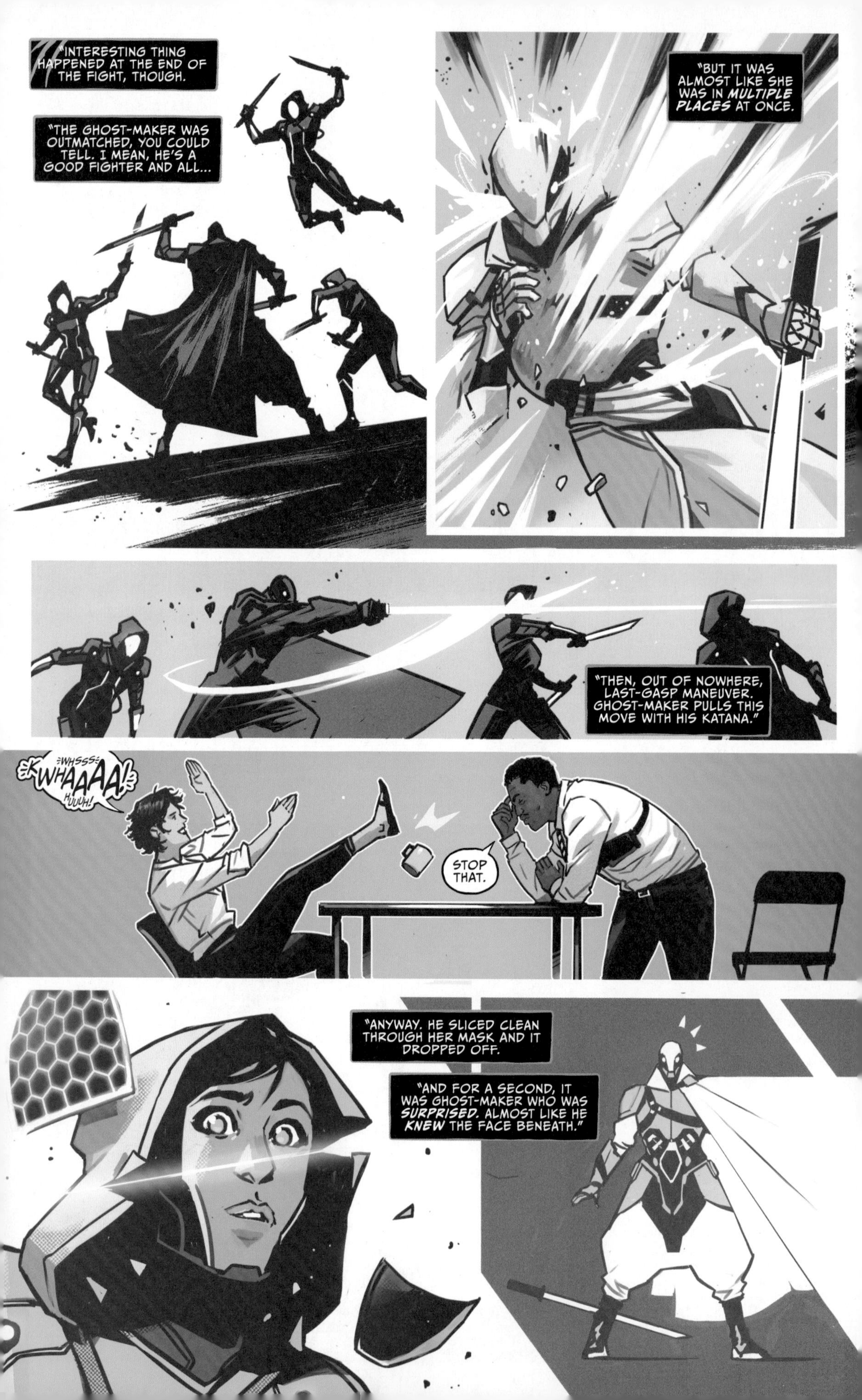

"INTERESTING THING HAPPENED AT THE END OF THE FIGHT, THOUGH.
"THE GHOST-MAKER WAS OUTMATCHED, YOU COULD TELL. I MEAN, HE'S A GOOD FIGHTER AND ALL...
"BUT IT WAS ALMOST LIKE SHE WAS IN MULTIPLE PLACES AT ONCE.
"THEN, OUT OF NOWHERE, LAST-GASP MANEUVER. GHOST-MAKER PULLS THIS MOVE WITH HIS KATANA."
WHSSS
KWHAAAA!
HUUUH!
STOP THAT.
"ANYWAY. HE SLICED CLEAN THROUGH HER MASK AND IT DROPPED OFF.
"AND FOR A SECOND, IT WAS GHOST-MAKER WHO WAS SURPRISED. ALMOST LIKE HE KNEW THE FACE BENEATH."

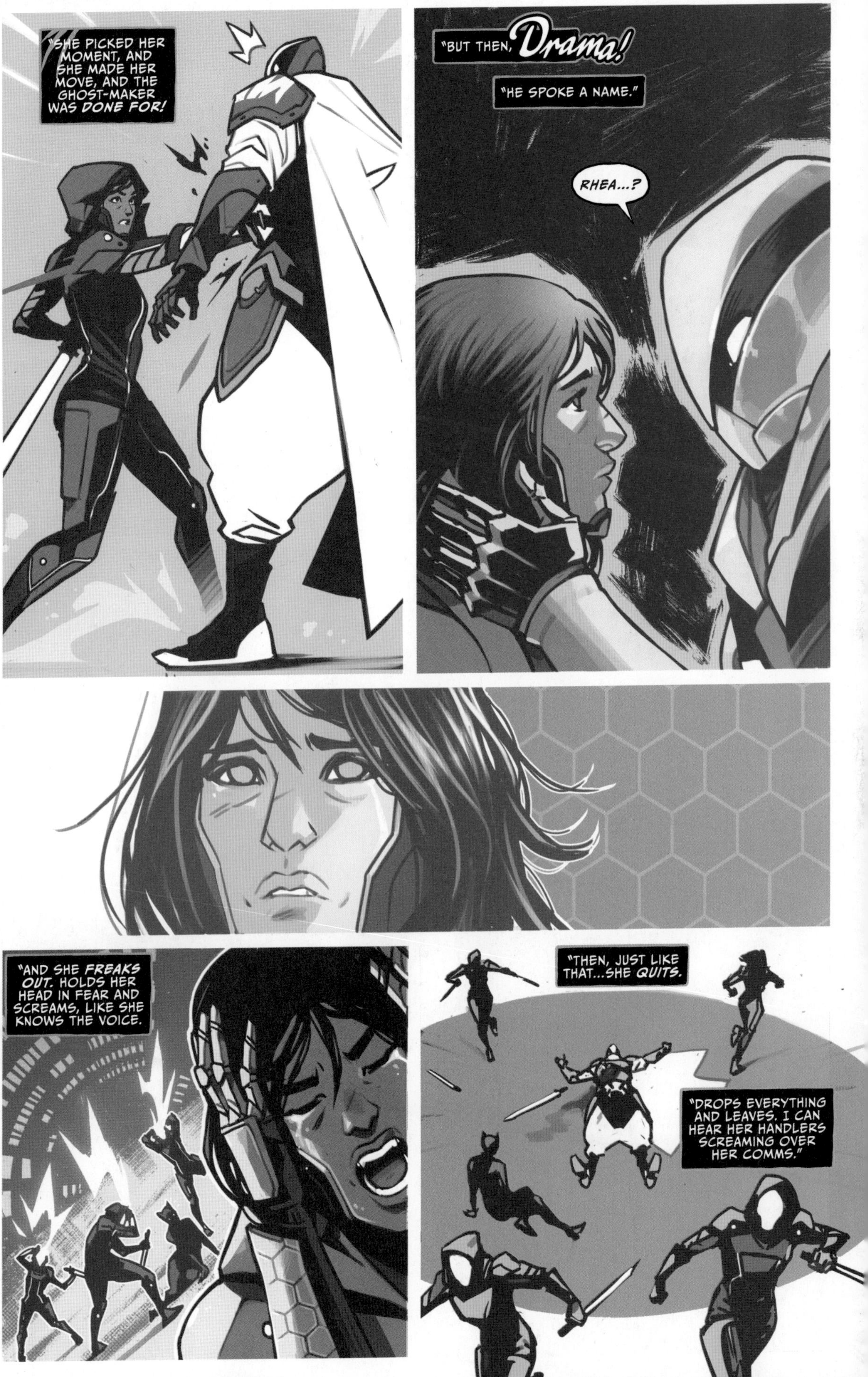
"SHE PICKED HER MOMENT, AND SHE MADE HER MOVE, AND THE GHOST-MAKER WAS DONE FOR!
"BUT THEN, Drama!
"HE SPOKE A NAME."
RHEA...?
"AND SHE FREAKS OUT. HOLDS HER HEAD IN FEAR AND SCREAMS, LIKE SHE KNOWS THE VOICE.
"THEN, JUST LIKE THAT...SHE QUITS.
"DROPS EVERYTHING AND LEAVES. I CAN HEAR HER HANDLERS SCREAMING OVER HER COMMS."

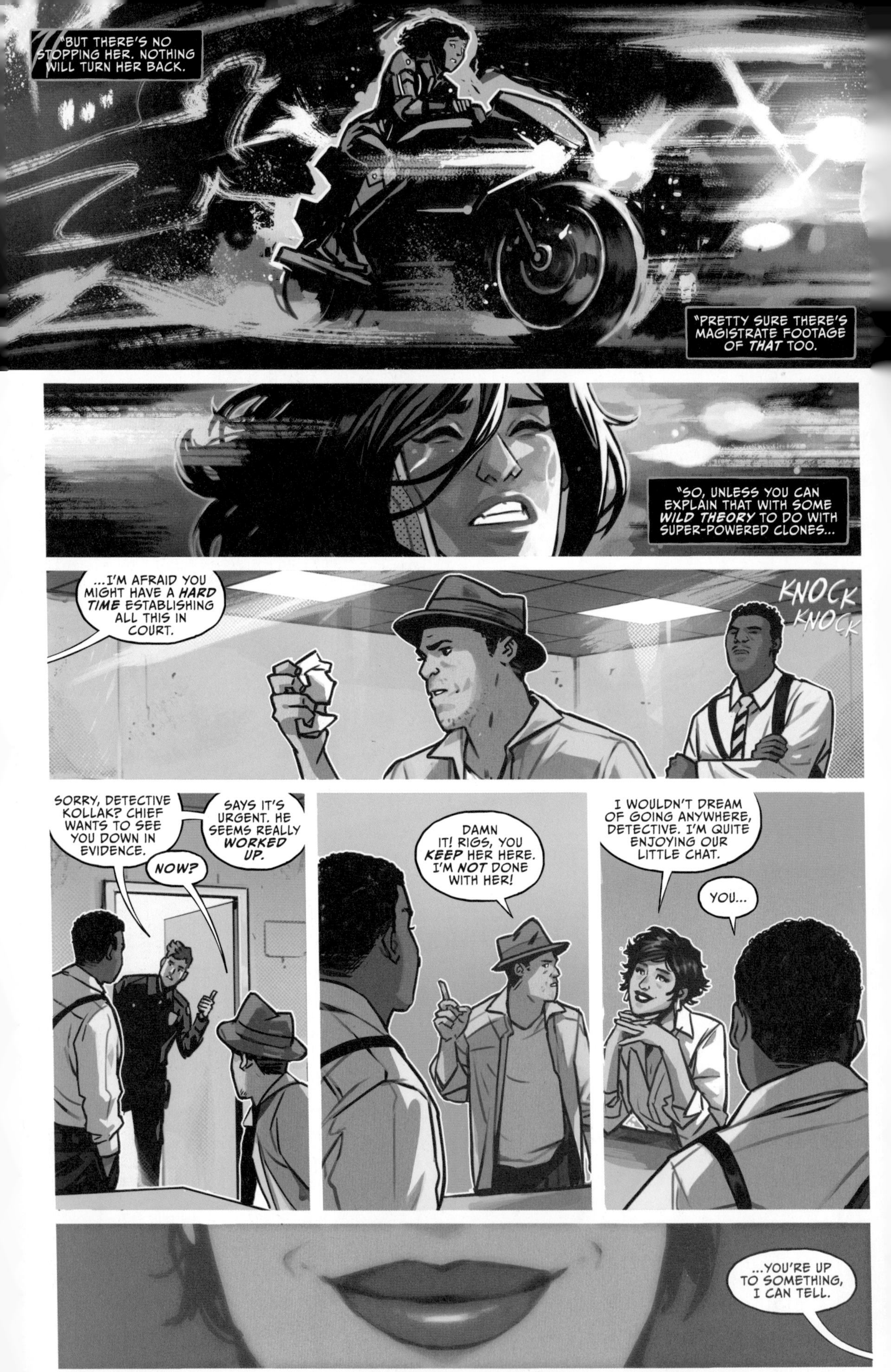
"BUT THERE'S NO STOPPING HER. NOTHING WILL TURN HER BACK.
"PRETTY SURE THERE'S MAGISTRATE FOOTAGE OF THAT TOO.
"SO, UNLESS YOU CAN EXPLAIN THAT WITH SOME WILD THEORY TO DO WITH SUPER-POWERED CLONES...
...I'M AFRAID YOU MIGHT HAVE A HARD TIME ESTABLISHING ALL THIS IN COURT.
KNOCK KNOCK
SORRY, DETECTIVE KOLLAK? CHIEF WANTS TO SEE YOU DOWN IN EVIDENCE.
NOW?
SAYS IT'S URGENT. HE SEEMS REALLY WORKED UP.
DAMN IT! RIGS, YOU KEEP HER HERE. I'M NOT DONE WITH HER!
I WOULDN'T DREAM OF GOING ANYWHERE, DETECTIVE. I'M QUITE ENJOYING OUR LITTLE CHAT.
YOU...
...YOU'RE UP TO SOMETHING, I CAN TELL.

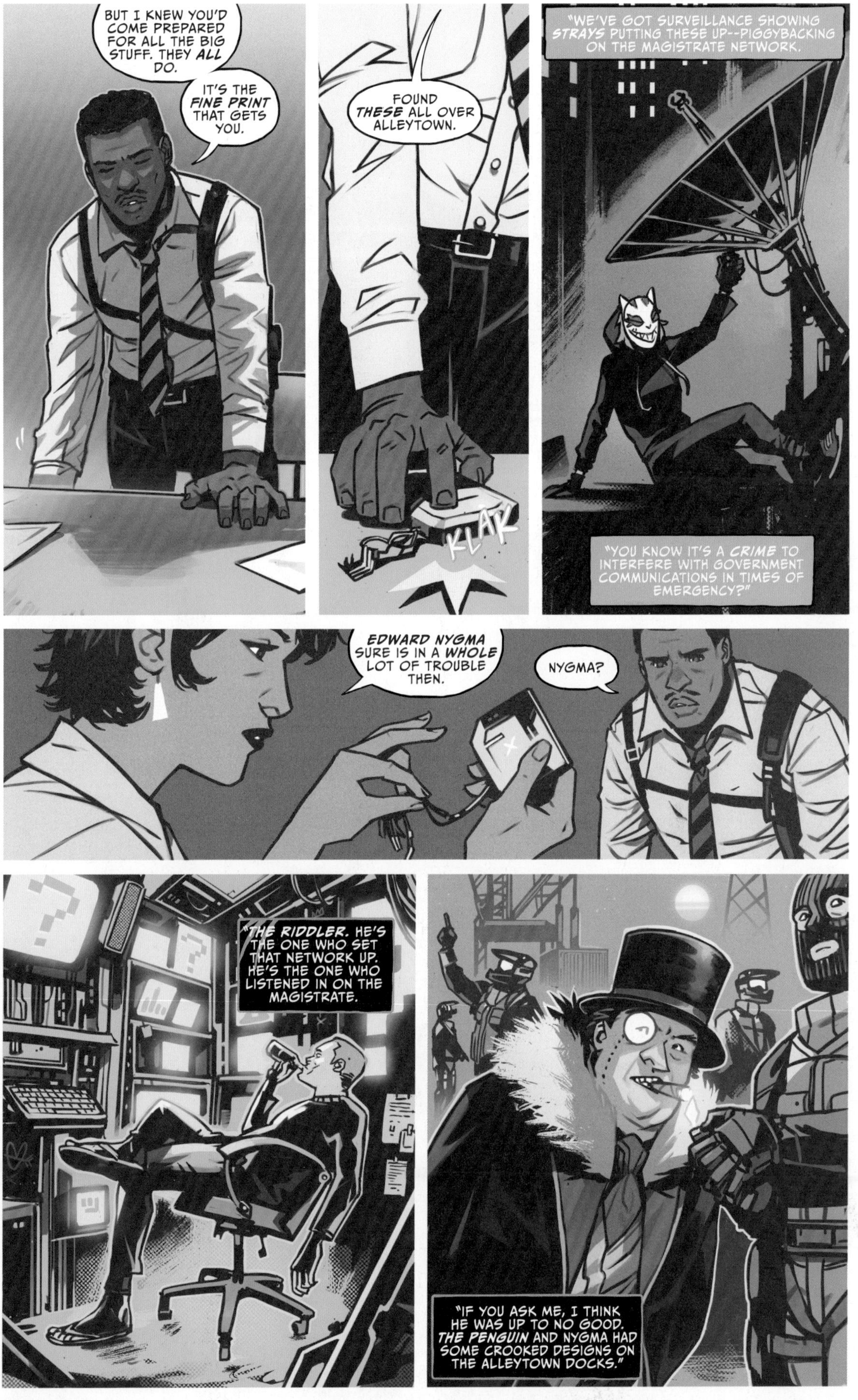
BUT I KNEW YOU'D COME PREPARED FOR ALL THE BIG STUFF. THEY ALL DO.
IT'S THE FINE PRINT THAT GETS YOU.
FOUND THESE ALL OVER ALLEYTOWN.
KLAK
"WE'VE GOT SURVEILLANCE SHOWING STRAYS PUTTING THESE UP--PIGGYBACKING ON THE MAGISTRATE NETWORK.
"YOU KNOW IT'S A CRIME TO INTERFERE WITH GOVERNMENT COMMUNICATIONS IN TIMES OF EMERGENCY?"
EDWARD NYGMA SURE IS IN A WHOLE LOT OF TROUBLE THEN.
NYGMA?
"THE RIDDLER. HE'S THE ONE WHO SET THAT NETWORK UP. HE'S THE ONE WHO LISTENED IN ON THE MAGISTRATE.
"IF YOU ASK ME, I THINK HE WAS UP TO NO GOOD. THE PENGUIN AND NYGMA HAD SOME CROOKED DESIGNS ON THE ALLEYTOWN DOCKS."

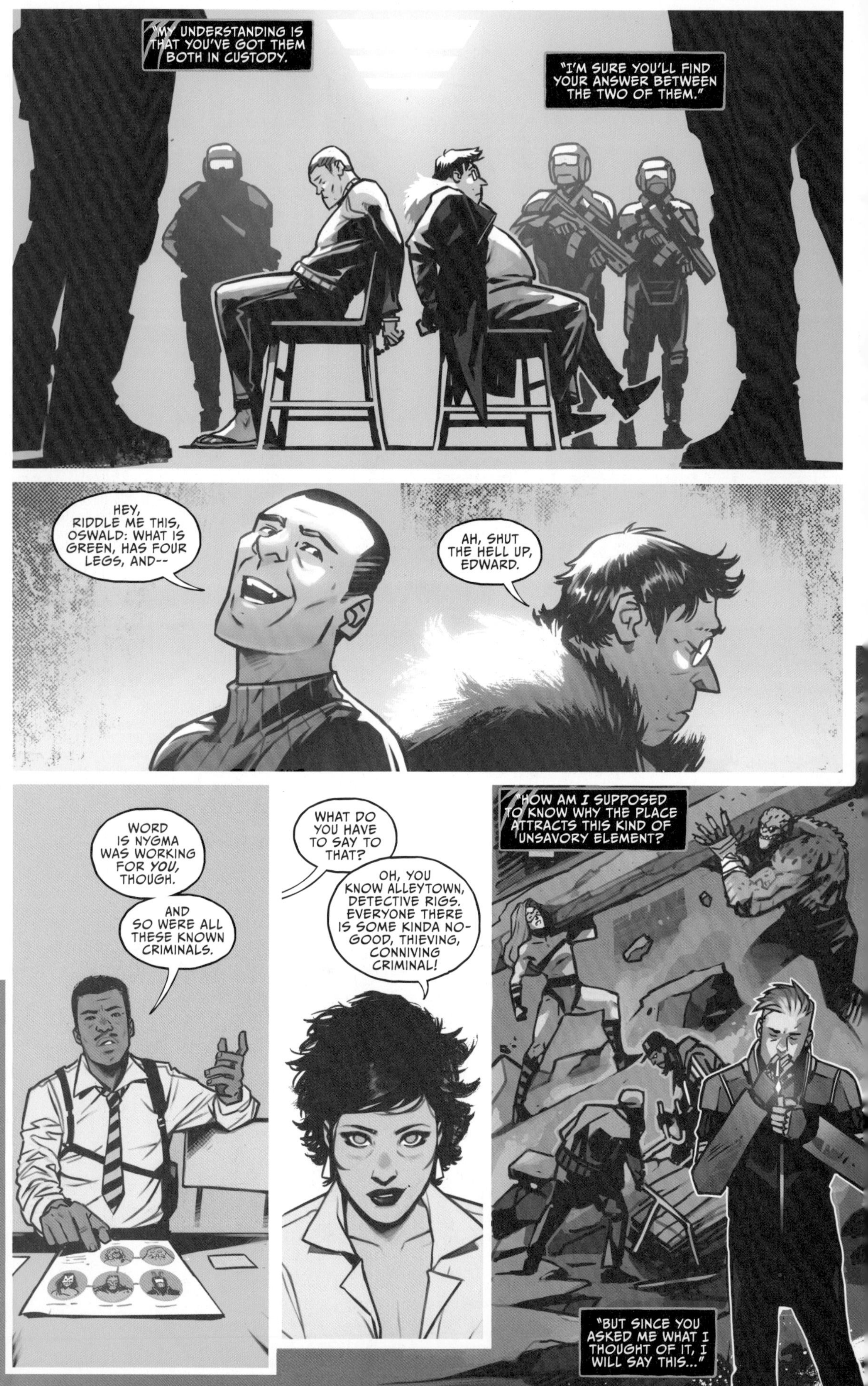
"MY UNDERSTANDING IS THAT YOU'VE GOT THEM BOTH IN CUSTODY.
"I'M SURE YOU'LL FIND YOUR ANSWER BETWEEN THE TWO OF THEM."
HEY, RIDDLE ME THIS, OSWALD: WHAT IS GREEN, HAS FOUR LEGS, AND--
AH, SHUT THE HELL UP, EDWARD.
WORD IS NYGMA WAS WORKING FOR *YOU*, THOUGH.
AND SO WERE ALL THESE KNOWN CRIMINALS.
WHAT DO YOU HAVE TO SAY TO THAT?
OH, YOU KNOW ALLEYTOWN, DETECTIVE RIGS. EVERYONE THERE IS SOME KINDA NO-GOOD, THIEVING, CONNIVING CRIMINAL!
"HOW AM *I* SUPPOSED TO KNOW WHY THE PLACE ATTRACTS THIS KIND OF UNSAVORY ELEMENT?
"BUT SINCE YOU ASKED ME WHAT I THOUGHT OF IT, I WILL SAY THIS..."

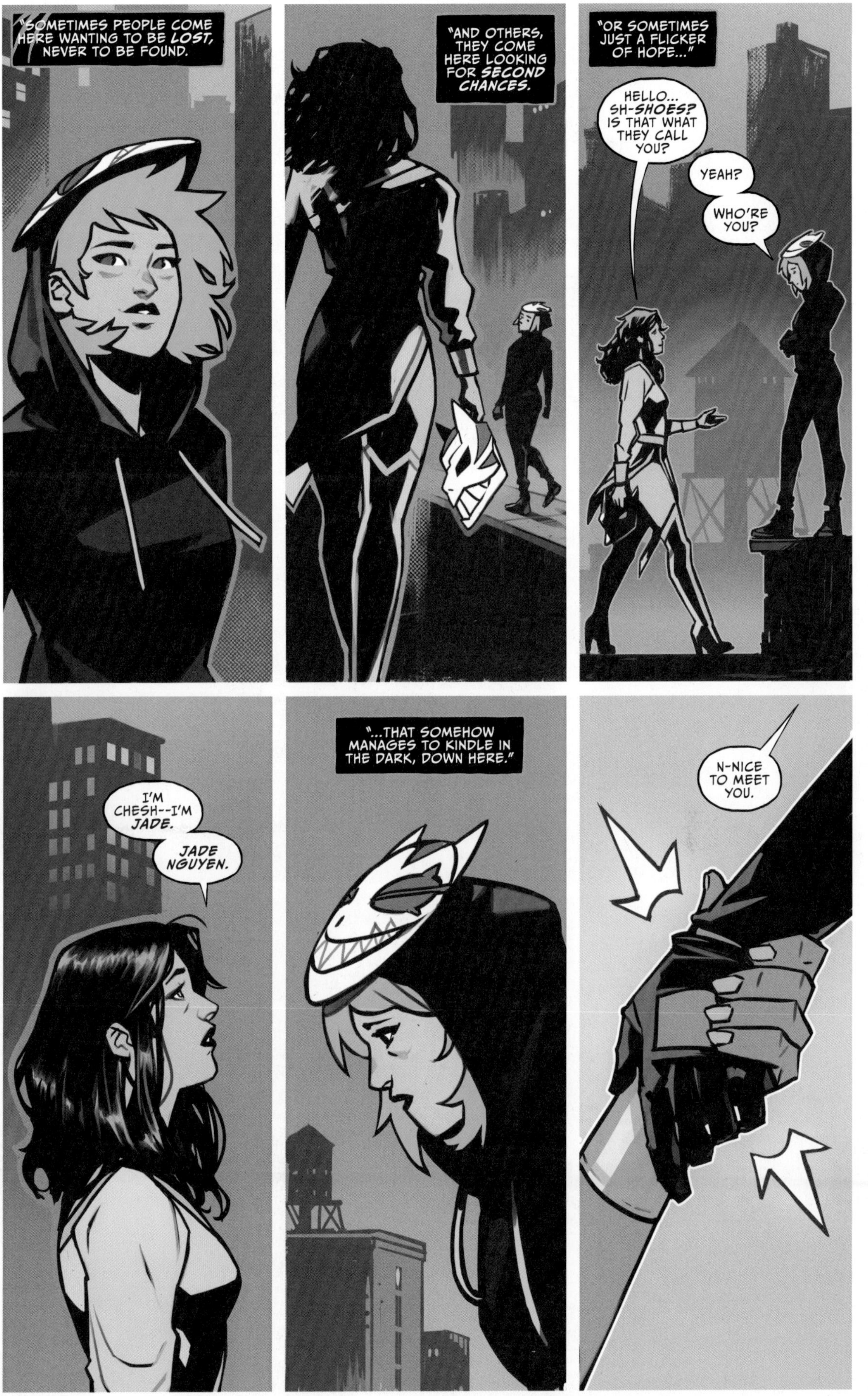
"SOMETIMES PEOPLE COME HERE WANTING TO BE *LOST*, NEVER TO BE FOUND.
"AND OTHERS, THEY COME HERE LOOKING FOR *SECOND CHANCES*.
"OR SOMETIMES JUST A FLICKER OF HOPE..."
HELLO... SH-*SHOES?* IS THAT WHAT THEY CALL YOU?
YEAH?
WHO'RE YOU?
I'M CHESH--I'M *JADE*.
JADE NGUYEN.
"...THAT SOMEHOW MANAGES TO KINDLE IN THE DARK, DOWN HERE."
N-NICE TO MEET YOU.

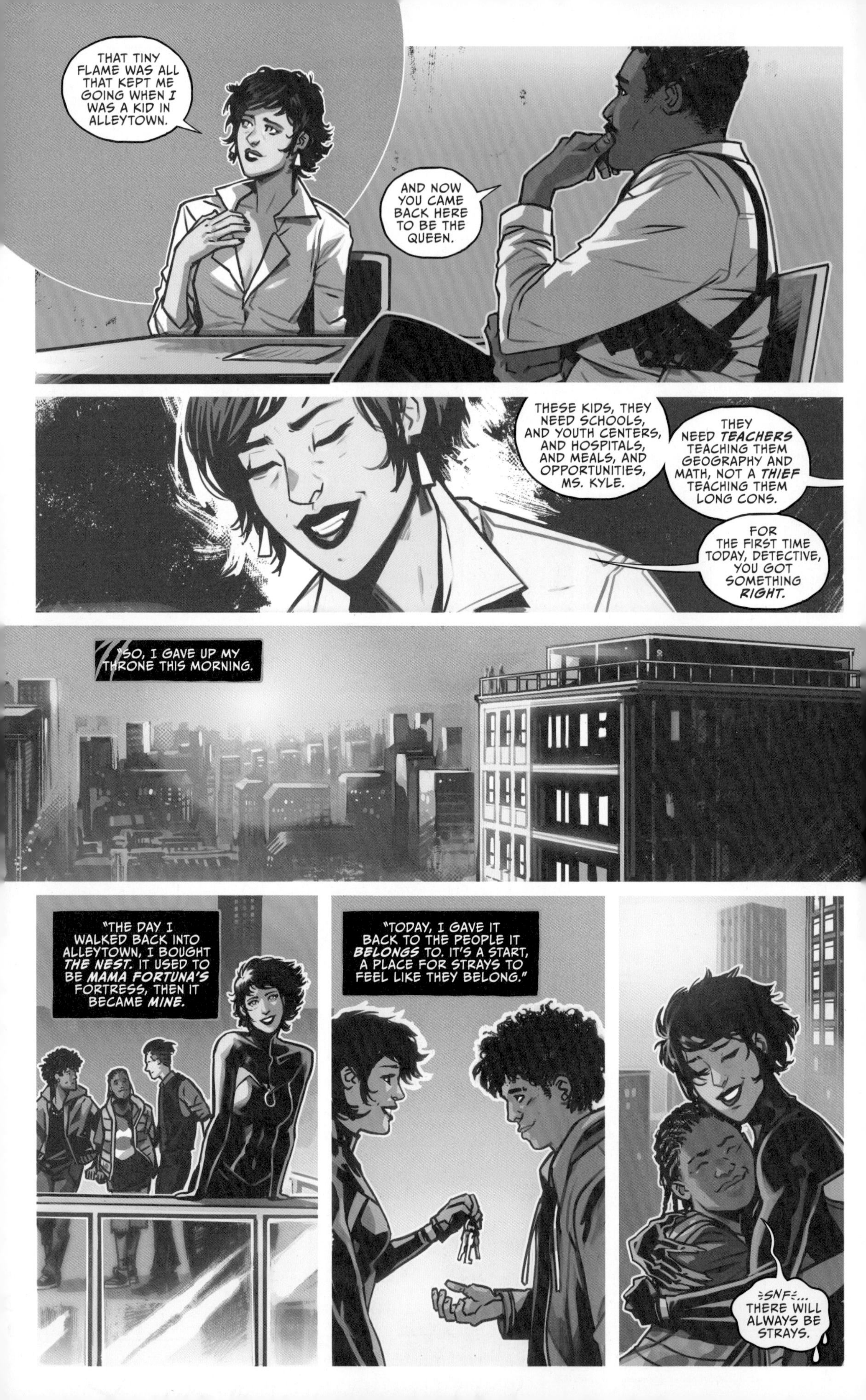
THAT TINY FLAME WAS ALL THAT KEPT ME GOING WHEN I WAS A KID IN ALLEYTOWN.
AND NOW YOU CAME BACK HERE TO BE THE QUEEN.
THESE KIDS, THEY NEED SCHOOLS, AND YOUTH CENTERS, AND HOSPITALS, AND MEALS, AND OPPORTUNITIES, MS. KYLE.
THEY NEED TEACHERS TEACHING THEM GEOGRAPHY AND MATH, NOT A THIEF TEACHING THEM LONG CONS.
FOR THE FIRST TIME TODAY, DETECTIVE, YOU GOT SOMETHING RIGHT.
"SO, I GAVE UP MY THRONE THIS MORNING.
"THE DAY I WALKED BACK INTO ALLEYTOWN, I BOUGHT THE NEST. IT USED TO BE MAMA FORTUNA'S FORTRESS, THEN IT BECAME MINE.
"TODAY, I GAVE IT BACK TO THE PEOPLE IT BELONGS TO. IT'S A START, A PLACE FOR STRAYS TO FEEL LIKE THEY BELONG."
SNF... THERE WILL ALWAYS BE STRAYS.

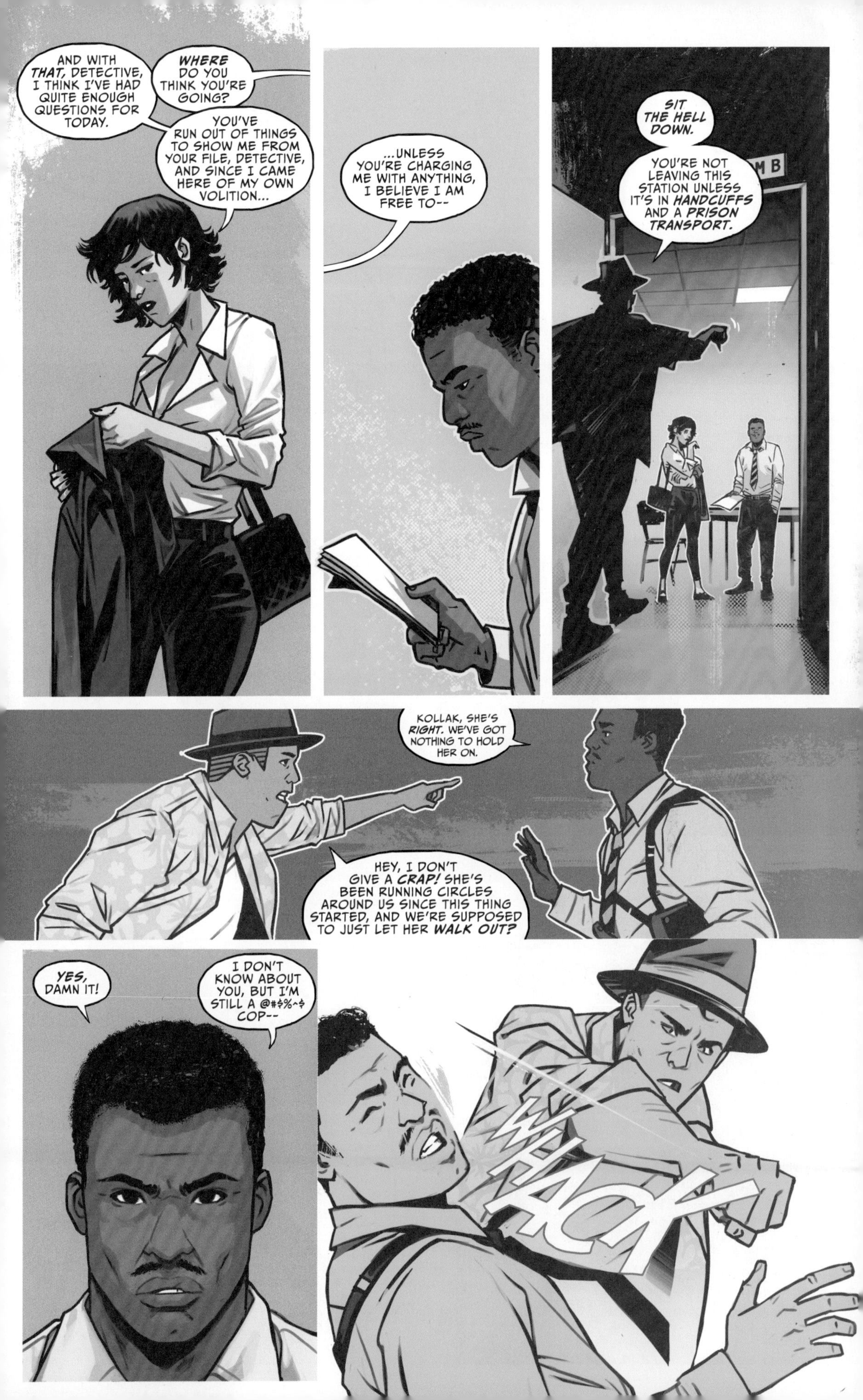
AND WITH *THAT,* DETECTIVE, I THINK I'VE HAD QUITE ENOUGH QUESTIONS FOR TODAY.
YOU'VE RUN OUT OF THINGS TO SHOW ME FROM YOUR FILE, DETECTIVE, AND SINCE I CAME HERE OF MY OWN VOLITION...
WHERE DO YOU THINK YOU'RE GOING?
...UNLESS YOU'RE CHARGING ME WITH ANYTHING, I BELIEVE I AM FREE TO--
SIT THE HELL DOWN.
YOU'RE NOT LEAVING THIS STATION UNLESS IT'S IN *HANDCUFFS* AND A *PRISON TRANSPORT.*
MB
KOLLAK, SHE'S *RIGHT.* WE'VE GOT NOTHING TO HOLD HER ON.
HEY, I DON'T GIVE A *CRAP!* SHE'S BEEN RUNNING CIRCLES AROUND US SINCE THIS THING STARTED, AND WE'RE SUPPOSED TO JUST LET HER *WALK OUT?*
YES, DAMN IT!
I DON'T KNOW ABOUT YOU, BUT I'M STILL A @#$%^$ COP--
WHACK

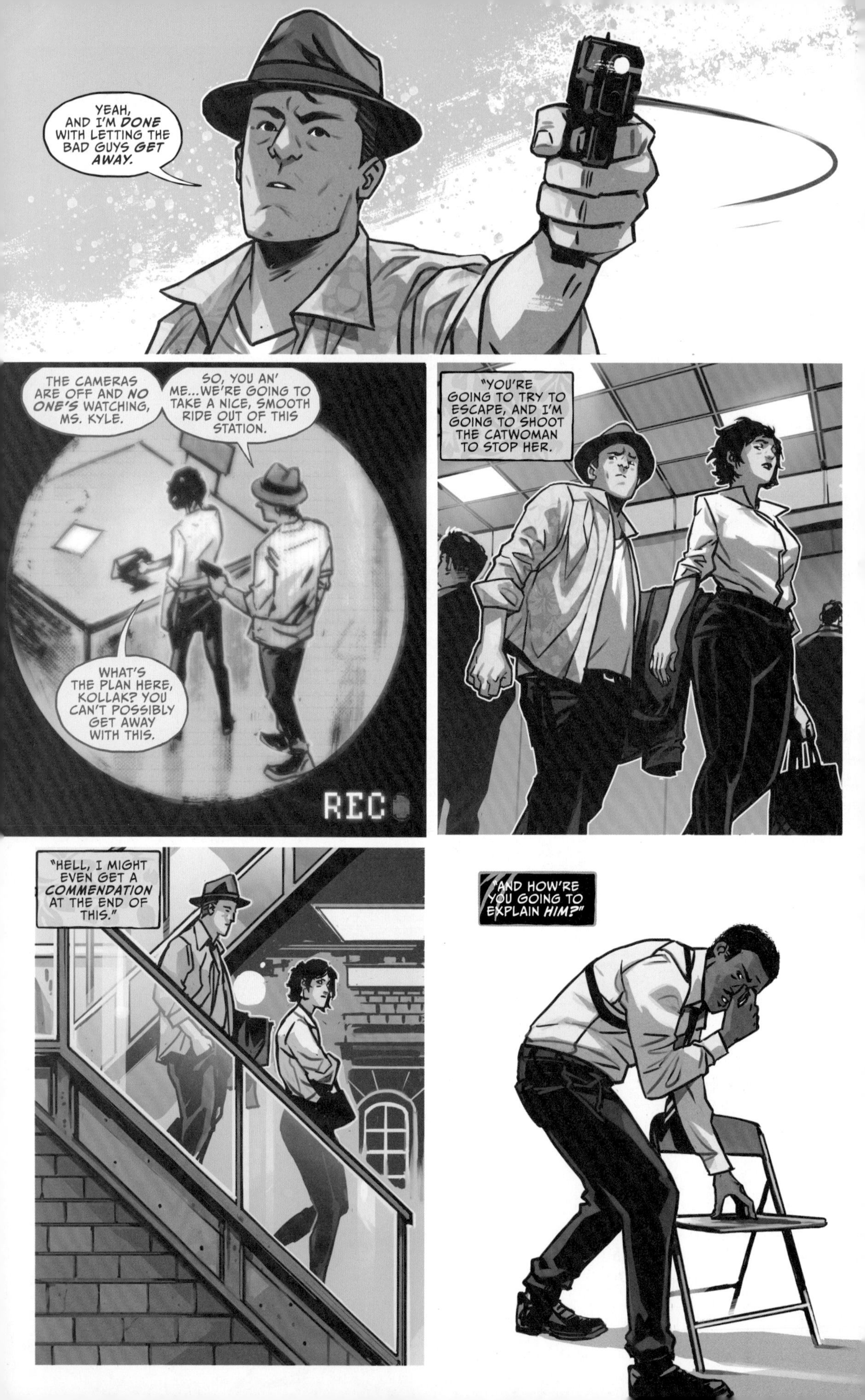
YEAH, AND I'M DONE WITH LETTING THE BAD GUYS GET AWAY.
THE CAMERAS ARE OFF AND NO ONE'S WATCHING, MS. KYLE.
SO, YOU AN' ME...WE'RE GOING TO TAKE A NICE, SMOOTH RIDE OUT OF THIS STATION.
WHAT'S THE PLAN HERE, KOLLAK? YOU CAN'T POSSIBLY GET AWAY WITH THIS.
REC
"YOU'RE GOING TO TRY TO ESCAPE, AND I'M GOING TO SHOOT THE CATWOMAN TO STOP HER.
"HELL, I MIGHT EVEN GET A COMMENDATION AT THE END OF THIS."
"AND HOW'RE YOU GOING TO EXPLAIN HIM?"

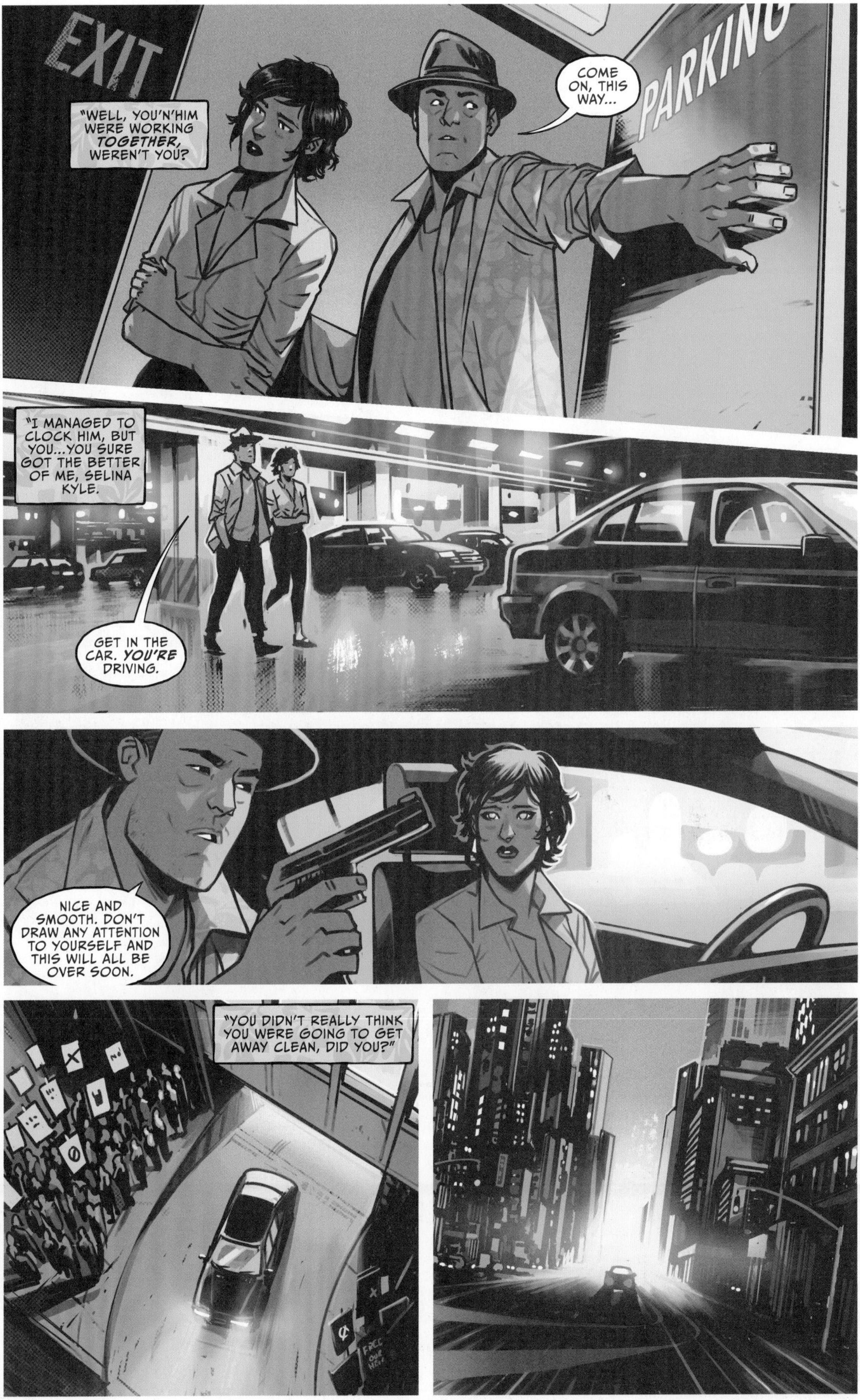
"WELL, YOU'N'HIM WERE WORKING TOGETHER, WEREN'T YOU?
COME ON, THIS WAY...
"I MANAGED TO CLOCK HIM, BUT YOU...YOU SURE GOT THE BETTER OF ME, SELINA KYLE.
GET IN THE CAR. YOU'RE DRIVING.
NICE AND SMOOTH. DON'T DRAW ANY ATTENTION TO YOURSELF AND THIS WILL ALL BE OVER SOON.
"YOU DIDN'T REALLY THINK YOU WERE GOING TO GET AWAY CLEAN, DID YOU?"

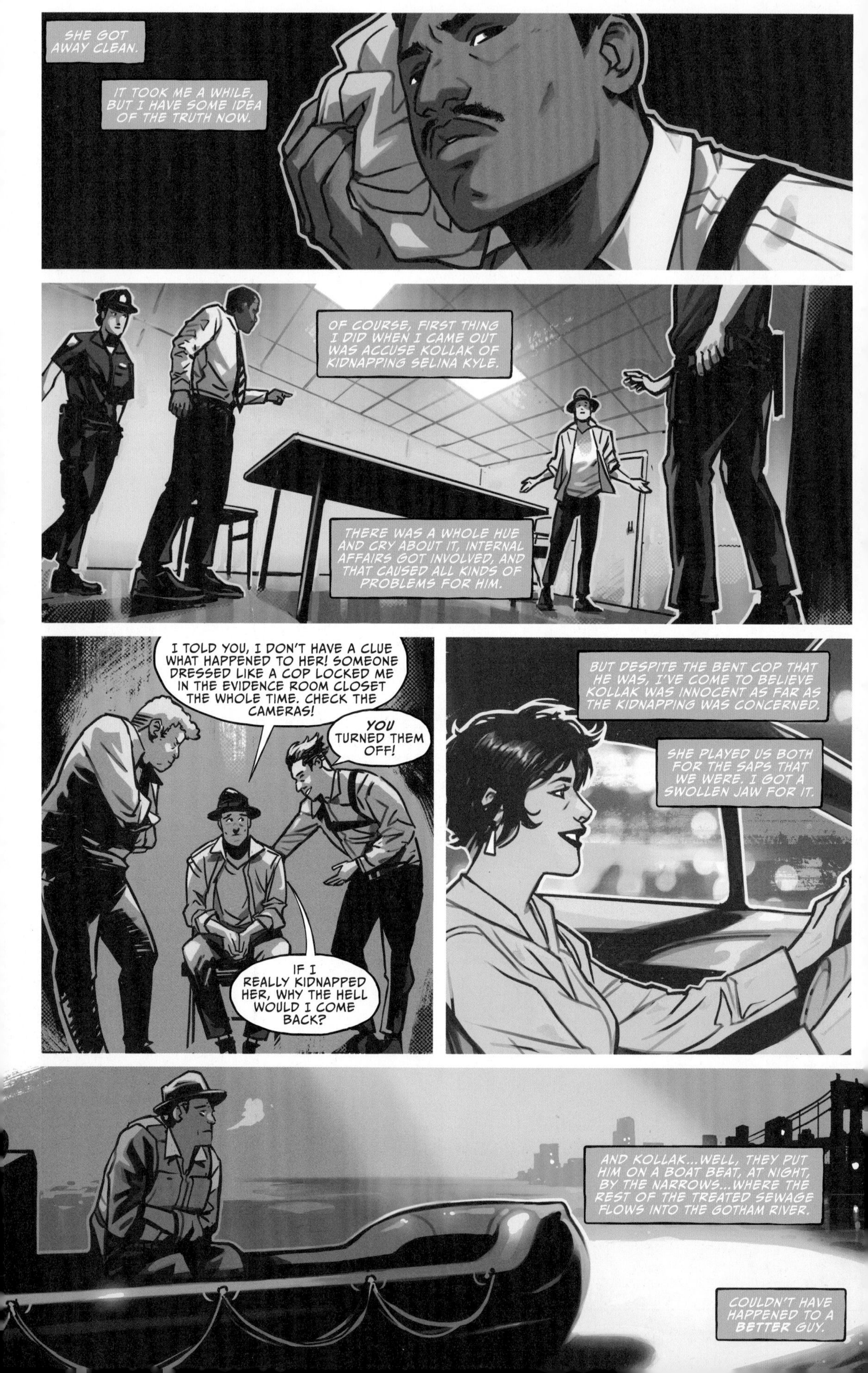
SHE GOT AWAY CLEAN.
IT TOOK ME A WHILE, BUT I HAVE SOME IDEA OF THE TRUTH NOW.
OF COURSE, FIRST THING I DID WHEN I CAME OUT WAS ACCUSE KOLLAK OF KIDNAPPING SELINA KYLE.
THERE WAS A WHOLE HUE AND CRY ABOUT IT, INTERNAL AFFAIRS GOT INVOLVED, AND THAT CAUSED ALL KINDS OF PROBLEMS FOR HIM.
I TOLD YOU, I DON'T HAVE A CLUE WHAT HAPPENED TO HER! SOMEONE DRESSED LIKE A COP LOCKED ME IN THE EVIDENCE ROOM CLOSET THE WHOLE TIME. CHECK THE CAMERAS!
YOU TURNED THEM OFF!
IF I REALLY KIDNAPPED HER, WHY THE HELL WOULD I COME BACK?
BUT DESPITE THE BENT COP THAT HE WAS, I'VE COME TO BELIEVE KOLLAK WAS INNOCENT AS FAR AS THE KIDNAPPING WAS CONCERNED.
SHE PLAYED US BOTH FOR THE SAPS THAT WE WERE. I GOT A SWOLLEN JAW FOR IT.
AND KOLLAK...WELL, THEY PUT HIM ON A BOAT BEAT, AT NIGHT, BY THE NARROWS...WHERE THE REST OF THE TREATED SEWAGE FLOWS INTO THE GOTHAM RIVER.
COULDN'T HAVE HAPPENED TO A BETTER GUY.

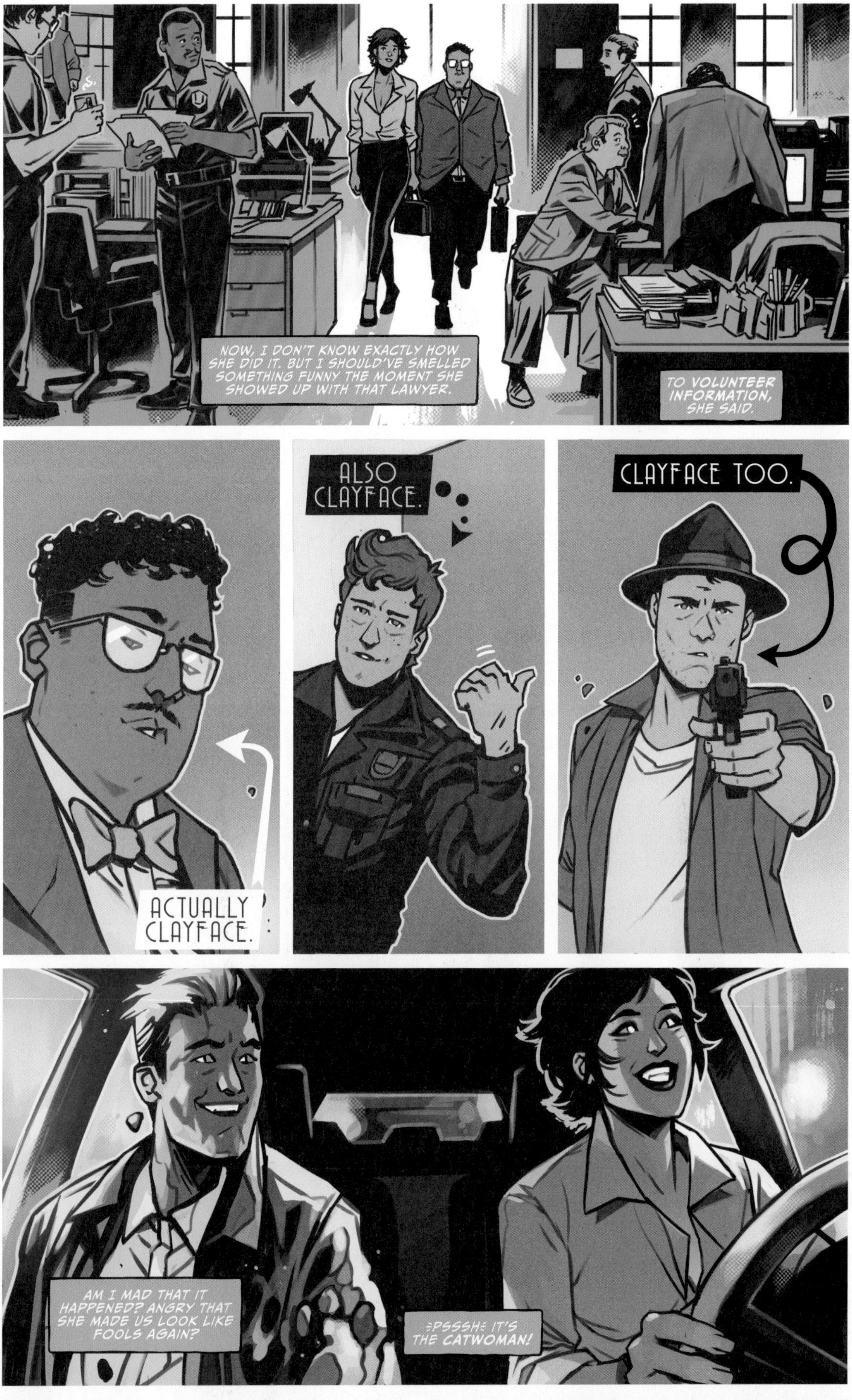
NOW, I DON'T KNOW EXACTLY HOW SHE DID IT. BUT I SHOULD'VE SMELLED SOMETHING FUNNY THE MOMENT SHE SHOWED UP WITH THAT LAWYER.
TO VOLUNTEER INFORMATION, SHE SAID.
ACTUALLY CLAYFACE.
ALSO CLAYFACE.
CLAYFACE TOO.
AM I MAD THAT IT HAPPENED? ANGRY THAT SHE MADE US LOOK LIKE FOOLS AGAIN?
PSSSH IT'S THE CATWOMAN!

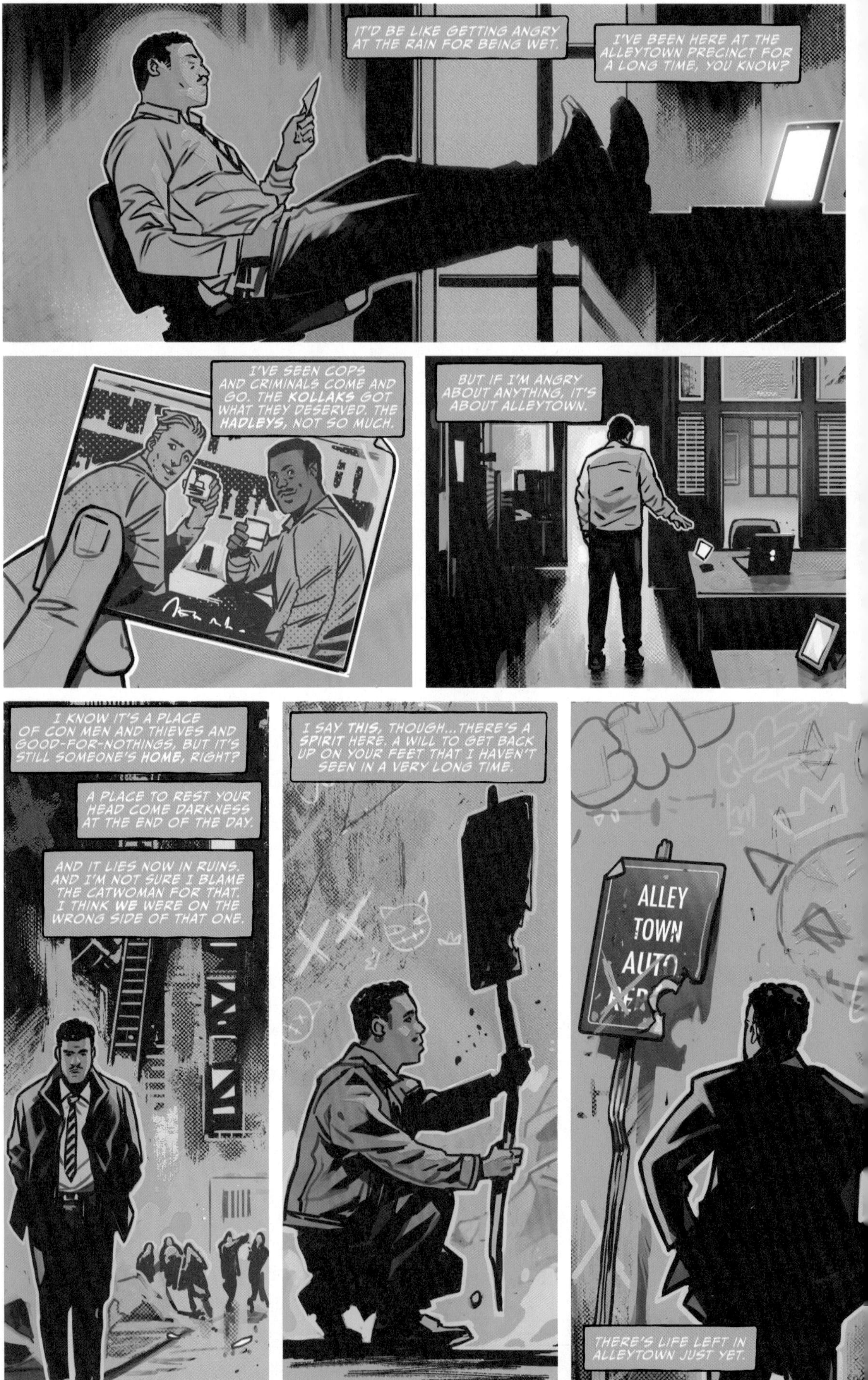
IT'D BE LIKE GETTING ANGRY AT THE RAIN FOR BEING WET.
I'VE BEEN HERE AT THE ALLEYTOWN PRECINCT FOR A LONG TIME, YOU KNOW?
I'VE SEEN COPS AND CRIMINALS COME AND GO. THE KOLLAKS GOT WHAT THEY DESERVED. THE HADLEYS, NOT SO MUCH.
BUT IF I'M ANGRY ABOUT ANYTHING, IT'S ABOUT ALLEYTOWN.
I KNOW IT'S A PLACE OF CON MEN AND THIEVES AND GOOD-FOR-NOTHINGS, BUT IT'S STILL SOMEONE'S HOME, RIGHT?
A PLACE TO REST YOUR HEAD COME DARKNESS AT THE END OF THE DAY.
AND IT LIES NOW IN RUINS. AND I'M NOT SURE I BLAME THE CATWOMAN FOR THAT. I THINK WE WERE ON THE WRONG SIDE OF THAT ONE.
I SAY THIS, THOUGH...THERE'S A SPIRIT HERE. A WILL TO GET BACK UP ON YOUR FEET THAT I HAVEN'T SEEN IN A VERY LONG TIME.
ALLEY TOWN AUTO
THERE'S LIFE LEFT IN ALLEYTOWN JUST YET.

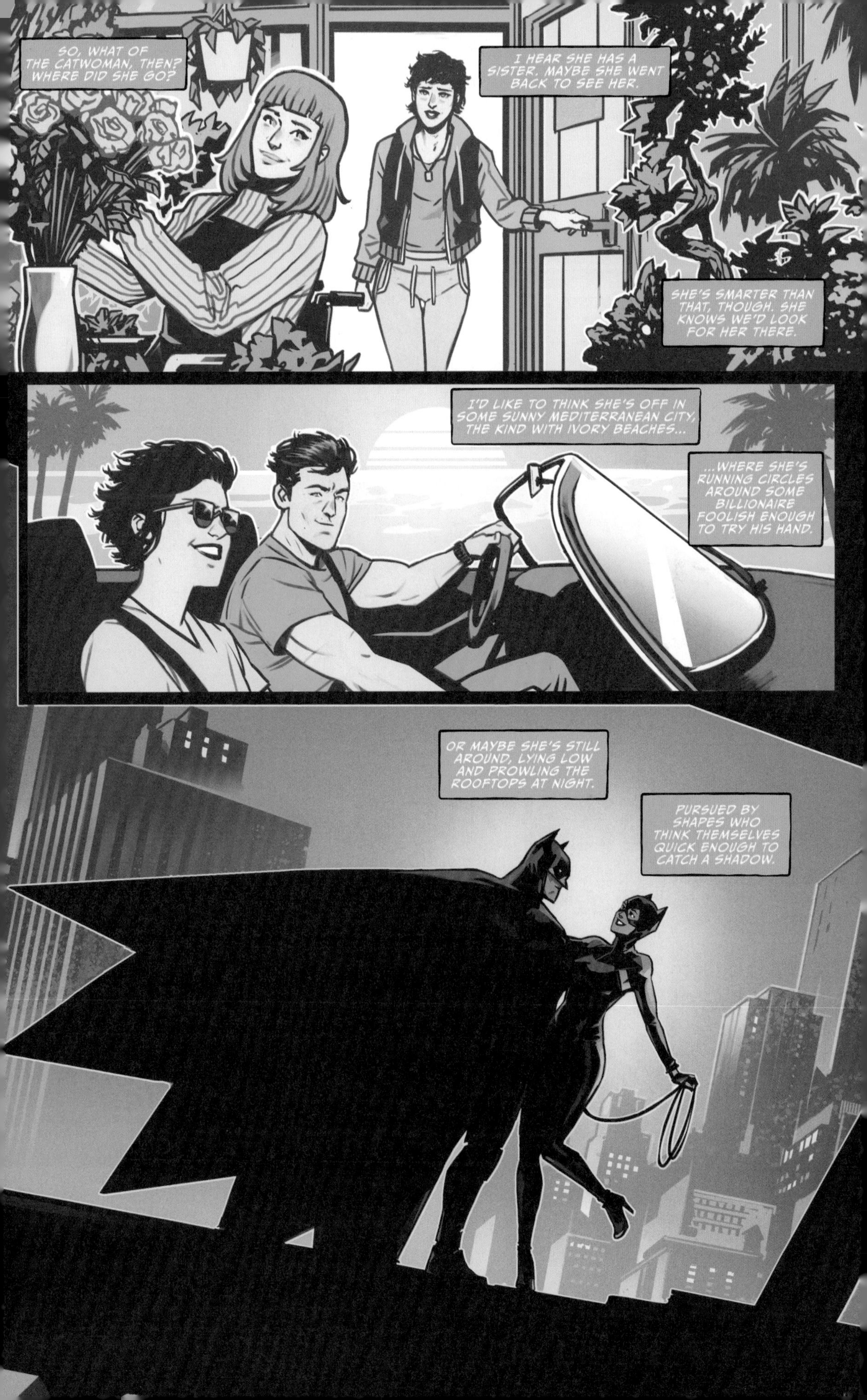
SO, WHAT OF THE CATWOMAN, THEN? WHERE DID SHE GO?
I HEAR SHE HAS A SISTER. MAYBE SHE WENT BACK TO SEE HER.
SHE'S SMARTER THAN THAT, THOUGH. SHE KNOWS WE'D LOOK FOR HER THERE.
I'D LIKE TO THINK SHE'S OFF IN SOME SUNNY MEDITERRANEAN CITY, THE KIND WITH IVORY BEACHES...
...WHERE SHE'S RUNNING CIRCLES AROUND SOME BILLIONAIRE FOOLISH ENOUGH TO TRY HIS HAND.
OR MAYBE SHE'S STILL AROUND, LYING LOW AND PROWLING THE ROOFTOPS AT NIGHT.
PURSUED BY SHAPES WHO THINK THEMSELVES QUICK ENOUGH TO CATCH A SHADOW.

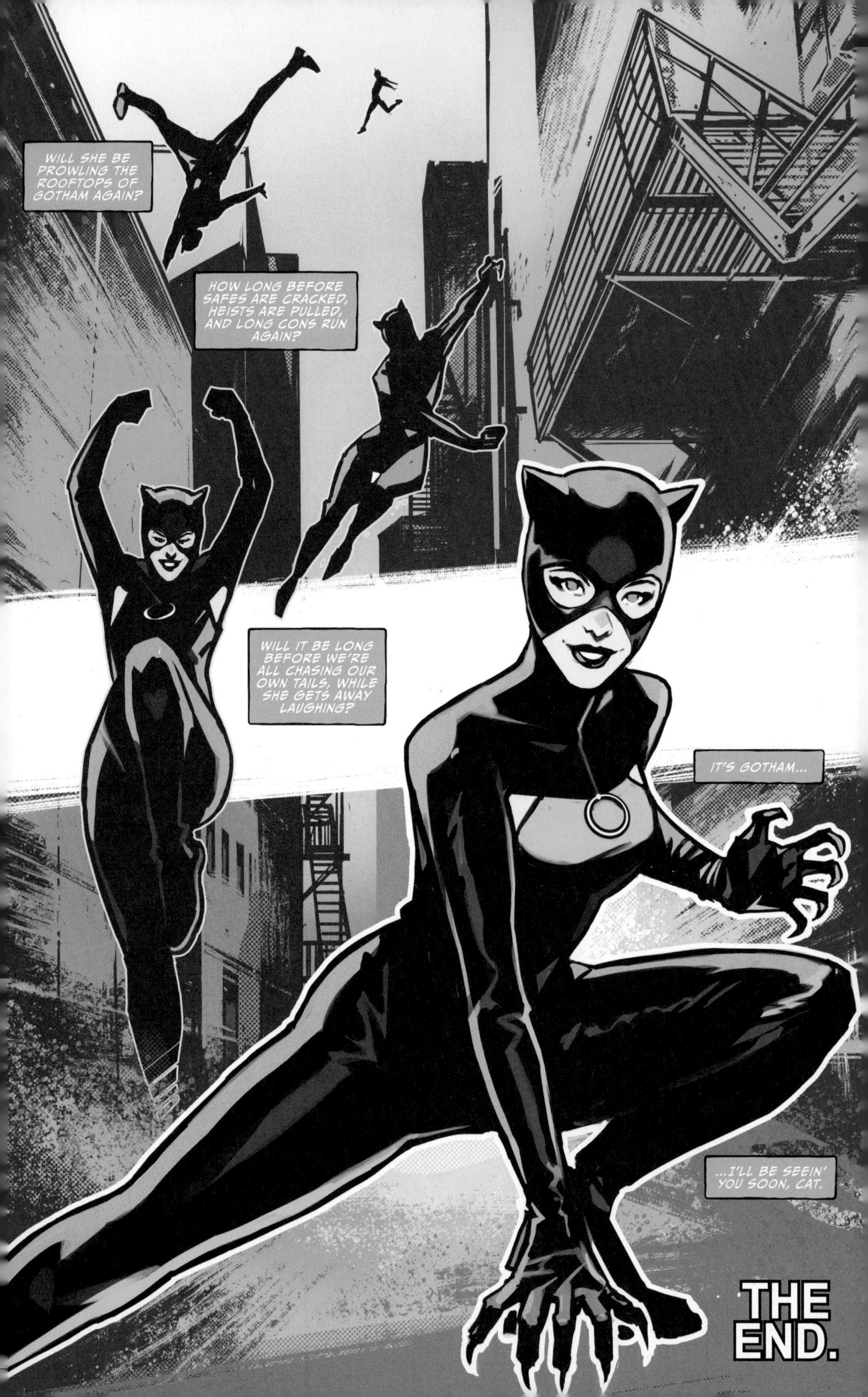
WILL SHE BE PROWLING THE ROOFTOPS OF GOTHAM AGAIN?
HOW LONG BEFORE SAFES ARE CRACKED, HEISTS ARE PULLED, AND LONG CONS RUN AGAIN?
WILL IT BE LONG BEFORE WE'RE ALL CHASING OUR OWN TAILS, WHILE SHE GETS AWAY LAUGHING?
IT'S GOTHAM...
...I'LL BE SEEIN' YOU SOON, CAT.
THE END.

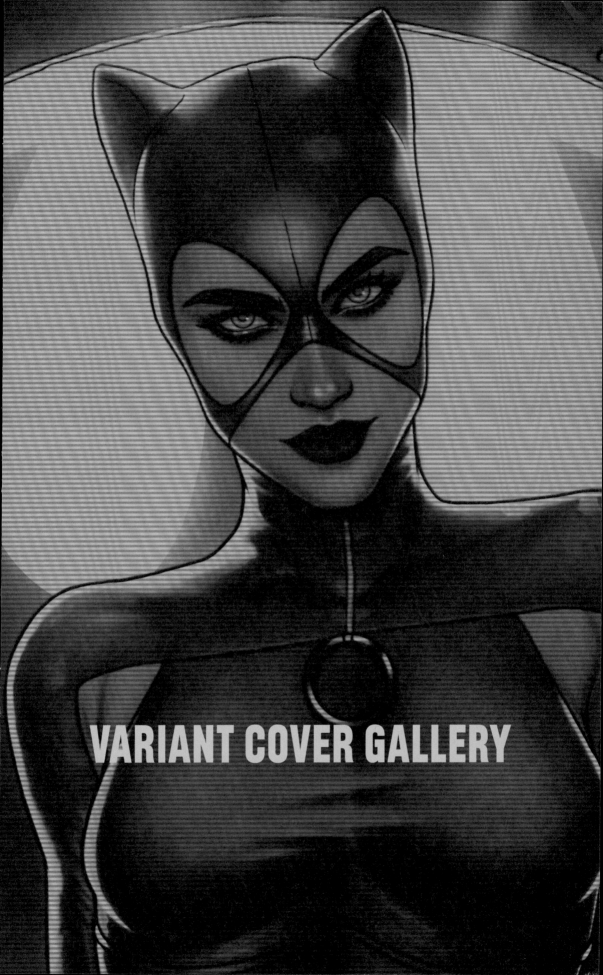

VARIANT COVER GALLERY

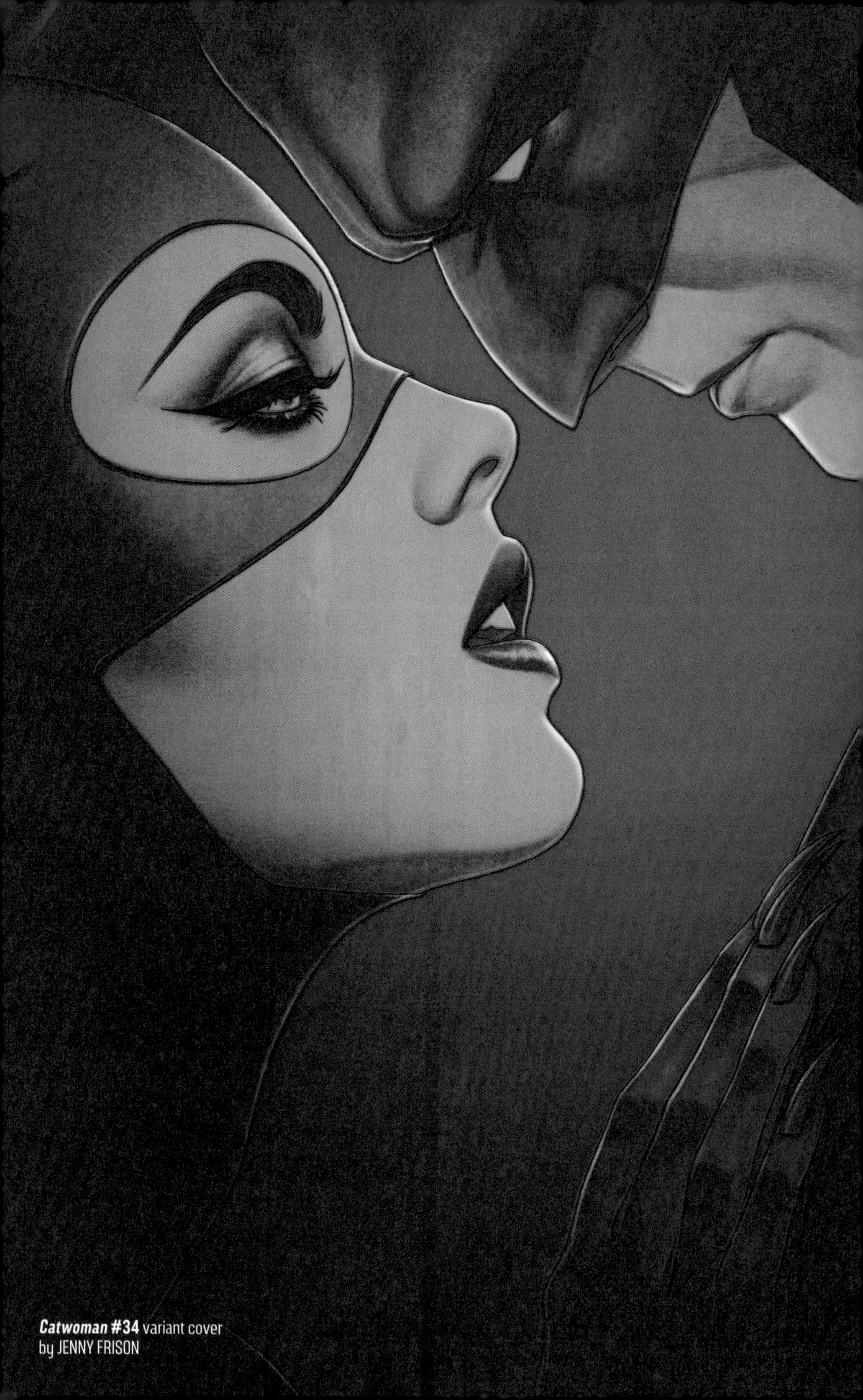

Catwoman **#34** variant cover
by JENNY FRISON

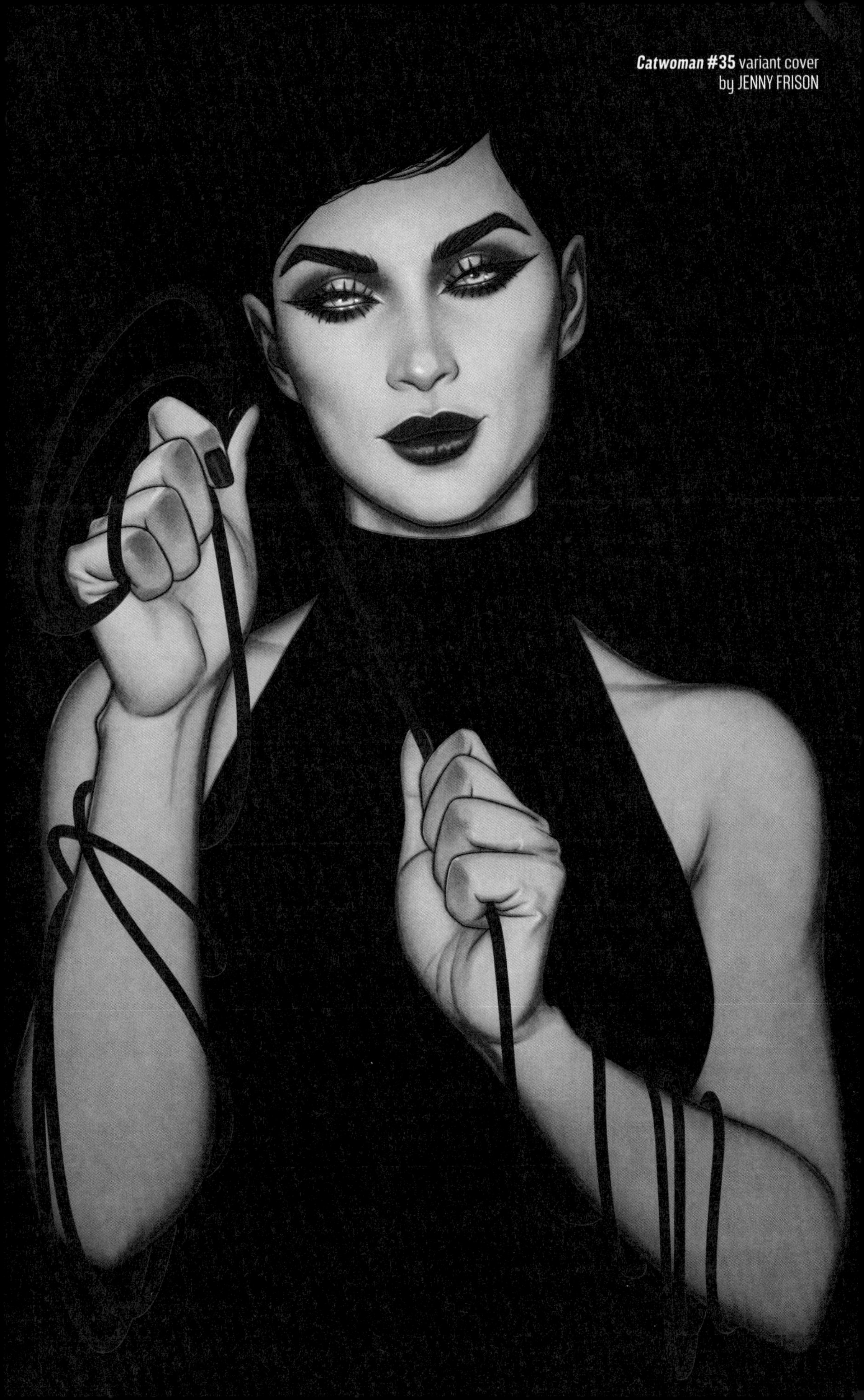

***Catwoman* #35** variant cover
by JENNY FRISON

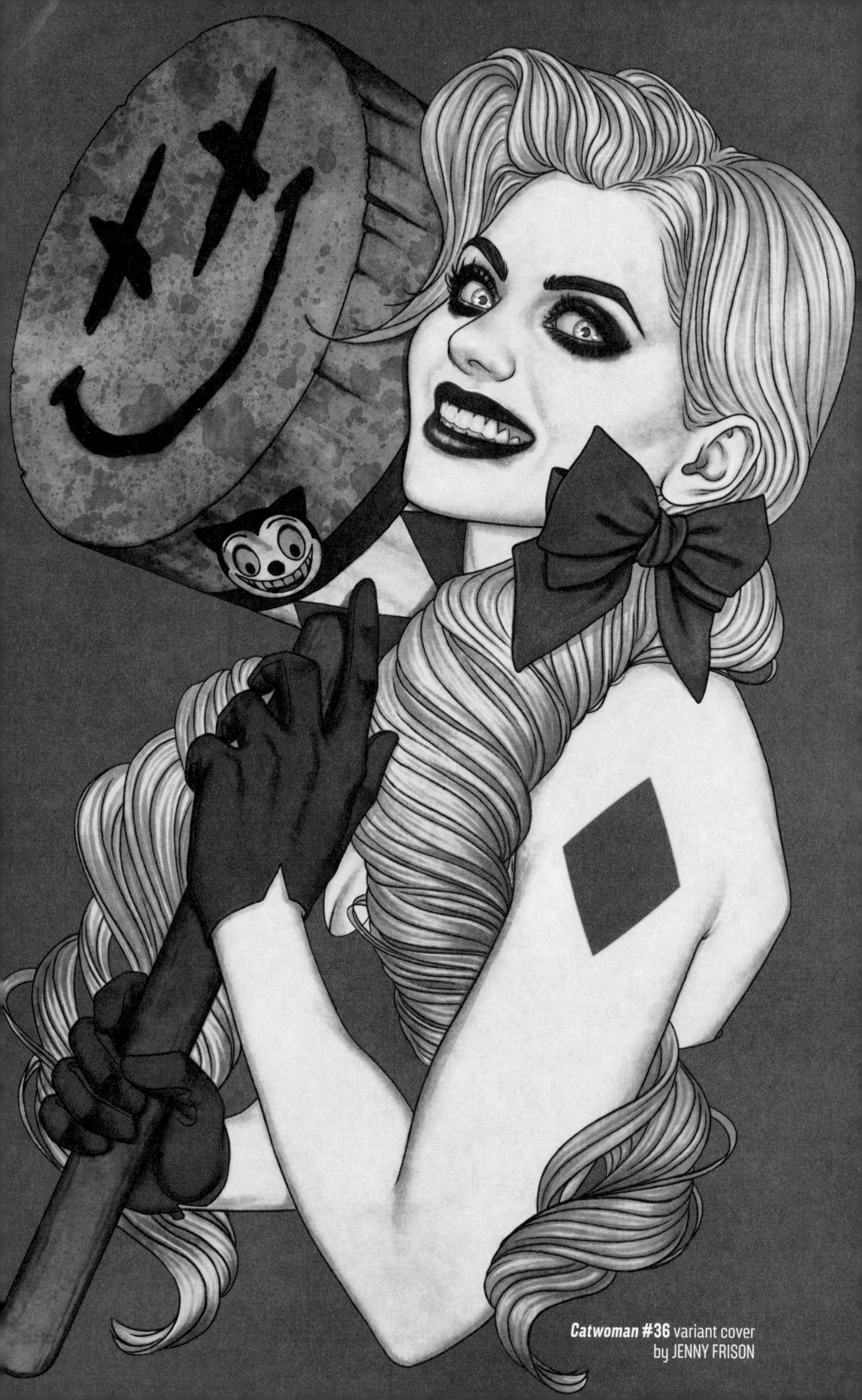

***Catwoman* #36** variant cover
by JENNY FRISON

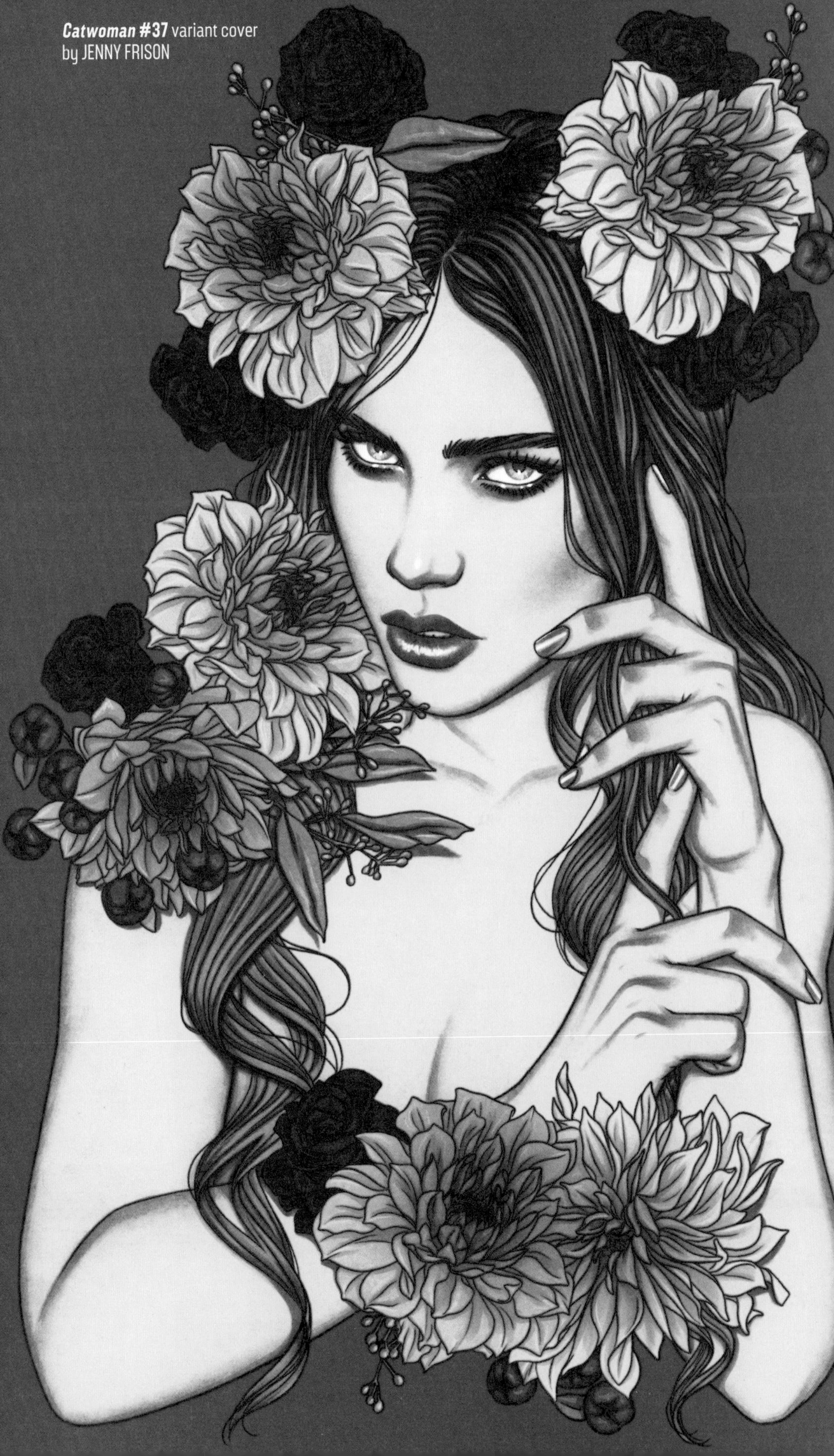

***Catwoman* #37** variant cover
by JENNY FRISON

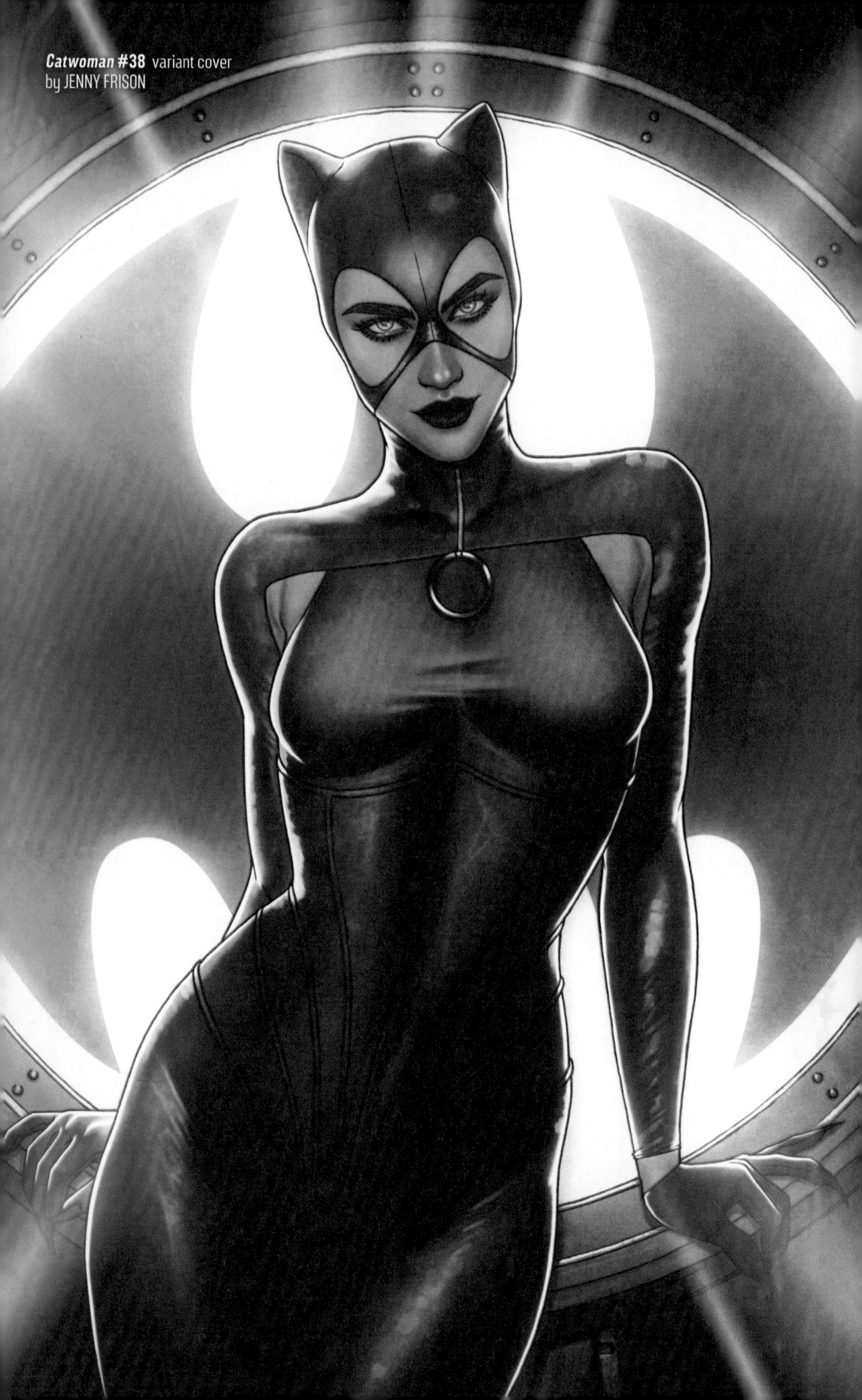

***Catwoman* #38** variant cover
by JENNY FRISON

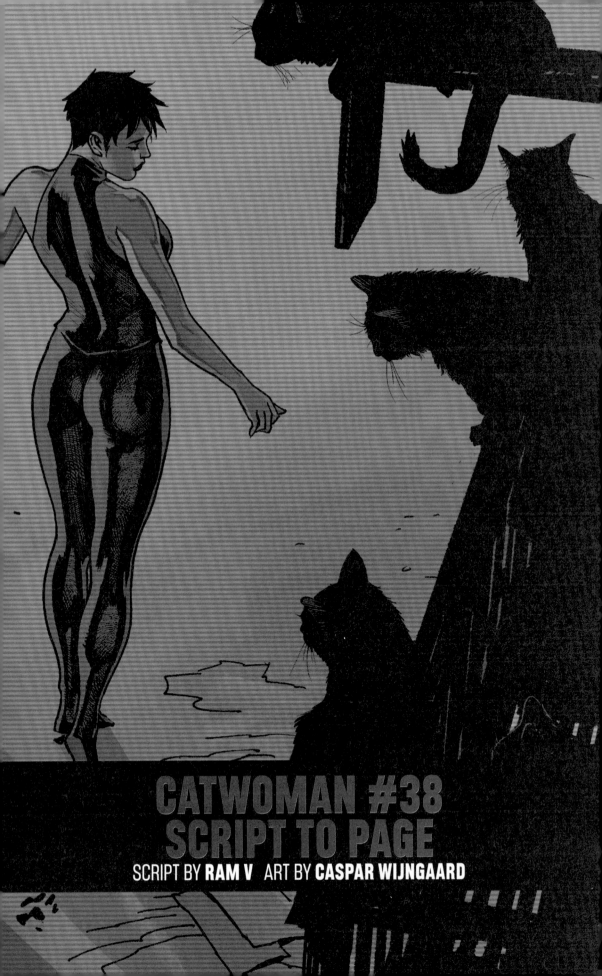

CATWOMAN #38
SCRIPT TO PAGE

SCRIPT BY **RAM V** ART BY **CASPAR WIJNGAARD**

PANEL 1

Big intro shot. The GCPD Alleytown precint building. Lots of police
presence outside. Riot gear cops. Vehicles. Choppers in the air.

There is a crowd of protesters in front of the building. Mostly The
Strays. Things are peaceful but the situation feels tense.

> LOCATION CAPTION
> GCPD BUILDING, ALLEYTOWN, GOTHAM.

PANEL 2

Detective Kollack, parting the blinds on a window to look outside and
sneer.

> KOLLACK
> Look at those fools, Rigs. Protesting,
> cheering on for a damn criminal.

> KOLLACK
> What's this goddamn city come to?

PANEL 3

Rigs is at a nearby table typing up a report, he speaks without
looking up from his typing. Kollack is poking his finger down on the
table as if to make an impassioned point. But he is being facetious.
So he smiles as he's doing it.

> RIGS
> You're kidding me, right? It's Gotham...

> RIGS
> ...this is how things have always been,
> Kollack.

> KOLLACK
> Well, not anymore, detective. Not on my
> watch.

PANEL 4

Rigs in the f/g is getting up from his table. Watching as Kollack
walks away with a file in hand in the m/g - we can see the door to an
interrogation room in the b/g.

> KOLLACK
> We've got a criminal to apprehend. Protect
> and serve! And all that!

> KOLLACK
> C'mon Rigs, where's your enthusiasm...?

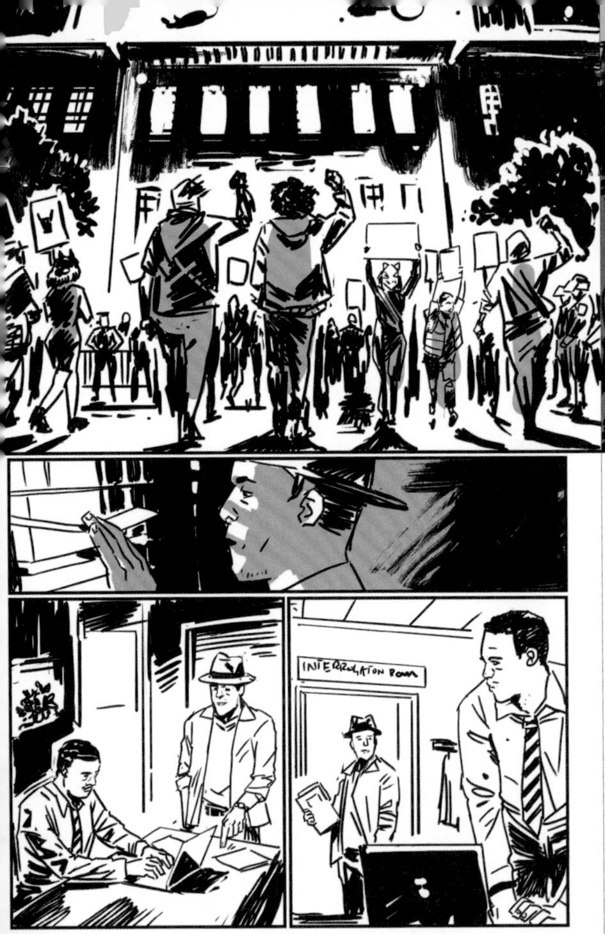

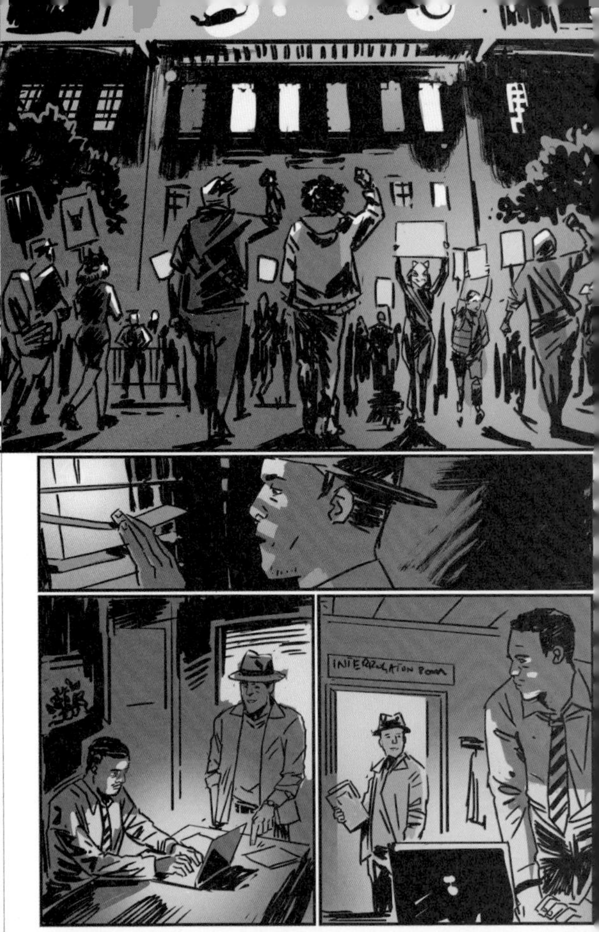

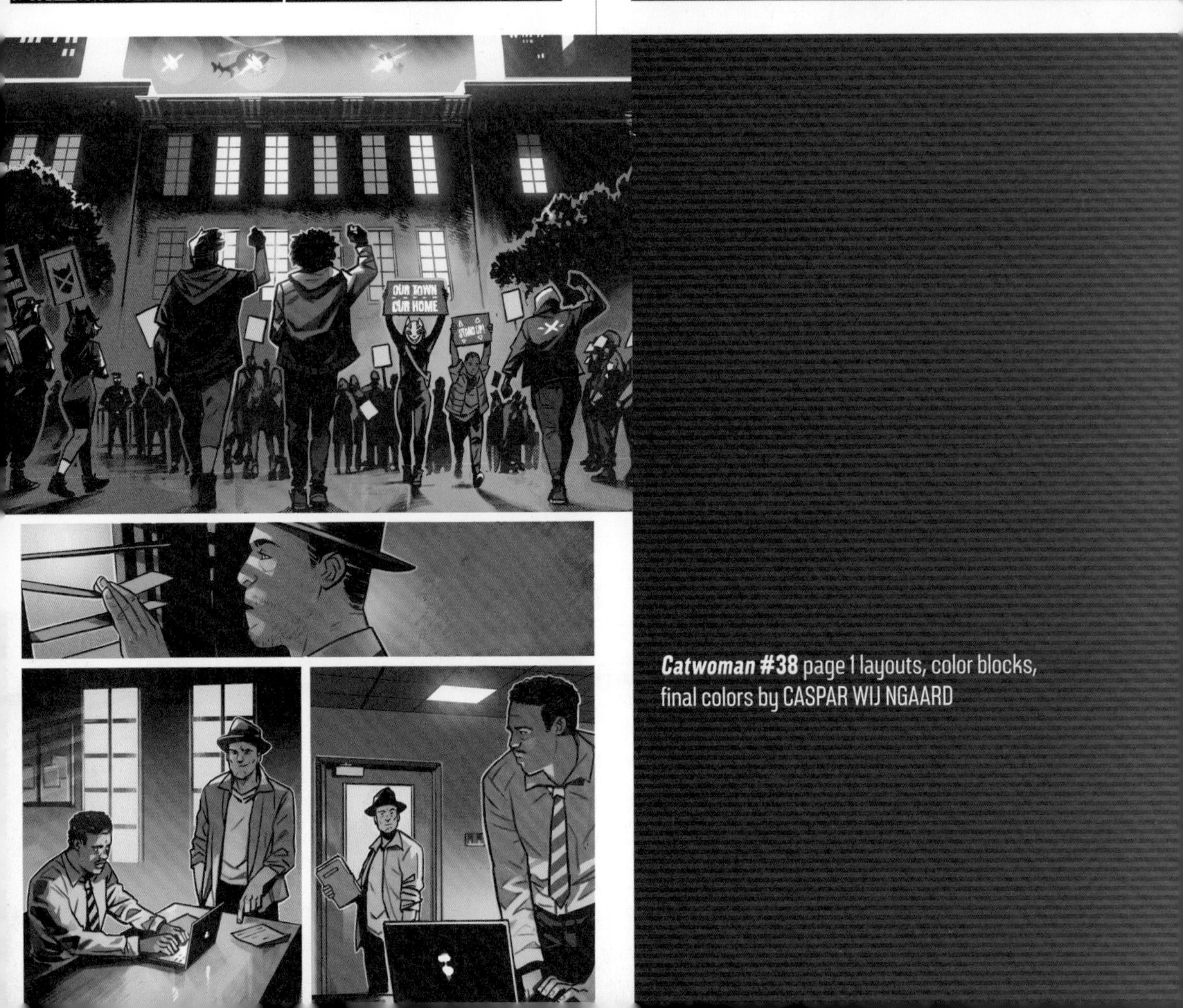
OUR TOWN
OUR HOME

***Catwoman* #38** page 1 layouts, color blocks, final colors by CASPAR WIJ NGAARD

PANEL 1

Close up on Selina at the funeral. Dark glasses on - wearing a hat
with a veil.

                        CATWOMAN V/O
              "I just wanted to say goodbye.

                        CATWOMAN V/O
              "Is that such a bad thing?

PANEL 2

Pull back to show the priest standing next to her but he is facing
the opposite direction, away from us so we only see his back.

It's a foggy morning in the cemetery.

                        CATWOMAN V/O
              "And as for who I was talking to...I met a
              priest at the service."

                        CATWOMAN
              You here to kill me, then? Finish what we
              started?

                        FATHER VALLEY
              Hahaha...It would be a fitting place to do
              it, no?

PANEL 3

Flip around for a surprise. It's Father Valley - dressed as an actual
priest. He's cut his hair shorter but still has his mirror glasses
on. Catwoman turns to a side so we can see a little bit of her face.

                        FATHER VALLEY
              But I think we shall let detective Hadley
              have his day. We can leave him at least
              that.

                        CATWOMAN
              I wish he'd never gotten involved.0

                        CATWOMAN V/O
              "To him, I made my confessions."

PANEL 4

On father Valley - close up. He's also pulling out a pocket bible
from his priestly garb. But it's been shot through with a bullet.

                        FATHER VALLEY
              <Biblical quote>

                        FATHER VALLEY
              I have never taken an innocent life before.

                        FATHER VALLEY
              So I came here to tell you this.

PANEL 5

Close up on their hands as FV hands the bible off to Selina.

                        FATHER VALLEY
              Beware Selina Kyle, of the many lives you
              have lived. They are all bought with the
              blood of the innocent.

PANEL 6

Selina watches from the f/g as Father Valley walks away from her into
the morning fog in that cemetery.

                        CATWOMAN V/O CAPTION
              "And he absolved me of my sins."

                        FATHER VALLEY
              I go now in penance for my mistakes. And you
              should pray, that our paths may never cross
              again.